Where to
FISH & HUNT
in North America

OTHER BOOKS BY JEROME KNAP

The Canadian Hunter's Handbook

101 Tips to Improve Your Fishing

The Hunter's Handbook

The Complete Outdoorsman's Handbook

Training the Versatile Gun Dog (with Alyson Knap)

Getting Hooked on Fishing (with David Richey)

Where to
FISH & HUNT
in North America

including Mexico and the Caribbean

JEROME J. KNAP

Pagurian Press Limited

TORONTO

Printed and bound in Canada
Library of Congress Catalog Card No. 74-80553
ISBN 0-919364-78-0

Distributed by:
PUBLISHERS MARKETING GROUP
A BAKER & TAYLOR COMPANY
Executive Offices
1515 Broadway
New York, N.Y. 10036
Distribution Center
Gladiola Avenue
Momence, Illinois 60954

FC-006

Contents

Introduction

There was a time when only the Teddy Roosevelts, the Zane Grays, or the scions of wealthy families could think of hunting in the wilds of Alaska or fishing for marlin off the Florida coast. But not today. Fishermen and hunters of just average means make long sojourns in pursuit of their favorite sport. This is the reason for this book.

Of course, no single volume can tell about all the hunting and fishing opportunities on this continent; nor can a single writer. But this was not the intention here. The task was to present a thumbnail sketch, the highlights of what each state, province, and even the islands in the sun and Mexico, have to offer to the sportsman. In addition, the addresses where an angler or hunter can get detailed information have been provided.

The seasons and licence costs, particularly in the sections on hunting, were those in effect at the time of writing. The reader, when planning a trip, should inquire about these details because they do change from year to year in the face of increasing demands for hunting. Fishing licence costs have not been included because, even for non-residents, they are not financially prohibitive. As far as seasons are concerned, most anglers know when these are. Fishing seasons, apart from a few special cases, are surprisingly uniform in the various regions of the continent.

The only other word of advice I can offer is to plan any long and expensive fishing or hunting trip early. A year is not too long. The best big-game guides, from Colorado to Alaska, are booked a long time in advance. The same applies to charter boats in Florida, Mexico, or even the Great Lakes in the peak of the season. Investigate the reputation of your outfitter, your guide, or charter-boat captain carefully before making a deposit. Since you will be unrolling a fair amount of folding green, you do not want to hire a man who does not know his business.

Fishing and hunting lure millions of men and increasing numbers of women into the outdoors. Deciding where to fish and hunt is not always easy. I hope that this book will help.

United States

ALABAMA

Alabama Department of Conservation and Natural Resources
64 North Union Street
Montgomery, Alabama 36104

Where to Fish

Bass may be Alabama's glamor fish, but it is the panfish — bream, crappies, and catfish — that provide the bread-and-butter fishing for most anglers. Panfish are found in every lake and river in the state.

One of the top bass lakes in the state is the 21,000-acre Smith Lake near Jasper, less than an hour's drive from Birmingham. This lake is the best spotted-bass water on the continent. The world record for spotted bass — an 8-pound 8-ounce fish — was caught here in 1968. Smith Lake has largemouth bass and rainbow trout as well.

However, all of the other impoundment lakes created by the Alabama Power Company such as Bankhead, Holt, Weiss, Lay, Mitchell, Jordan, Martin, Logan, and Yates have good fishing. Martin is known for its spring bass fishing.

Further information on these lakes can be obtained from the Advertising Department, Alabama Power Company, P.O. Box 2641, Birmingham, Alabama 35202.

Several of the Tennessee Valley Authority lakes — Wheeler, Wilson, and Pickwick — in northern Alabama also have excellent fishing for smallmouth and largemouth bass, as well as crappies, sauger, and white bass. Lake Eufaula, on the Alabama-Georgia line, is famous for its big bass. This lake has many marinas, camping parks, and motels around its shores. A number of competent guides operate on it. The Eufaula Chamber of Commerce can provide a list of guides and information on accommodations.

Alabama's big lakes are not the only fishing spots. Many of the small lakes and ponds have fine bream and bass fishing. Incidentally, bream means bluegills to Alabamans and they call them "brim". A giant bluegill of 4¾ pounds has been caught in this state. Fee fishing for channel cats has also recently caught on.

Alabama has some fine saltwater fishing. Mobile Bay is the saltwater fishing

8

center for both offshore and inshore fishing. The main game species are: cobia, sailfish, kings, the finely flavored red snapper, and the tough-fighting tarpon. Charter boats can be hired at Bayou La Batre, Orange Beach, and Dauphin Island. The best billfish fishing is in the summer.

Alabama is very conscious of what sport fishing means to its tourist trade. The Alabama Bureau of Publicity and Information keeps itself informed daily on the best fishing. In fact, if you want to know where the fish are biting in Alabama, you can phone the Bureau of Publicity free, by dialing a Watts line (1-800-633-5761).

Where to Hunt

Alabama is the only state where a hunter may take a buck a day. The state boasts a deer herd of 500,000 scattered all over the 67 counties. However, Alabama also has fine dove, quail, rabbit, and squirrel gunning and its wild turkey flock exceeds 300,000 birds. Good duck hunting is found along the Mobile Delta, while the Tennessee Valley has some fine Canada goose and duck shooting.

The deer season generally starts in mid-October for archers, who can take deer of either sex. For the gun hunter, the season starts in mid-November and lasts until early January. Gun hunters are restricted to bucks only. Much of the best deer hunting is on private land, frequently under lease to hunting clubs. For non-residents without contacts, there are a number of public hunting areas. Good areas are Coosa, Black Warrior, Cahaba, Covington, and Demopolis but Choccolocco near Anniston, and Hollins near Talladega-Goodwater are regarded as even better bets by the state game authorities. The latter two areas have fairly heavy hunting pressure.

In a number of southern Alabama counties, tom turkeys are legal game. There are both spring and fall seasons. March 20 is usually the opening date for the spring season, when the harvest of gobblers approaches the 30,000 mark. The fall turkey season opens mid-November and runs for two months.

Quail, doves, rabbits, and squirrels are scattered throughout the state in suitable habitats. The best of the quail hunting is again on private plantations, some of which cater to hunters on a package-deal basis. For hound-dog music fans, raccoons, foxes, and opossums are fairly abundant.

The licence costs in Alabama are reasonable. A non-resident all-game licence costs $25.15; small game only is $10.15; a 7-day all game is $10.15; and a 7-day small game, $7.15. A special licence at $3.15 is needed to hunt deer and turkey in the public management areas.

Smallmouth Bass

9

ALASKA

Alaska Department of Fish and Game
Department A
Subport Building
Juneau, Alaska 99801

Where to Fish

The 49th state is one of the last frontiers of unexploited fishing on this continent. Alaska is blessed with over twelve million acres of water surface. Trout and salmon are the main quarry. Of the salmon, the huge king or chinook salmon and the coho provide most of the action. Among the trout, the angler has a choice of rainbow or steelhead, cutthroat, Dolly Varden, or lake trout. As one would expect, Alaska also has fine arctic char and arctic grayling fishing. The crown for the most elusive fish in the Alaskan waters must go to the inconnu or sheefish, a huge and savage member of the whitefish family.

The rainbow trout is the most sought-after fish in Alaska. The best rainbow trout waters, according to the Board of Fish and Game, are Lower Talarik Creek, the Gibraltar River and Gibraltar Lake, the Iliamna River, the Kulik River, the Kvichak River from Lake Iliamna to the Kaskanak Flats, the Newhalen River, and the Alagnak or Branch River. A stretch of the Nyakuk River from the outlet at Tikchik Lake downriver for a few miles is also good. The Copper River from its mouth to the falls has a fine fishing reputation.

These rivers are designated as "trophy trout" waters, and the fish certainly run big — 12 to 18-pound rainbows are common. Special creel limits are in force here. An angler may keep only five rainbows, only one of which may be over 20 inches. This restriction is designed to protect the big breeding fish.

Alaska has many other streams with fine steelhead fishing. Many of the streams also have Dolly Varden as an added bonus. Some have arctic char and cutthroat trout. Most of Alaska's lakes also have lake trout. For trophy grayling fishing, the waters in the Ugashik area are the best.

Most of Alaska's top fishing waters lie in wilderness areas. Flying in with pontoon-equipped aircraft is the only way to reach them. Most have no accommodation, so anglers have to camp out. Air-taxi services are available in most Alaskan centers. Lake Hood in Anchorage is an example of a big seaplane base. Dillingham and King Salmon are others. These centers can be reached by commercial flights.

The favorite tackle of Alaskan anglers is medium spinning outfits and No. 8 or No. 9 flyrods. The spinning lures should be in the ⅝-ounce class. The fly selection should include large flies in streamer patterns and bucktails in fluores-

---

The mountain country of Alaska, British Columbia, and the Yukon offers outstanding big-game hunting for such species as sheep, mountain goats, caribou and, of course, the lordly moose.

cent colors. Peacock patterns in brown and grizzly are also often used. Sinking lines and lines with sinking tips are a must. The leaders should be strong — 8 to 12-pound test. For grayling, small dark patterns such as Nos. 10 and 12 Black Gnat are the best. Grayling can also be taken on tiny spinners.

The best fishing months in Alaska are June, late August, and September.

Where to Hunt

To a hunter, Alaska means big game. The two are synonymous and for good reason. The 49th state offers some of the finest big-game hunting on the continent.

Moose and caribou are Alaska's most widely distributed and most abundant big-game animals. The best moose herds exist in the Anchorage and Fairbanks regions and the Sustina Valley. Caribou are found over most of Alaska, including the Alaska Peninsula. It would be difficult for a guided non-resident hunter after a general bag not to get a caribou or moose.

Alaska's best Dall-sheep country lies in the Wrangell Mountains and in portions of the Alaska range with top trophy heads in the Chugach Mountains and Brooks Range. The best mountain-goat range lies in the upper slopes of the Chugach, Wrangell, and Talkeetna Mountains.

Bears are Alaska's other outstanding trophies. Now that the polar bear is completely protected, the big brown is the top bear trophy. The Alaska Panhandle is a good area for these giant bruins, but the Alaska Peninsula is perhaps even better. Grizzlies occur throughout the mountain regions of the state. A hunter could run into a record-book grizzly just about anywhere. Black bear are very widely distributed in the 49th state, particularly along the coast.

Not many hunters know that Alaska also has some fine elk and deer hunting. The elk herd on Afogank and Raspberry Islands is in good shape. The deer hunting in southeastern Alaska for the Sitka blacktails is outstanding in some local areas. Alaska also has a limited bison hunt in the Big Delta area. Walrus and muskox are the other two big-game animals but both are protected. However, there is a distinct possibility that a limited muskox season will be held in the future in areas where these shaggy bovines are over-grazing their winter range.

One of Alaska's top big-game trophies is one that has not received much recognition — the wolf. This is unfortunate. To bag a wolf in a fair chase is a feat of no small stature.

Alaska also offers some outstanding small-game hunting. Its waterfowling rivals that of the Canadian prairies. Outstanding goose hunting can be had at Yakutat and Cold Bay, as well as in most of the Alaska Peninsula. The Alaska Peninsula also has fine duck hunting, as does Susita Flat near Anchorage. The best brant shooting in Alaska is near Port Heiden.

Ruffed, spruce, blue, and sharp-tailed grouse are all found in Alaska but are in the "fool-hen" category and make poor shotgunning. A handgun or a rifle is a more sporting way to take these birds. The limits are generous, 15 birds per day. Ptarmigan — willow, rock, and white-tailed — are also found in Alaska and, during the high cycle years, hunting for these Arctic grouse is very popular. The limits are also very generous — 20 birds per day. Snowshoe hare is Alaska's chief small-game mammal and in many areas there is no bag limit.

Alaska's game is managed in area units, with the seasons and sometimes the bag limits, varying from unit to unit. The big-game season is in early fall with caribou and deer as early as August 1, followed closely by the goat season, then sheep and moose. Bear seasons open on September 1 and stay open until June of the following year. Seasons on wolves, coyotes, and wolverines open on September 1 and close at the end of April. Usually the upland game-bird seasons open in early August and stay open until the end of April the following year. The snowshoe-hare season is usually open the year around, while migratory birds, governed by federal laws, generally have a season from early September until freeze-up.

At the time of writing, non-resident hunting licences cost $20. Big-game tags for brown or grizzly bear and sheep are $50; bison and moose, $100; black bear, elk and goat, $75; caribou and wolf, $50; deer and wolverine, $25. Non-resident hunters must be accompanied by a guide when hunting sheep and brown and grizzly bears.

ARIZONA

Arizona Game and Fish Department
Department F, 2222 West Greenway Road
Phoenix, Arizona 85023

Where to Fish

Arizona is rarely thought of as fishing country, but it is. The large impoundments in the arid regions of Arizona have outstanding bass fishing, while many of the mountain streams have very fine trout and even grayling fishing.

San Carlos Lake near Globe and Roosevelt Lake in the Salt River chain are two of the top largemouth bass waters in the state. The best fishing is from March to June and again in the late fall from October to December. The fish generally run 2 to 4 pounds, but bigger lunkers are landed frequently. The biggest bass are taken by busting the brush on the bottom.

Striped bass have been introduced into the Colorado River. The top striper hotspot is from the Davis Dam down to Lake Havsu City. Night fishing is generally the best. Minnow-action lures are the favorite baits.

Arizona also has some fine smallmouth bass fishing in streams across the mid-section of the state. The Black River between the San Carlos Indian Reservation and Fort Apache is excellent for smallmouth. Many stretches of this picturesque stream are for backpackers only. The angler has to descend 600 feet into a canyon. Medium-sized spinners and streamers such as Mickey Finn and Supervisor are the favorites.

The White Mountain area is the center of Arizona's trout fishing. It has many fine trout streams and excellent trout lakes, including Big and Crescent, just below Baldy Peak. The lakes have rainbows, brookies, and grayling. Late spring and early fall are the best times. For detailed trout fishing information in this area, write to White Mountain Apache Enterprise, Whiteriver, Arizona 85941.

The Mongolon River country also has some fine trout waters. Chevelon Creek below the rim has good rainbow and brown-trout fishing. Again this is a back-packing proposition. Two other good streams are Cibecue Creek in the Fort Apache Indian Reservation and Canyon Creek in the Tanto Forest reaches. Occasionally the browns in the Cibecue run up to 6 pounds.

Another fine trout lake is Wheatfields on the Navajo Indian Reservation. The lake is not particularly well known, but it produces fine fishing for rainbows and cutthroats of up to 3 or 4 pounds. Ashurst Lake, in the Coconino Plateau about 20 miles south of Flagstaff, is another fine rainbow trout lake. Another good bet is Long Lake, also in the Coconino Plateau.

Arizona's biggest trout come from Willow Beach, a 12-mile stretch of water between Hoover Dam and Willow Beach Marina on the Colorado River. Clear water and beautiful vistas are the trademarks of this part of the Colorado, but the action comes from the big rainbows. The local record is 21 pounds, and fish in the 4 or 5-pound class do not really attract too many second looks. The best time to fish here is in the winter or spring.

For an angler who prefers a mixed bag, the best water is Lake Powell on the Utah line. Largemouth bass, walleyes, and rainbow trout provide action here, with the added bonus of beautiful scenery. Another good bet for a mixed bag is the lower Colorado River near Yuma. The backwaters of the Imperial Dam back up some 20 miles into the arid countryside of southwest Arizona. This water produces fine catches of largemouth bass plus assorted panfish such as bluegills, warmouth, and black crappies. But this stretch of the Colorado is probably best known for its catfish. Flatheads of up to 30 pounds are caught every year, and the state record of 41 pounds 12 ounces came from here. However, the best-eating catfish are the 4 to 8-pounders, and these are very common.

Where to Hunt

Hunters new to the dry Arizona countryside are surprised at the variety of game that this seemingly barren country produces. The principal upland game birds are: three species of quail, two species of doves, wild turkey, and band-tailed pigeons. The drought of recent years has been hard on Gambel's quail but birds can be found in fair numbers around irrigated areas and water courses leading into desert reservoirs. The valley of the Gila River, southwest of Phoenix, is good. The best scaled-quail gunning is found in the grassy plains and rolling highlands near Arivaca and in the farming belt south of Klondyke and Fort Grant. The beautiful Mearn's quail are found in the grass country south of Tucson, with Patagonia, Sonoita, San Rafael Valley, and Garder Canyon repu-ted as being very good.

The season for Gambel's and scaled quail generally begins in early October, with Mearn's quail opening in early December. The season on all three species runs until the end of January. Incidentally, a good dog is needed for the tight-holding Mearn's.

Undoubtedly doves offer the fastest upland gunning in Arizona. The season starts in September with the attractive white-winged dove being the main quarry. By the end of the month, the whitewing migrates south to Mexico. In the December dove season, the mourning dove is the quarry.

The best places for doves are in farming country, particularly if it is well irrigated. Maricopa, Picacho, Gila Bend, Buckey, and the area between Yuma and Parker all offer fine gunning. The dove's close relative, the band-tailed pigeon, is found in the high country in oak stands. The best turkey country in Arizona is in the South Kaibab, North Kaibab, and White Mountains.

Irrigation projects, stock ponds, and the major rivers in Arizona also provide some fine waterfowling. Waterholes south of Flagstaff, White Mountains, Cholla Lake near Winslow, and the Colorado River Valley are good bets during the early season. The Colorado River also has fairly good goose hunting. When the northern mallards, pintails, canvasbacks, and redheads come down in December, the best gunning is found in the desert waterholes.

There is also a fine selection of big game in Arizona. The most numerous animal is the mule deer. Good deer country is Kaibab Forest, with the season running into late November, but Black Rock Mountain and Mount Turnbull are even better. Hidden Rim and Grand Wash Cliffs, also in the Arizona Strip country, are good too. The general season, bucks only, runs from late October and early November.

The diminutive Coves whitetails are found in southeastern Arizona and east of Nogales. Good whitetail country also lies in Greenlee County and areas around Tombstone and the Fort Huachuca Military Base. The Baboquivari Mountains are also reputed to be good.

Arizona has a stable but not particularly large elk herd. A top place to get a bull is the Fort Apache Indian Reservation. A special $100 permit is needed. The Flagstaff-White Mountain areas are also good. The seasons vary in the various management units, with open season coming in late September in time for bugling.

The pronghorn herd in Arizona is restricted, but the Chino Valley, north of Prescott, is a fine bet. The open plains north of Flagstaff and north of the White Mountains also offer good possibilities.

Javelina, the little desert pig, is probably Arizona's most unusual big game. The late February season is short and by special permit only. The Nogales and Baboquivaris areas are good. The Pinal Mountains and the Chiricuahua foothills are also highly regarded, but probably the best place to bag a desert pig is on the San Carlos Indian Reservation.

Aside from varmints such as coyotes, foxes, and bobcats, Arizona has two other big-game mammals — black bear and cougar. The best bear hunting is on the Fort Apache Reservation, while the best mountain-lion country lies in the

Prescott Ranchlands. Hound packs are needed for the cougars. There are guides specializing in cat hunts in Arizona.

Without a doubt Arizona's top big-game trophy is the desert bighorn. Of course the limited open season is by special-draw permit and your chances of getting one, particularly if you are a non-resident, are very low. If you do get a permit, your chances of bagging a trophy ram are excellent. The desert mountains are the best places to hunt for the sheep. Guides specializing in sheep hunts are available.

A non-resident hunting licence costs $30 with tags for bighorn sheep being $250; elk, $75; antelope, $50; black bear, $25; javelina, $20; turkey and cougar, $10; deer, $4.

ARKANSAS

Hunting and Fishing Information
Arkansas Game and Fish Commission
Little Rock, Arkansas 72201

Where to Fish

The Ozark country of Arkansas has some of the best fishing waters in the mid-south. Fishingwise, Arkansas is a mixed-creel state. Bass, panfish, and catfish are the most sought-after species; but rainbow trout, trophy browns, and walleyes add glamor to the fishing scene.

Most of Arkansas's lakes are man-made impoundements on big rivers. Bull Shoals is probably the best known of these. It is a picturesque lake with high bluffs, wooded shores, and rocky beaches. But it is the lunker largemouth bass that attract the anglers. A fair number of 7 to 8-pound bass are caught here every season. The lake record is 14 pounds.

Aside from largemouths, Bull Shoals has smallmouth bass, crappies, and white bass. The white bass run in March and bring fishermen by the droves. Fall and spring are the best times for largemouths.

Lake Norfork is another good fishing lake. It boasts the same species as Bull Shoals. Norfork has over 20 public usage areas for fishing and boat launching. Other good bass lakes are Beaver Reservoir near Fayetteville and Greer's Ferry near Herber Springs. Nimrod Reservoir is well known for its excellent crappie fishing.

In recent years one of the most productive lakes in the state has been Millwood in southwestern Arkansas. Sections of this lake are heavily wooded, and that is where the bass and crappies congregate. Also Lake Dardanella has been producing top catches.

River float-trips after trout or smallmouth bass are one of Arkansas's angling trademarks. White River below Bull Shoals Dam is the best stream for a float-trip after rainbows. The towns of Bull Shoals, Flippin, Mountain Home, and Cotter have guides and outfitters who specialize in such trips.

Many of the smaller trout streams in the state are not suitable for float fishing and camping overnight, and some are too small for any boat. Here are some of the better trout streams in the state: the Norfork River from the dam to White River; the Little Missouri below Narrows Dam; the Spring River below Mammoth Spring; and the Little Red below Greer's Dam.

Many of the Arkansas rivers are too warm for trout. But they do have many scrappy smallmouths. Although trout are the glamor fish of Arkansas's rivers, it is the smallmouth bass that are the most widely distributed. The scrappy smallmouth is found in all the Ozark watersheds. Some of the best bass rivers are the Eleven Point, the Strawberry, the Caddo, the Black, the King, the War Eagle, the Saline, the Cossatot, and the Current and Ouachita.

One of the best-known smallmouth streams is the Buffalo, but state experts do not consider it the most productive. A couple of the best, but little known smallmouth rivers are the Crooked Creek which flows from Harrison to Yellville and the Mullberry.

Of course Arkansas also offers excellent panfish and catfish angling. One of the more interesting and offbeat species of fish is the giant alligator gar. This fish occurs in muddy, slow-moving rivers such as the Red River near Texarkana, the lower Ouachita, and the Arkansas; but the best one is the lower White. The best gear for gar is saltwater tackle with large fish such as dead suckers for bait. The gar can weigh up to 300 pounds, but 100-pounders are more common.

Aside from the state Game and Fish Commission; the Parks, Recreation and Travel Commission, State Capital, Little Rock, Arkansas 72201, is a good source of additional fishing and camping information.

Where to Hunt

Arkansas is a deer, duck, and other small-game state. The best whitetail range lies in the southern and southwestern part of the state, but the deer there tend to be on the small side. The place to bag a big buck is northwest and north-central Arkansas. Most of the deer hunting is on private land but the land held by the big paper companies is generally open to hunting. The public hunting areas of Piney Creek, Muddy Creek, Shirley Bay, and Cut-Off Creek all have whitetails as well. The split seasons vary with about a week in mid-November and then again a week in mid-December. Archery seasons start October 1 with a primitive-weapons hunt about two weeks later.

The wild turkey has made a strong comeback in all suitable habitat throughout the state. The Ozarks and Ouachita Mountains south to the Arkansas River are the top places for gobbler hunting. The spring season runs for about three weeks in April while the fall season runs for the same time in October. Arkansas is still a fine duck state, but the draining of marshes and other wetlands for agriculture has reduced the number of ducks. The duck gunning in the flooded timber between Little Rock and White River in the east-central part of the state is outstanding. Waterfowl management areas of Bayou Meto, Wattensaw, Dagmar, and Hurricane Lake are well known for their mallard concentrations. Rivers and creeks throughout the state also have good duck shooting for mallards and woodies. Most of Arkansas is in the Mississippi flyway. There are a number of duck-hunting guides operating in the state.

Dove is the other important migratory-game species. The birds are spread out over the farming areas, particularly where combines leave grain scattered on the fields. Petit Jean, Hope, and Fort Chaffee Game Management Areas have good dove shooting. The river bottoms of the White and Arkansas Rivers are well worth trying.

Quail, cottontail, and squirrel hunting has its ups and downs but it is generally good in areas with good cover. The abandoned farms in the rolling Ozark uplands are a good bet for bobwhites, as are some of the cut-over forest lands owned by the paper companies in the southern part of the state. The hunting on these cut-overs is hard because of the thick cover. Cottontails are found in similar cover. The bobwhite season runs from early December to mid-February, while the rabbit season runs from early October to mid-February. The limit on both species is eight per day. The best squirrel hunting is in the hickory and oak stands in the Ozark and Ouachitas Mountains. The season runs from early October to the end of January.

A non-resident licence costs $20, with tags for wild turkey and deer being $10.

CALIFORNIA

Conservation Program Officer
California Department of Fish and Game
1416 Ninth Street
Sacramento, California 95814

Where to Fish

California offers tremendous variety for the fisherman. Its 1000 miles of coastline offer excellent saltwater fishing opportunities. Its mountain country has clear-flowing trout streams. The salmon and steelhead runs are strong in many of the rivers in the northern half of the state. And as if this were not enough, there are many lakes and rivers with fine fishing for warm-water species such as bass. There is little doubt that California will break the record for largemouth bass soon.

Fort Bragg is a small port with tremendous fishing for king salmon during late May to early August and then for coho in the late summer and early fall. The winter saltwater fishing here is mostly for ground fish. Other fishing centers are Humboldt Bay, Trinidad Head, and Crescent City. Salmon with bottom fish provide most of the action. The Klamath River is well known for its salmon run, attracting thousands of anglers.

The area around Capitola, Princeton, and Santa Cruz is known for its albacore, salmon, and rockfish. Striped bass also provide hot action in the summer, with a peak run in August.

San Francisco Bay is the top striped-bass area of California. The stripers arrive in the Bay in April, but the best fishing is in the summer. Salmon also produce action. The tasty halibut is another sought-after fish.

Monterey Bay must be one of the most scenic fishing ports in California. But besides scenery, it boasts outstanding ground-fish angling for such species as snappers and cod. Morro Bay is another top saltwater-fishing area. Good albacore fishing lies to the south, and good salmon fishing to the north.

The Channel Islands area is another hotspot. The variety of ground fish is tremendous. This is largely because of the rocky habitat found on the ocean bottom here. One of the favorite local fishing sports is jigging for grouper with fresh bait. This is deep fishing — and I mean deep — 500 to 700 feet down.

Albacore, yellowtail, and marlin migrate through the Channel Islands area during proper seasons. Yellowtails come first in mid-spring. They are followed by bass, bonito, and barracuda. The albacore come through in July and August. They are the glamor fish of the area and attract many anglers. The big-game buffs have to wait until September and October when the striped marlin come through.

Southern California also has much sizzling saltwater action. In the San Diego area are the Coronado Islands. Actually they lie in Mexican waters, but are within easy reach of San Diego boats. Yellowtail fishing is superb here. And in late winter, white sea bass provide hot action. Later in the season, albacore get most of the play, plus such exotics as yellowfin and bluefin tuna.

Another good fishing area is Santa Monica Bay. During the winter months sand bass, halibut, white sea bass, barracuda, yellowtail, and bonito provide most of the action. One local hotspot for big bonito is around Rocky Point. And in the fall, good runs of bluefin tuna do come in at times. The fish run a good size — 20 to 35 pounds.

Most of the long-range fishing is done out of San Diego. Trips of up to two weeks down the Baja coast and even into the Sea of Cortez are common. Charter boats and party boats are available in all of the areas and ports mentioned.

California also boasts some excellent freshwater fishing. Seven species of trout can be caught in California streams and lakes. Bighorn Lake in Fresno County is a good bet for the beautiful golden trout. The eastern brook trout is found in many of the alpine lakes and mountain rills. Lakes Tahoe and Donner have lake trout. Donner Lake also has kokanee salmon. One of the top rainbow waters in California is the stretches of the Sacramento River in Shasta County. But steelhead are found in most of the rivers draining into the Pacific north of San Luis Abispo County. Certainly Klamath River steelheads are legendary. The run begins in late August, but September and October are better.

Warm-water panfish are abundant in many California rivers and lakes. The main panfish species are bluegills, black crappies, and yellow perch. White catfish are popular sport fish in the San Joaquin Delta. Channel cats are found in the Colorado River.

However, bass are California's top warm-water fish. Smallmouths are found in a number of streams, with the Russian River being considered the best. Spotted bass are also found in a number of streams. Cosumnes is the best one.

Largemouth bass occur throughout much of the state. The San Diego area has two top bass lakes — Miramar and Murray. Not much farther away are San Vincente and El Capitan Reservoirs. Other top waters are the Lower Otay Reservoir, Lake Sutherland, Lake Henshaw, Vail Lake, Lake Wohlford, Comanche Lake, and Clear Lake. In most of these lakes, 10-pound largemouths are not regarded as particularly noteworthy fish.

Shad is another popular sport fish in many California rivers. When the shad run is in from the ocean, word among fishermen spreads like wildfire. The Yuba River is one hotspot. The fish even go up as far as the Feather River. Generally the run begins in late May, but the peak occurs in mid-June.

Where to Hunt

California, with its wide range of habitats, offers a wide variety of game. You can hunt everything from bandtailed pigeon to wild pig in California. Deer — mule deer and blacktails — are California's primary big game. The seasons vary from region to region, and even from county to county in some instances. In some areas the season starts in early August and, for bow hunters, even in early July. The limits in some areas are two bucks per season. The best areas are the west side of the state down into Santa Barbara County in the early season, while the eastern half of the state into Fresno County is the best bet in the late season. California also has a week-long antelope season but it is restricted to residents only.

Wild pig can be hunted in the southwestern part of the state below Monterey and in the northwest, Santa Rosa, and Eureka. There is no limit and no closed season on the porkers — they are regarded as an agricultural menace.

Bear hunting in California is confined to the forested northern half of the state. Trinity and Siskiyou Counties are the best for bagging a California bruin. The limit is one adult bear per year. Cubs and sows with cubs are fully protected. Aside from black bear, cougar is the other big-game carnivore.

Small game is quite abundant in many parts of California. Some fine waterfowl gunning, with liberal seasons, is found in the state. Most of the major valleys have good shooting near water. The Sacramento Valley is the best. Doves are also numerous in California.

All three species of quail — mountain, desert, and California — are popular game birds. The seasons vary but in some areas open in late September. Marin, Napa Solamo, Lassen, Modoc Humboldt, and Del Norte Counties are all good but Mendicino and Lake Counties are reputed to be the best. The limits vary from six to ten birds per day.

Chukar partridge has caught on quite well in the dry mountain terrain of California. Seasons also vary, but generally start in late October. The limit is four birds per day. Modoc and Lassen Counties are the best bet, with the area between Honey Lake and Madeline in Lassen County being tops.

Wild turkey has also made a strong comeback in California. A fall season of a week or so in late November is held in Colusa, Lassen, Nevada, Santa Barbara, Yuba, Monterey, Trinity, Shasta, and parts of other counties. Some of these counties also have a spring season for gobblers from late April to early May. One bearded turkey per season is the limit then. The fall season is open for two weeks in mid-November.

Rabbits and tree squirrels are found over most of the state with suitable habitat. The rabbits consist of cottontail, brush, and pygmy species, as well as jackrabbits. There is no closed season or limit on jacks but the others have seasons through most of the fall and winter with limits of five per day. The southwest coastal region of the state is the best rabbit country. Tree-squirrel seasons are similar to those on rabbits but the limit is generally four per day. The forested northwest part of the state is the best squirrel country.

A non-resident hunting licence costs $35, with a deer tag at $25, a bear tag at $1, a pheasant stamp at $2, and a state duck stamp at $1.

COLORADO

Information and Education Office
Colorado Game, Fish, and Parks Division
6060 Broadway
Denver, Colorado 80216

Where to Fish

Fishing in Colorado generally means trout. The state has thousands of miles of trout streams and over 2000 lakes. The Grand Mesa country of Colorado is long on striking scenery, good campsites, and fine fishing. The best streams and lakes in this area can be reached only on horseback or shanks' mare. However, there are some accessible lakes with good fishing, such as Weir, Johnson, Alexander, Island, Carp, and Eggleston. Some of the better streams are Ward, Leroux, and Surface. Summer comes late at high altitudes. The best time to fish here is during July and August. For detailed fishing information on this area, write to Grand Mesa National Forest Headquarters, Delta, Colorado.

One of the most noteworthy lakes in Colorado is Trappers Lake in the Flat Top primitive area of the White Mountain National Forest. This is probably the best cutthroat lake in Colorado. The lake has a 10-inch limit, and no live or fresh bait can be used — only artificials.

There are other lakes and streams in the White Mountain with excellent fishing for brook trout, cutthroat, and lake trout. Other good lakes in Colorado are Grandby, which has kokanee salmon and trout; and Twin Lakes near Leadville which has big lake trout.

Several of the reservoir lakes in the state have fine trout fishing. Steamboat Lake, north of Steamboat Springs, produces fine rainbow trout fishing in its 1000 acres. Miramonte Reservoir, south of Norwood; Echo Canyon Reservoir, south of Pagosa Springs; and Ruedi Reservoir, east of Basalt; all have fine trout fishing.

One of the top rainbow and brown trout streams on the eastern slope is the

Cache la Poudre River in the Roosevelt National Forest. Another good stream is the South Platte. It is also a brown and rainbow water on which some reaches are restricted to fly and lure fishing. The South Platte is easily accessible below the Cheesman Reservoir.

The western slope also has some fine trout streams such as the Yampa, the White, the Eagle, the Gunnison, and the Rio Grande. However, the best known trout stream on the western side of the Divide is Roaring Fork. This may well be the finest rainbow and brown trout water in Colorado. The stretch around the ski resort of Aspen is reserved for fly fishing only.

Trout completely overshadow warm-water fish species in Colorado. The best bet for largemouth bass, white bass, panfish, and catfish is Sterling Reservoir in eastern Colorado. This lake is also the best walleye water in the state.

Where to Hunt

Elk and deer are Colorado's two principal big-game animals. The elk season runs from late October to mid-November. In some areas cow elk can be taken on a special permit, but other areas are open only for bulls with a rack of four points or better. The best elk areas in the state are the Grand Mesa, east of Grand Junction, the Rio Grande and San Juan National Forests in southwest Colorado, the high plateaus along the White River Plateau north of Glenwood Springs, Piceance Basin west of Meeker, and the area from Del Norte to Durango.

The deer season takes place in mid-October and generally it is bucks only. Some of the best mule-deer hunting is found in the areas recommended for elk but the deer usually are found at lower elevations than elk. The best areas for mule deer are the Piceance Basin and the Uncompahgre Plateau west of Montrose.

Colorado has a very limited bighorn-sheep hunt on draw-permit system and a limited antelope hunt. The big-horn hunt is generally restricted to residents only. The antelope season opens for about a week in late August. The hunter's success for pronghorns is high. The best areas are the rolling plains in eastern Colorado and around the South Park area, near Fairplay in central Colorado.

The other two big-game mammals are black bear and mountain lion. The bear and cougar season is open during the deer and elk season, but there is also a spring season which begins on February 1 for cougar and on April 1 for bear. Cougar and bear are found throughout the wilderness areas of the state but neither are particularly abundant.

Although most hunters tend to think of Colorado as big-game country, the state also offers some fine shotgunning. The duck season opens in mid-October and runs to mid-January. Colorado uses the point system for bag limits with mallard hens and the rarer waterfowl species receiving the most protection. The goose season opens in early November and closes with the duck season.

The best areas for ducks are in the northeastern plains along the South Platte River and in the San Louis Valley of southern Colorado, while the best Canada goose hunting lies in southeast Colorado in the Arkansas River Valley near

Tamar and Eads. The area around Fort Collins is also fine goose country. All the better spots are under season-long leases, but some of the landowners do lease pits on a daily basis.

Pheasant, chukar, blue grouse, sage grouse, quail, and dove are also hunted. The white-tailed ptarmigan is the state's most unusual game bird. It is found in the high mountain peaks. The pheasant season usually begins on the third Saturday in November, with the best area being in the plains country in northeastern Colorado. The sage and sharptail-grouse season begins in early September and stays open for two or three days. The sage and blue grouse are found in the rolling sagebrush hills and timbered slopes respectively, in the northwest part of the state. Dove gunning is scattered throughout the state, as is rabbit hunting.

For non-residents Colorado offers a package licence which includes all big game, except pronghorn and bighorn, plus small game and fishing for $135. A small-game licence costs $15 for non-residents. Big-game licences can be purchased separately, with elk costing $75, while deer, antelope, and cougar cost $50, and bear $25.

CONNECTICUT

Wildlife Unit
Connecticut Department of Environmental Protection
State Office Building
Hartford, Connecticut 06109

Where to Fish

The small state of Connecticut has surprisingly good fishing. The state's biggest river, the Connecticut, has a tremendous run of shad in late May or early June. The shad run in the Connecticut is surpassed only by the run in Florida's St. Johns River. The shad run attracts anglers in hordes. The shad are very sporty fish when caught on light tackle.

Connecticut's trout fishery is largely a hatchery product. The Board of Fish and Game lists all the lakes and streams that are stocked with trout every year. Incidentally, the Board publishes a very useful pamphlet called *Access to Connecticut Fishing Waters*. The trout fishing in the early season is quite good, but the better streams tend to be crowded. Two of the top trout streams are the Housatonic River in northwestern Connecticut and the Farmington River west of Hartford. Two of the top trout lakes are Mashapaug Lake in the northeast and Wonosopomuc in the northwest. Mashapaug Lake holds the state record for brown trout — a 16-pound 4-ounce fish.

Another salmonid found in the state is the little kokanee salmon. The kokanee has been stocked in East Twin Lake near Salisbury. The favorite way to catch these 18-inch pink-fleshed salmon is by trolling with small minnows.

Bass are the bread-and-butter game fish of Connecticut. Smallmouths and bigmouths are found throughout the state in many of the ponds and small lakes. The most famous of these is Glasgow Pond in Griswold County.

There are a number of mixed-creel lakes in the Nutmeg State. Candlewood

Lake near the New York State border has rainbows, largemouth bass, and a variety of panfish, such as white and yellow perch and bluegills. Panfish and bass are abundant. The earlier mentioned Mashapaug Lake also has largemouth and smallmouth bass. Indeed, the state records for both fish come from this lake. The Timble Islands off Stony Creek are another hotspot. When blues and stripers are on a feeding binge, the action can be hot.

For a mixed bag, the Niantic Bay is a good bet. Almost all species of fish found in Long Island Sound waters can be caught here. The catch can be anything from flounder to squeteague.

Connecticut's coastline also offers some fine saltwater angling action. Stripers and blues provide most of the fishing. The Thames River offers good striper action in April. The power station at Monetville is one local hotspot. Out in open water, the Norwalk Islands are a good place for blues and stripers. The Stratford Shoals off Stratford are another. Bartlett's Reef near New London is an excellent area also.

Charter boats can be hired in all the ports. In some ports, big party boats operate daily. New London is the main charter-boat base.

Largemouth Bass

Where to Hunt

Connecticut is a small-game state. Waterfowl hunting is quite good because the state has three major river valleys, many small inland marshes, and an uneven coastline. Most of the better shooting spots are on private land but the state has several special waterfowl Game Management Areas. The island off Norwalk, Great Island on the Connecticut River, and the marsh behind Selden Neck are three top spots.

Upland game-bird shooting offers pheasants, principally a put-and-take situation, plus bobwhites, ruffed grouse, and woodcock. Good pheasant covers are Salmon River and Day Pond State Parks. A top woodcock cover is the southern portion of the Pachaug State Forest. Ruffed grouse are scattered throughout the state in all suitable cover while quail are restricted to the coastal areas which are free of heavy snowfalls. Squirrels and rabbits are also scattered throughout the state in suitable cover. The bushytails generally go underharvested.

Connecticut, surprisingly, has a fair deer herd, but only landowners can hunt the animals on their lands. There are a couple of exceptions: a farmer can give a permit to hunt deer on his land to up to five people during the November-December season and bow hunters can hunt on all state lands during the December season. The bow licence costs $5.35 in addition to the regular hunting licence, which for non-residents costs $13.35.

DELAWARE

Delaware Board of Game and Fish Commissioners
Dover, Delaware 19901

Where to Fish

Delaware is basically a saltwater fishing state. Its undulating coastline creates a fine habitat for many species of marine fish. But Delaware also has fine freshwater fishing. Trout fishing is largely a put-and-take proposition. Brandywine Creek is one of the best trout streams in the state. One of the local hotspots on this river is below the dam at Alapocas Woods. Other trout streams are White, Clay, Mill, and Pike Creeks.

There are a number of small lakes and ponds in Delaware with excellent largemouth bass, panfish, and chain pickerel populations. Lake Como near Smyrna is one of the top lakes for bass, pickerel, yellow perch, crappies, and bluegills. Others are Lumis Pond, Becks Pond, and Silver Lake. Primehook Marsh is regarded by many as the top pickerel water in the state. All these waters have public access. The only other noteworthy freshwater fishing action is in the Delaware River during the shad run.

Outstanding saltwater fishing is found along the coast from Cape Henlopen south to Fenwick Island. Warm water from the south and cold water from the north overlap here, bringing with them both cold and warm-water fish species.

Inshore party boats have a long season for sea trout, cobia, fluke, perch, snappers, and striped bass. Headboats also have good fishing for ground fish. Striped bass probably have the biggest following in Delaware. They can be taken by surfcasters in several areas. The entrance to Delaware Bay is good. The locally favored spots are Indian River Inlet, Rehoboth Bay, and the Lewes area. Boat casters can take stripers anywhere in Delaware Bay.

Boats, both party and charter, are available at Indian River Inlet, Mispillion Lighthouse, and Bowers Beach. There are a number of boat-launching sites in the main fishing areas. Marinas in these areas also have small boats and outboards for rent. There are even public camping parks in many of these places, where anglers can park their trailers or pitch their tents.

Migrating game fish such as striped bass, white marlin, bluefish, bluefin tuna, albacore, bonitos, and others pass by the Delaware coast. The tuna and billfish require a run of 30 miles or more offshore. In the winter months, cod provide most of the action. Indian River Inlet is the local hotspot. As the cod fishing peters out in April, Atlantic mackerel start their run which lasts four or five weeks. Diamond jigs are the best bait for these fish.

Towards spring weakfish start to run. There is also a fall run of these fine sportfish. In the spring tautog also start to bite around the sea jetties. Bluefish arrive in May and stay in Delaware waters until fall. May is also a good time for big black drum. The drum can grow to a good size, up to 80 pounds.

Yellow Perch

Where to Hunt

Shotgunners do not lack hunting opportunities in Delaware. As one would expect, the Chesapeake Bay coastline offers some fine waterfowling. The southwest tidewater and the Delaware Bay areas are two fine duck hunting spots. Delaware also has some of the finest Canada goose hunting in the United States. The big corn fields attract and hold the honkers. Areas near Bombay Hook Refuge and Nanticoke Wildlife Area are a good bet — so are corn stubbles near the Maryland border close to Blackwater and Remington Farms refuges.

Sea ducks and scaup are overlooked by most hunters. The best places for sea ducks and scaup are in the coastal waters south of the Chesapeake and Delaware Canal.

Delaware also offers some fine marsh-bird gunning. Rail hunting is excellent and these long-legged birds are rarely hunted. The same is true of gallinules and coots — by coots I mean 'marsh hens', not sea ducks. Parts of the coastal tidewater offer very fine snipe gunning for those tough enough to slug through the mud. Not many hunters venture after snipe.

Upland game-bird shooting means quail, ringnecks, dove, and woodcock. Bobwhites are found over much of the state, but Kent and Sussex Counties with their big soybean and corn fields are the best bet by far. The quail season runs from late November to the end of February. The limit is eight bobwhites per day. Pheasants are fairly well restricted north of the Chesapeake and Delaware Canal.

Woodcock pass through Delaware on their way south. A hunter who times the flight well can have some very fine hunting. Woodlands near the coast are the best places for these relatives of the snipe. The most popular game bird in terms of birds bagged is the dove. These birds are found throughout the state, especially in the corn and grain farming areas.

Delaware also has some fine rabbit covers and squirrel woods. The bunny season runs from about Thanksgiving to the end of January. The best area for rabbits is Kent and Sussex Counties. With its marshes and corn fields, Delaware has a high population of raccoon and opossum for the hound men.

White-tailed deer are the only big game in the state. Although the deer herd is not large, it is thriving. The animals, being well fed on grain and corn, are big. Kent County has the best deer hunting in the state. The limit is one deer per season. Only shotguns, bows, and primitive (muzzle-loading) weapons are allowed.

For a tiny state, Delaware has a fair number of public hunting areas, including some for waterfowl only. The non-resident hunting licence costs $25.25.

FLORIDA

Information and Education Director
Florida Game and Fresh-Water Fish Commission
Bryant Building
Tallahassee, Florida 32304

Where to Fish

Florida is a tremendous fishing state. It boasts the best bass lakes in the nation, as well as outstanding saltwater fishing, both big game and inshore.

On the north gulf coast, Panama City is one of the top locations for billfish. White and blue marlin and sails offer fine action. A run of 50 miles or more into the gulf is needed to reach the best waters. May to October is the best time for billfish. Such species as amberjack, barracuda, redfish, and king mackerel can be taken closer to shore. And a fisherman can wade the flats for tarpon and sea trout.

Destin is another center for billfish, cobia, and wahoo. Hundreds of marlin and sailfish are taken here every year. The Fort Pierce area also has a fine billfish run. Generally this run is best in December and January.

It is hard to pick out the best tarpon water in Florida, but certainly Boca Grande is one of the best. Big tarpon congregate here in the summer, with June being the best month. The tarpon run big here, 100 pounds plus. The Florida Keys also have outstanding fishing. For big-game fishing, it would be hard to beat Key West in December. Dolphin, sailfish, and bonito provide most of the action. There is also good tarpon fishing in February. Marathon and Islamorada have fine bonefish angling plus tarpon and billfish. Nearly all of the Keys have good fishing on their doorstep.

On the Atlantic Ocean side, the Indian River is famed for its big sea trout. They can be caught from boats or by wading. The snook and jack crevalle fishing is also good in this area in the spring and summer months. Most of the big tourist centers such as Palm Beach, Pompano Beach, and Miami have good fishing.

Visiting anglers should investigate the fishing piers in all of the major Gold Coast centers. Most piers charge a small daily fee, but this is a lot cheaper than fishing from a boat. The fishing can be very good. Many of these piers have tackle and bait shops and even snack bars and shelters, in case of inclement weather. The fish depend on the season, but they can be anything from Spanish mackerel to groupers and snappers.

The freshwater angler can also find a lot of action in Florida. Largemouth bass is the fish. Lake Jackson near Tallahassee is one of the best bass lakes in the country. The local experts say that more 10-pound bass come out of this water than any other lake. Lake Okeechobee is another fine bass water. This lake also has outstanding crappie fishing, particularly on the north side during the winter months. February is the peak of the crappie season. Other top bass lakes are Hatchineha, Kissimmee, Tohopekaliga, and Tsala Apopka.

The Ocala National Forest has many smaller lakes that contain fine bigmouth

27

bass and panfish. The Loxahatchee Basin just west of Florida's Gold Coast is another excellent bass and panfish spot. This is a National Wildlife Refuge with several public boat-launching ramps. Fishing is allowed here from sun-up to dark.

Some of Florida's rivers also produce fine fishing action. The St. Johns River is well known for its shad run from December to April. The best shad fishing is found from Lake Monroe to Puzzle Lake. The St. Johns also has some striped bass, plus largemouths and panfish. The bass and panfish action is the hottest during winter and spring.

Another fine river is the Apalachicola with big striped bass and sturgeon. The best striper and sturgeon fishing is Woodruff Lock and Dam on the Georgia line. Largemouth bass, bream, crappie, and catfish also provide action. The Homosassa River is well known for its bass and bream fishing. Saltwater species such as tarpon and sea trout are caught in the lower reaches.

In Florida all of the best fishing areas — salt and freshwater — have ample supplies of boats for rent or charter. Bass guides operate on the big lakes. Generally Florida charter-boat captains are knowledgeable fishermen. Guides are also available for bonefish and tarpon in the top areas.

Where to Hunt

Florida is a fine hunting state, particularly for the shotgunner. Migratory birds of many species are available. Duck hunting is quite good in many areas of the state, but much of it is on private land leased to duck clubs. Some of the best areas open to the public are the Apalachee Game Management Area in Jackson County, the Aucilla Preserve, and the Everglades Game Management Area.

Dove hunting is exceptionally good. The bird is found throughout the state with the farming areas being the best. Woodcock, snipe, marsh hens, and gallinules are some of the other migratory game birds found in the state. All are little hunted.

Quail is the most popular game bird in Florida and the state boasts of top bobwhite gunning. The limits are generous — 12 birds per day. Unfortunately, much of the best bobwhite country is privately owned. However, there are places open to those who look for them. The best quail areas lie in the northern part of the state. Jackson County west of Tallahasse is another. Charlotte County on the lower west coast is also good.

Florida also boasts the second biggest turkey flock in the United States. (The top honor goes to Texas.) Good turkey-hunting areas are not hard to find and many are open to hunters who do not have an 'in'. The best place to bag a gobbler is in the Aucilla Game Management Area and in Levy and Glades Counties.

The tarpon is one of the top game fish of the world. It is found in the brackish water of the Gulf Coast and the Caribbean.

Rabbits — cottontails and marsh rabbits — plus squirrels, gray and fox, are abundant in Florida. Rabbits are so abundant that there is no closed season and no limit. Squirrels are found in the hardwood forests and the limit is 10 grays and two fox.

Big game in Florida means bear, wild hog, and deer. Bear are not numerous in Florida. There is little real wilderness left to harbor the bruin. Some 50 are bagged each year. Wild hogs are plentiful in several areas. There are a number of good places to bag a porker. Gulf and Calhoun Counties are excellent and the Gulf Hammock Game Management Area in the Glades is also a good bet.

The deer is the top big-game animal in Florida. The state has a large deer herd and allows each hunter two deer per season. Deer are found almost throughout the entire state. But the best deer-hunting country lies in Okaloosa-Walton Counties, Liberty and Wakulla Counties, Dixie and Levy Counties, Brevard and Volusia Counties near Cape Kennedy, and the Ocala National Forest in Marion County. The season for deer, wild pig, wild turkey, quail, and squirrel opens wide in early November. The closing date varies from one area to another. There is also a spring turkey season for gobblers.

Florida was one of the pioneers in setting up public game-management areas and has a network of thirty-eight. A visiting hunter should not have difficulty in finding a place to hunt.

A non-resident hunting licence is $26.50, but a 10-day licence is available for $11.50. An alien hunting licence costs $50.00.

GEORGIA

Public Relations and Information Department
Georgia Department of Natural Resources
270 Washington Street
Atlanta, Georgia 30334

Where to Fish

Georgia has an exciting variety of fish to tempt the angler. The Blue Ridge Mountains in the northern part of the state have many hundreds of miles of cool, clear trout streams for brookies, rainbows, and browns. Most of these streams are stocked, but native fish exist in some. The best fishing lies in the headwaters that can be reached only by hiking. The West Fork of the Chattooga River is a top pack-in trout stream in Georgia.

The largemouth bass is the most important game fish in the state. Some of the top bass lakes are: Sinclair on the Oconcee River between Eatonton and Miledgeville; Seminole in the southwest corner of Georgia; Lanier northeast of Atlanta; Clark Hill on the South Carolina-Georgia border; Hartwell, just north of Clark Hill; and Walter F. George just south of Columbus. The latter lake is about 10 years old and lately has been yielding many big bass.

Many of these lakes have white and striped bass as well. Clark Hill, Sinclair, and Lanier have good white-bass fishing. Of these, Clark Hill is the best. The peak fishing season is during the spawning run in March and early April. Clark Hill also has outstanding crappie fishing, although crappie and bream fishing is good in most of Georgia's lakes and ponds.

The famous Okefenokee Swamp has some fine fishing for bass, but the chain pickerel is even more numerous here. The pickerel run a good size and on light tackle they provide scrappy sport. The freshwater angler should not overlook Georgia's bigger rivers. The Flint River has fine smallmouth fishing. The Altamaha in south Georgia is good for largemouths, bream, and catfish. The Altamaha's two main branches, the Ogeechee and Ocmulgee, also have fine fishing for bass and bream. Other rivers worth fishing are: Frederica, Chimney, Barbers, Forest, Half Moon and Kilkenne. These rivers have fine runs of striped bass and shad in the spring.

Georgia's saltwater fishing is also excellent — striped bass fishing is good in many of the bays in the fall, surf fishing for channel bass is excellent in October and November, and spotted sea trout are abundant during the fall in many of the bays and rivermouths.

Offshore fishing is good for a wide range of species including dolphin, bonito, amberjack, cobia, bluefish, and striped bass. Sailfish are also caught. One of the top producing areas in recent years has been Sapelo Reef east of Cabretta Inlet. (The reef is well marked.)

Charter and party boats operate out of Jekyll Island, Brunswick, Savannah, and other ports. Most of the top fishing areas have public boat-launching facilities. The Game and Fish Commission publishes a list of saltwater and freshwater fishing camps, including the services offered, such as guides and charter boats.

Where to Hunt

Although deer are fairly abundant and distributed throughout the state, Georgia is basically a small-game state. It has the best bobwhite gunning on the continent. The best quail country lies in southwest Georgia in the plantation belt. Unfortunately, the better bobwhite hunting is very jealously guarded by the landowners.

Southeast Georgia also has good quail hunting, but the birds are found in thicker wooded cover. It is easier to find a place to hunt than in the southwest plantation belt. The best bets are timber company lands, most of which allow hunting. There are a number of public quail-management areas in the state. These allow quail hunting two days a week, usually on Wednesdays and Saturdays, throughout the season.

The dove is the state's most popular game bird. It is found throughout the state, but the farming areas are the best. Georgia also has some grouse hunting, but it is restricted to the high hill country where both walking and shooting are very difficult. Consequently, grouse are not hunted much in Georgia.

Squirrels are a very popular game species in Georgia, as they are throughout the south. They are found in all mast-producing hardwood forests. The mountain country is good, but the coastal plain of southern Georgia is even better. Cottontails are found throughout the state but are most numerous in the agricultural areas.

Georgia also has some duck shooting, mainly in the coastal areas. But the duck hunting here is not nearly as good as in Louisiana, Arkansas, or Florida. Georgia's turkey hunting is good. The best areas are the Piedmont National Wildlife Refuge north of Macon and the Clark Hill Management Area near Augusta.

Deer hunting in Georgia is quite good and is getting better. Parts of the state allow antlerless deer but generally it is bucks only. One of the best areas for deer is the Oconee National Forest and the surrounding forest industry lands. The Piedmont National Wildlife Refuge in the Oconee Forest has deer hunting by permit. The mountain country in the northern part of the state is also good. The Chattahoochee National Forest allows public hunting, as does the State Wildlife Management Area in the forest, but the management areas have a deer season of only one week.

The coastal area of Georgia also has fine deer hunting. Most of the deer covers are thick heavy forests and swamps. Hunting is difficult and dogs are generally used. Some of the hunting is on private land but forest industry lands in the area allow public hunting.

Quail, turkey, and rabbit seasons open in late November, while squirrel and deer open in early November. There is also a spring turkey season. The grouse, raccoon, and possum season opens in mid-October.

An all-game non-resident hunting licence costs $25.25, while a big-game only licence is $10.25. A ten-day licence costs $15.25.

HAWAII

Hawaii Division of Fish and Game
530 South Hotel Street
Honolulu, Hawaii 96813

Where to Fish

Stated briefly, Hawaii is a fisherman's paradise. It has good deep-sea fishing the whole year around. Bill fish are the principal quarry, with blue, striped and black marlin, sailfish, and swordfish being the main species. An 1100-pound blue marlin has been taken in Hawaiian waters.

Yellowfin tuna is another game fish that is abundant. They also run a good size. The yellowfin is a tremendously strong fighting fish. However, the most plentiful fish in Hawaiian waters is the dolphin.

Although billfish and yellowfin are found around all of the islands, Berber's Point and the Waianae Coast are two very well-known fishing areas. Penguin Banks is another. The Kailua-Kona fishing grounds are famous for their marlin. The local hotspot for yellowfin is the beautiful "Garden Island" of Kauai.

Other fish species around the islands include wahoo, skipjack, bonito, and a variety of bottom fish such as jack cravelle, amberjack, barracuda, gray, red, and pink snappers, and several others.

The center of Hawaii's bonefish fishing is Kauai. There are a number of charter boats here that specialize in bonefishing. The one-time world-record bonefish of 19 pounds 2 ounces came from Kauai.

Visiting anglers can enjoy excellent fishing by surfcasting or spinning from rocky points on many of the islands. Such do-it-yourself fishing is much cheaper than chartering a boat. The most often caught fish on the beaches is, of course, bonefish. But jack crevalle and many smaller species are also caught.

Charter boats are available in all the major harbors. Honolulu's Kewalo Basin has the biggest charter fleet, particularly for big-game fishing. The port of Kailua-Kona also has a fair-sized fleet. Lahaina on Maui has a fleet which specializes in bonito, wahoo, and bottom fish.

Freshwater fishing in Hawaii is limited. Native freshwater fish are rare. However, several mainland species have been introduced into some of the reservoirs and irrigation waters. Kauai has some trout fishing. Bass are doing well in some of the rivers of Kauai, but all the other islands have bass in impoundments as well. The best bass fishing is probably in the Wahlawa Reservoir, about thirty miles from Honolulu. Channel cats are also flourishing in some of the irrigation waters and reservoirs.

The Hawaii Visitors Bureau, 2270 Kalakaua Avenue, Suite 801, Honolulu 96815, publishes a very useful booklet called *Fishing in Hawaii*. It is available without charge.

Where to Hunt

Many hunters do not think of Hawaii as a hunting state. The surf, the sandy beaches, and the comely maidens with swaying grass-clad hips evoke other images, but the Hawaiian islands offer some of the finest hunting anywhere. None of the game on current seasons is native. It has all been introduced.

All of the major islands of the Hawaiian Archipelago have game. The island of Hawaii is the biggest and has probably the best hunting — for feral sheep, wild goats, pigs, and upland game birds.

Sheep are the top game of the island with the big rams making outstanding trophies. There are three game-management areas on the island that provide public hunting for sheep almost the year around. The vast Parker Ranch also allows public hunting but on a fee basis.

The mouflon, the beautiful wild sheep of the European mountains, has been introduced to the archipelago. But only on Lanai is it plentiful enough to allow an open season. This island also has a limited season on pronghorns.

Wild goats and pigs are found on almost every island. The seasons are open the year around in many areas. The limits are generous — two pigs and one goat per day. The horns on some of the billies are quite spectacular and make fine trophies. The boars can go to 400 pounds, but 200-pounders are the norm.

Deer are also found in the state. The islands of Lanai and Molokai have a season on axis deer. There are a number of areas open to public hunting on both these islands. Also the Puu-O-Holu Ranch on Molokai caters to hunters on a fee basis. Blacktailed deer have been introduced to Kauai, the most northern island, and are open to limited hunting.

The Hawaiian islands offer outstanding bird shooting. Although waterfowl are fully protected because many of the native species are endangered, many species of upland game birds are abundant. There is fine dove shooting for barred, lace-necked, and mourning doves. Ring-necked pheasant, chukar, francolin, and quail hunting is also good on many islands.

The non-resident hunting licence costs a very reasonable $15. There are several hunting outfitting services in Hawaii that can arrange for guides and dogs — indeed entire hunting trips for vacationing hunters.

IDAHO

Idaho Department of Fish and Game
600 South Walnut Street
Boise, Idaho 83707

Where to Fish

Idaho is trout country. There are over 2000 lakes in the state, and nearly all have trout. There are also over 35,000 miles of streams. Besides trout there are salmon — coho, chinook, and kokanee. Smallmouth bass, channel cats, and sturgeon round out the fishing menu.

Pend Oreill Lake in the Panhandle of Idaho has superb fishing for kamloops, rainbows, cutthroat, Dolly Varden, kokanee, and smallmouth bass. Trolling is the most popular way of fishing here. There is plenty of accommodation in the small communities around the lake, plus many campsites. Another big lake in this area is Priest, which is famous for its big lake trout.

Several of the big impoundments also offer fine fishing. The Magic Reservoir, located near the junction of highways U.S. 20 and U.S. 93, has good rainbow-trout angling. But bring your camping gear. There is no accommodation. The Blackfoot Reservoir in southeastern Idaho is a good bet for big cutthroat and rainbows. Again bring your camping gear. The Anderson Ranch Reservoir northeast of Mountain Home is good for rainbows, kokanee, and smallmouth bass.

The Island Park Reservoir, in the northeastern corner of the state, is one of the most famous of the Idaho lakes. Rainbow trout, kokanee, and coho offer excellent fishing. Actually this entire area of Idaho is outstanding. There are many fine trout streams here, but the best ones generally require some hiking. Two well known streams are Hotel Creek and Henry's Fork of the Snake River.

Idaho has fine stream fishing. For steelhead, the Salmon River between Riggins and Whitebird is hard to beat as fly water. Another good stretch, particularly for spin fishermen, is from the Middle Fork to Challis. The Clearwater is probably as good as the Salmon. The best stretch lies between Spalding and Kooskiah. October and November are the top months for steelheaders.

34

The previously mentioned Henry's Fork is an excellent fly-fishing stream with good hatches in the summer months. The rainbows here run big. The Silver Creek is another fine trout stream with some "fly fishing only" stretches, but public access is a problem in some areas. Another good fly-fishing river is the Teton near Driggs. This river is best floated. The scenery is breathtaking and the cutthroats generally are hungry. Guides are available.

The Big and Little Lost Rivers are two fine trout streams for brook trout, rainbows, and whitefish. The best fishing on the Big Lost is north of Arco. A couple of other fine trout streams are Loon Creek and Warm Springs Creek. These can be reached from Sunbeam. Both are camping propositions. This is also a good way to reach the Middle Fork of the Salmon.

The Salmon River has a good run of salmon in June. When the salmon run is on, you can expect plenty of competition for the best holes. The Salmon River also has a good steelhead run in the fall. However, timing the peak of the run is not easy. Cutthroats, rainbow trout, and whitefish provide fine angling action in the "River of No Return". A float trip on this river is an exciting adventure for any fisherman. Guides are available.

The 1000-mile long Snake River also has fine fishing. The Hell's Canyon area can be fished primarily from a boat. There is a fall run of chinook and steelhead, but rainbows and smallmouth bass offer angling in the summer. There are also channel cats and sturgeon. Guides are available.

Local experts advise that non-residents often make the mistake of heading straight for the big-name streams and ignoring the smaller brooks. Many of these hold fine trout. Public access may be a problem, but many of the ranchers in out-of-the-way places will allow fishing with permission, if the angler appears to be responsible. Ask in the small communities about local fishing. Also, obtain good topo maps and study them carefully. The Department of Fish and Game publishes a number of fishing bulletins, booklets, and maps.

Where to Hunt

Idaho is one of the top five hunting states in the United States. It has some excellent big-game hunting and some outstanding bird shooting. Because of its sparse population, its hunting pressure is, by eastern standards, light.

For the big-game hunter, elk is the top attraction. The high country in remote areas, far from the road, is the place to get a trophy bull. Some of the best areas are the Upper North Fork of the Clearwater, Little North Fork of the Clearwater, Upper South Fork of the Clearwater, and the areas bordering the Salmon River between Middle Fork and French Creek. The Middle Fork is also good. As well, the Lochsa and the Selway drainage areas are highly regarded by state experts.

The best time to plan an elk hunt is in September during the rut or later in the season when the snow has moved the elk out of the high country and the animals have become concentrated in the more sheltered areas.

Mule deer is Idaho's more common trophy and the state boasts a big herd. The southern half of the state is the best for deer. The eastern portion of southern Idaho is the place to hunt if you are after a top muley trophy. All the management units along the Idaho-Wyoming border are a good bet. However, the units along the Idaho-Utah border are also good. The areas north of Snake River, Big and Little Lost Rivers, and Birch Creek are very good as well. The Boise River drainage north of Boise is also well regarded.

The state has limited hunting for bighorn, mountain goats, and antelope — all on a draw basis with quotas for the different management areas. The pronghorns are found in the rolling plains country, while sheep and goats are in the remote mountain areas.

Idaho's bird shooting is excellent. There is some fine duck hunting on the main rivers and stock ponds in the ranching country. No specific areas can be singled out. The state is also one of the best places to bag a sage grouse. Range fires and sage-spraying projects to seed grass for cattle have restricted the range of these big grouse drastically. But Owyhee County, south of Snake River near Grasmere, is still good sage-grouse country. The drainages of the Blue and Mary's Creeks are also good.

The three exotic game birds of Idaho are the chukar, the pheasant, and the speedy little hun. Chukar hunting in Idaho is excellent in the arid hilly regions. Hell's Canyon from Weison to Lewritan is a good bet. The main stream of the Salmon River from Whitebird to the mouth is also good. The ring-necked pheasant, another of Idaho's exotic game birds, is restricted to the well-watered farm country. Permission to hunt pheasants is not too difficult to obtain from landowners. The identification card from the Idaho Landholder Sportsmen's Council helps to gain pheasant hunting access. It is wise, even for a non-resident, to join the organization. The Hungarian partridge is found in the drier grain-farming areas throughout the state. Idaho has the best hun gunning in the United States. A dog is a must to find these speedy little game birds. Idaho also has valley quail in some of the more sheltered areas in the farming country. Grouse — Franklin, ruffed grouse, and blue grouse — are found in the forested areas of the state. Coyotes, jack-rabbits, and cottontails are also found in Idaho. The cottontails are of several species, but are not hunted very much.

The season for big game opens in mid-September and later, depending on the management unit. A packhorse trip into the remote country with a good outfitter is the best way for a non-resident to maximize his chances of a successful hunt. The upland bird seasons generally begin in late September.

The general non-resident hunting licence is $135 with the deer tag at $2; black bear, $2.50; elk, $3; antelope tag, $5; moose, goat, bighorn sheep, and cougar $10 each. There is a special licence just for deer at $75 and one for just black bear at $25. Special permits are required for controlled hunting areas. These can cost up to $25 for such species as moose or sheep.

ILLINOIS

Illinois Department of Conservation
102 State Office Building
Springfield, Illinois 62706

Where to Fish

The coho is the glamor fish in Illinois. And certainly the introduction of coho into Lake Michigan has revitalized sport fishing for Illinois anglers. In the early spring, coho, along with the odd steelhead, brown, or even chinook, can be taken by casting from piers and walls. South Chicago to Waukegan is the main fishing area.

By mid-May, the salmon move out into deeper offshore water. Trolling then becomes the chief fishing method. There is a free public boat ramp on the Little Calumet River, south of 130th Street in Chicago.

However, the largemouth bass is the main game fish for Illinois anglers. It is found throughout the state and many of the reservoirs have excellent bigmouth fishing. Sangchris Lake southeast of Springfield has 100 miles of irregular shoreline for fine fishing. Besides bass, the lake also has fine white crappie and channel cat fishing. Other panfish are present as well. Baldwin Lake, north of Baldwin, is another reservoir lake. It also has largemouth bass plus white bass, crappies, bluegills, and bullheads.

Kinkaid Lake, just a mile north of Grimsby, has to rate as one of the most picturesque of Illinois's man-made lakes. It is deep and clear. Largemouth bass is the main sport fish, but northern pike were introduced in 1971 and are thriving. Kinkaid is expected to produce trophy pike in a few years. Crappies, bluegills, and channel catfish are also present.

In southern Illinois, the most important lake is the Carlyle, just fifty miles east of St. Louis. Crappies and channel cats are the most sought-after fish here, but the lake also has good bass, as well as bluegills, bullheads, and flathead catfish. White bass are also becoming well established. Rend Lake is the newest reservoir in southern Illinois. It has been stocked with largemouths, bluegills, and northern pike. The Department of Conservation biologists feel that eventually Rend will have excellent angling.

Horseshoe Lake is better known for its Canada geese than its fishing. But the stands of gum trees and bold cypress provide the ideal spawning habitat for bluegills. These tasty panfish grow big and fat here. Crappies and largemouth bass are an added bonus.

Central Illinois has good fishing in Lake Shelbyville, nestled in the Kaskaskia Valley. The lake is only about an hour's drive east of Springfield. Crappies, bluegills, white bass, smallmouths and largemouths, several species of catfish, walleye, and northern pike are found here.

The Fox Chain O' Lakes in the northeastern part of the state also provides good fishing action. This is again mixed-creel water, with anything from largemouth bass through panfish, catfish, walleyes, and pike.

The Crab Orchard National Wildlife Refuge just east of Carbondale has three lakes — Crab Orchard, Devil's Kitchen, and Little Grassy — open to public fishing. They are basically bass lakes, with good crappie, bluegill, and channel-cat fishing.

Some of the best walleye fishing in Illinois is found on the upper Mississippi between East Dubuque and Rock Island. The walleye's close cousin, the sauger, is available here, along with bass, panfish, catfish, and a variety of coarse fish.

All these waters have public access and boat-launching sites. Many have campgrounds, and accommodation is available near all these fishing spots.

Where to Hunt

The "Land of Lincoln" is basically a shotgunning state — even the deer must be taken with a smoothbore; however, muzzle-loading rifles, and, of course, bows and arrows can also be used. The cottontail is the most abundant and popular game species in the state. It is found in suitable habitat throughout Illinois, but the southern portion of the state below Route 40 and also between the Mississippi and Illinois Rivers, south of Route 136, are the best areas.

Squirrels — both fox and gray — are found in the state and, among hunters, they follow the cottontail in popularity. More fox squirrels are bagged each year than grays. The timber country of northwestern and southwestern Illinois has the best squirrel range.

The dove is the state's most popular game bird. The major river valleys are all good areas for doves. The southern part of the state is generally regarded as being better dove country because the birds stay there somewhat longer before moving on southward.

Bobwhite is a well-distributed game bird in Illinois. However, the northern and northwestern parts of the state are on the northern fringe of the quail range and the gunning is spotty. However, south and southwestern Illinois are fine quail country. The area around Menard is excellent. A good, wide-ranging dog is needed to find the coveys.

Pheasant hunting in Illinois is not spectacular, but in restricted areas it is quite good. McLean, Champaign, Livingston, Ford, and Iroquois Counties are the best bet. But some pheasant hunting is found as far north as McHenry County and farther. Some of these counties also have scattered coveys of Hungarian partridge, which can be hunted at the same time as the pheasants.

Illinois has some fine waterfowl hunting — particularly near the major refuges. The best duck hunting is found along sections of the Illinois River; parts of the Mississippi Valley are also good. A couple of local hotspots are the Carlyle Reservoir near Carlyle and Oakwood Bottom near Grand Tower.

Goose hunting is centered around Horseshoe Lake, Union County, and Crag Refuges in the southern counties. The honkers winter on the refuges, flying out early to feed. There are many daily-fee goose clubs operating around these refuges. The State of Illinois also operates a public hunting area on a daily-fee permit basis.

All of Illinois is open to archers for deer, but gun hunters are restricted to about 87 counties. The deer season is split with a few days in mid-November and a few days in early December. The archers have a much longer season, but it is also split. A deer licence costs $5.00. Deer hunting in Illinois is restricted to residents only.

Small game and waterfowl seasons open as early as August 1 for squirrel, and mid-November for cottontails, bobwhites, pheasants, huns, ducks, and geese. The dove season generally opens in mid-September. A non-resident hunting licence costs $15.50.

INDIANA

Indiana Division of Fish and Wildlife
607 State Office Building
Indianapolis, Indiana 46204

Where to Fish

Michigan City is Indiana's coho-fishing hub. During the last two or three years, the coho fishing has been outstanding. All the charter-boat captains have been doing a brisk business. The peak months are April to June, and then again in September and October. Besides coho, the charter boats also get good catches of chinook and lake trout, with the odd steelhead and big brown to sweeten the creel.

The Little Calumet River and Trail Creek are two other hotspots for salmon during the spawning run. The chinook run has been particularly strong in recent years. Some of the other streams have also been getting salmon and steelhead runs from September through November.

The yellow perch has again returned as an important sport fish in Lake Michigan. The perch runs in Indiana's portion of the big lake have come on strong in recent years. When these jumbo yellow perch come in, they attract hordes of anglers.

In its 1000-plus lakes Indiana has good inland fishing as well. Largemouth bass are the most important fish species. But, of course, chunky panfish produce more action. Bluegills and crappies are the most important panfish. Catfish, both channel cats and bullheads, are also popular with Hoosier anglers. Pike and walleye also occur in some Indiana waters. And trout, mostly rainbows, have been stocked in a number of the cooler lakes.

Lake Monroe, south of Bloomington, is a major largemouth bass lake. But it also has excellent bluegill and crappie fishing. Boats are available for rent on the lake. There are several public accesses plus campgrounds. Flatbelly Lake near North Webster has fine panfish angling for bluegills and red-eared sunfish. No gasoline motors are allowed on this 450-acre lake. Oliver Lake north of Wolcottville in La Grange County is a large-mouth bass lake that has also been stocked with rainbows. The area between Terre Haute and Linton has several reclaimed strip-pit lakes which offer fine bass and bluegill fishing. These lakes are under the control of the Indiana Coal Association, P.O. Box 210, Terre Haute 47808, which has fishing information on these lakes. The Quick Reservoir in Scott County has bluegills, bass, and walleyes.

Raccoon Lake, east of Rockville, has a fine run of white bass plus good crappie fishing in the spring. Bischoff Reservoir, southeast of Batesville, has good action in the spring for bluegills, crappies, and red-eared sunfish.

For those who prefer river fishing, Indiana has many fine streams, several of which can be floated for an exciting fishing trip. One of the better streams for a float trip is the Tippecanoe which ranks as Indiana's top smallmouth bass stream. It also has good channel-cat fishing. The Pigeon River in the northeast part of the state is stocked with rainbow trout and also has smallmouths and rock bass. Canoes can be rented on both these rivers.

The Kankakee River near South Bend is a good bet for walleyes and northerns. The Fawn River in the northeast tip of Indiana is a scenic stream, with good smallmouth action plus rock bass and northerns west of Orland. The reaches around Greenfield Mills have trout as well. The previously mentioned Little Calumet River, east of Chesterton, has rainbow trout and runs of salmon. Southern Indiana also has one fine smallmouth bass stream, the Little Blue River near Fredricksburg. Big rock bass are an added bonus.

Where to Hunt

The Hoosier State is basically small-game country. However, deer are increasing in many parts of the state where enough forest land exists. The whitetail harvest in Indiana is about 3,000 animals per year. The best places to bag a buck in Indiana are Owen, Greene, Putnam, Bartholomew, and Brown Counties. The northeast tip of the state — Steuben and La Grange Counties — also yields big bucks.

The number-one game is the cottontail. The bunny is found over the entire state, but the southwestern counties of Parke, Gibson, Dubois, and Pike are the best. Bushytails — both gray and fox — are the number-two game for Hoosier hunters. Again, every county has some good squirrel woods. The best areas are the forested river valleys.

Waterfowling in Indiana is not outstanding. Duck hunters in Indiana depend almost solely on migrating birds. There are a number of public duck-hunting areas in the state, the best being Kankakee, Willow Slough, and Hovey Lake.

The pheasant is the glamor game. Although clean farming is not conducive to good pheasant populations, Indiana does have some fine ringneck hunting and the birds have been increasing since the mid-60's. Newton, Benton, and Warren Counties are the best. The bobwhite quail is an underharvested game bird, according to state game biologists and, for this reason, Hoosier hunters are allowed to take a generous 10 birds per day. There are local hotspots for quail in all of Indiana's counties, but the southeast part of the state is best. Posey and Vanderburg Counties are generally regarded as the top quail producers, while

Washington, Scott, Shelby, and Cass Counties are also good. Many hunters do not realize that Indiana has a bit of grouse gunning in the northern part of the state. The grouse hunting would be better if there were more suitable cover.

The non-resident small-game licence costs $16.25, while a non-resident deer licence is $25.75. The small-game seasons open in mid-fall.

IOWA

Information and Education Department
Iowa State Conservation Commission
300 Fourth Street
Des Moines, Iowa 50319

Where to Fish

Iowa is better known for its agriculture than for its fishing. It has both. The Mississippi and its big tributary, the Missouri, flow through the state. On top of this there are many fine lakes, both natural and man made, plus many smaller rivers and some fine trout streams.

Trout fishing in Iowa is mostly confined to the northern portion of the state, in the hilly country where over 40 spring-fed streams meander through farms and forests. The trout are rainbows and browns. The top trout streams are: Bloody Run, Trout River, French Creek, North Bear Creek, South Bear Creek, Waterloo Creek, and Little Paint Creek.

The north and northwestern parts of Iowa also have several dozen lakes made by the glaciers during the last ice age. These lakes are all cold and clear. Some of these lakes are big — anywhere from 1000 to 6000 acres.

Three of the top glacier-made lakes are Spirit, East Okoboji, and West Okoboji. These have good pike and panfish angling, and excellent walleye fishing in the spring and fall. Spirit and West Okoboji also have white bass and smallmouths.

Clear Lake in Cerro County is best known for its fine white-bass fishing, but it has good fishing for northern pike and crappies. Another fine white-bass water is Storm Lake in Buena Vista County. This lake also has good crappie fishing.

Iowa has good largemouth bass fishing. Many of the best bass lakes are man made, but some are natural. Among the top largemouth bass lakes are MacBride, Wapello, Manawa, Geode, Nine Eagles, Beeds, Union Grove, Rathbun, Anita, Miami, Blue, and Prairie Rose. Big Creek Reservoir, Iowa's newest lake, will also be good. It has been stocked recently.

Smallmouth bass are not as widely distributed in Iowa as largemouths, but there are several good waters for these fine-fighting gamesters. The previously mentioned West Okoboji is one, but the Turkey River, the Volga River, the Maquoketa River, the Iowa River from Alden to Steamboat Rock, and the Cedar River from Otranto to Cedar Falls are all good bets.

Walleye, along with their smaller cousins the saugers, produce fine fishing in several Iowa waters. A few have already been mentioned earlier. Both the Mississippi and the Missouri have fine walleye fishing in several areas. The Missouri oxbows can also provide worthwhile action. The Iowa River below the dam has a good reputation. The Des Moines River above Boone is good. Black Hawk Lake is also very good in the spring and fall.

Northern pike fishing is good in a number of lakes, some of which have already been mentioned. Others are: Five Islands, Browns, Blue, Red Rock, and Upper Pine. Some of the rivers also have northerns. The West Fork of the Cedar River is good. The Wapsipinicon above Independence is a good bet. The Mississippi above Davenport is also very productive.

Panfish of several different species and the smaller catfish are widely distributed over the state. You can find them in almost all creeks and rivers, lakes, and ponds. In Iowa the channel catfish is a very popular game fish. It is stocked in many larger farm ponds, plus the impoundment lakes. It also occurs naturally in many Iowa waters. Good channel-cat fishing can be had in such rivers as the Mississippi, the Missouri, the Des Moines, the Iowa, the Cedar, the Raccoon, the Skunk, and others. Lakes Darling, Black Hawk, and Clear also have lots of channel cats.

The Iowa Conservation Commission has free fishing literature on request.

Where to Hunt

Iowa has excellent pheasant hunting. The gaudy ringnecks find Iowa's corn fields to their liking and, they can be hunted over nearly all of the state, except for the extreme southeast. However, the highest pheasant populations are found in the north-central, east-central and southwestern parts of Iowa.

Bobwhite quail is Iowa's second most-important upland game bird. Reasonably good quail populations can be found in the southern portion of the state as far north as Interstate 80. However, the very southern Iowa counties are definitely the best. Another covey bird, the Hungarian partridge, is also found in Iowa, but its range is restricted to the northwest portion of the state.

The pheasant and hun season starts in early November and lasts until the end of January. Three cock pheasants and two huns per day are the limits. Despite the rather liberal ringneck season, Iowa game biologists find that there is still a surplus of cock birds in the spring. The bobwhite season opens in late October and also runs until the end of January. The limit is eight birds per day.

Ruffed grouse may also be hunted in Iowa. The season is generally all of November with a two-bird limit. Ruffed grouse are restricted to the wooded hills of northeastern Iowa.

Waterfowl hunting in Iowa is surprisingly good. Corn attracts and holds the birds for a time as they migrate down the Mississippi Flyway. The state maintains a large number of first-rate public shooting areas for ducks and geese. The best goose hunting is found in the Missouri River Valley.

Gray and fox squirrels and cottontails are all popular game in Iowa. The rabbits are found over the entire state where there is proper cover, but the southern portion is the best. The fox squirrel is found all over the state in timbered areas, while gray squirrels tend to be more abundant in eastern Iowa. The rabbit and squirrel season generally opens in September.

Deer also thrive in Iowa and some 11,000 animals are harvested annually. Only shotguns and bows and arrows are allowed, and the hunting is restricted to residents only. Deer are found throughout the state, with the biggest bucks in corn country and the greatest number of deer found in counties that are more heavily wooded.

A non-resident game licence — except deer, of course — costs $25. Iowa has an excellent hunting-information packet designed for the non-resident.

KANSAS

Kansas Forestry, Fish, and Game Commission
Box 1028
Pratt, Kansas 67124

Where to Fish

The fertile soil of the Kansas prairies also means fertile waters. The fish growth rate in Kansas reservoirs is outstanding. Northern pike reach 20 pounds in five years. It is the big impoundments that have made the Sunflower State such fine fishing country.

Here is the rundown on some of the top producing reservoirs: Tuttle Creek near Manhattan produces outstanding catches of crappies, but its 15,000 acres also harbor northern pike, walleye, white bass, and largemouths. Catfish are also well represented, with channel cats, flatheads, and bull-heads. There are a dozen public camping and picnicking areas around the lake.

Perry Reservoir north of Topeka has over 160 miles of shoreline which provide excellent habitat for largemouth bass, crappies, white bass, and northerns. Walleyes are found in the deeper holes. The lake also has channel cats. There are campgrounds and a marina on the lake.

Pamona Reservoir, northeast of Lyndon, is a scenic 4000-acre lake. It has good largemouth bass fishing plus walleye, crappie, white bass, and catfish. One walleye hotspot is around Dragon Park. The crappie fishing is excellent, with catches of over 100 crappies a day on record. Pamona has a couple of marinas; there are also two state parks — Vassar and Carbolyn — with full camping facilities. The Corps of Engineers operates a few additional recreation areas.

Milford Reservoir near Junction City is the biggest and newest lake in Kansas. It boasts big walleyes, big largemouths, and respectable northerns. It also has crappies, white bass, bluegills, and channel cats. The fishing in recent years has been good, with many reported catches of 30 bass a day. The flooded timber areas around the outlet creeks such as Quimby, Curtis, Franum, Mall, and others are the places to nab the big bass.

The lake has a marina, plus a dozen public boat-launching ramps and public usage areas, some with camping facilities.

Other reservoirs with fine fishing are: Wilson north of Russel, Cedar Bluff south of Ogllah, and John Redmond near Ottumwa. They have the general run of Kansas fish species, but Cedar Bluff has smallmouth bass, while Wilson also has spotted bass. Striped bass have been stocked in John Redmond, but the lake is a good bet for big channel cats. All these reservoirs have camping facilities, marinas, and public boat-launching ramps.

Another good producer is the Cheney Reservoir for white bass and crappies. This lake is close to Wichita and gets heavy fishing pressure. The Council Grove Reservoir has big pike. The state record comes from there. The county state lakes, such as the ones in Pottawatomie and Marion Counties are also good bets for bass, panfish, and channel cats.

Not all Kansas fishing is in big reservoirs. The farm ponds that dot the Kansas landscape offer good fishing, but to gain access one must have an "in" with a farmer. There are some pay-as-you-fish channel-cat ponds as well.

Kansas rivers should not be overlooked. The smaller streams such as the Pawnee, Elk, Fall, Delaware, and Wakarusa, among others, offer fine catches of panfish, bass, and bullheads. Big catfish are found in the big rivers. The Neosho River is perhaps the best bet for huge cats. The best stretch to fish is between Burlington and St. Paul.

Where to Hunt

Pheasants, bobwhite quail, and doves are the most important game birds in Kansas, but the real glamor bird is the prairie chicken. The mourning-dove season is the first to open in early September. The bird has a state-wide distribution and the best hunting is near grain stubbles and bean fields. Towards the evening, waterholes are good too. The prairie chicken season opens in early November. Both greater and lesser prairie chickens are found in Kansas. The top gunning for these prairie grouse is in Lyon, Coffey, Woodson, and Osage counties.

The bobwhite and ringneck season opens in early November. The eastern half of the state is better for quail, while the western half is better for pheasants. Finney County is the best bet for bagging a limit of ringneck roosters. Allen, Bourbon, Wilson, Neosho, and Woodson Counties are the best for bobwhites; while Republic, Clay and Washington Counties offer both pheasant and quail gunning.

Rabbits, cottontails, and jacks, as well as squirrels (both fox and grays), are the chief small-game mammals. Rabbits are very numerous and have no closed season. The squirrel season opens in early June and closes in late December. The bushytails are distributed over most of the state with the best gunning in the timbered river bottoms.

Kansas has good waterfowl shooting. The area between Quivira and Cheyenne Bottoms is good for ducks and geese. This is chiefly stubble hunting. Many of the best spots are tied up, but a hunter who does a bit of scouting should have no trouble in finding a place to hunt. Two good hotspots for ducks are the Kirwin Reservoir and Marais de Cygne. Glen Elder Reservoir is also good.

Both mule deer and whitetails are found in Kansas. The season is short but the hunter success rate is good. Unfortunately, the special-draw deer permits are restricted to residents only. The High Plains area in northwest Kansas is mule-deer country. Whitetails are widely distributed in the "Sunflower State" and are found in wide shelter belts, woodlots, and brushy ravines. Red Hills is another deer hotspot.

A non-resident hunting licence costs $15 plus $1 for an Upland Game-Bird Stamp.

KENTUCKY

Kentucky Department of Fish and Wildlife Resources
State Office Building Annex
Frankfort, Kentucky 40601

Where to Fish

The Blue Grass State has superb bass fishing. Smallmouths in particular grow big. The world-record smallmouth of 11 pounds 15 ounces was taken in Dale Hollow Lake. But largemouth bass, spotted bass, and white bass fishing is also good. In addition, Kentucky has walleyes, rainbow trout, muskies, panfish, and catfish of several species.

The big lakes provide most of the angling in Kentucky. Dale Hollow, south of Burkesville on the Kentucky-Tennessee line, has 4300 acres of fishable water. Rainbow trout are stocked annually. But Dale Hollow is famous for its small-mouth bass. Catches of four and five-pound bass are common.

Kentucky Lake on the Tennessee River is a 158,000-acre reservoir. Large stringers of jumbo crappies in April and May attract anglers from far and wide. But this lake also has walleye and striped bass. These anadromous fish have been doing well in the big lake, with twenty-pound fish being boated; and that is big for landlocked stripers. Kentucky Lake is one of the world's biggest impoundments.

Herrington Lake, in the beautiful blue-grass country near Danville, is rich in limestone, which produces bumper crops of bass, particularly whites. When the spring run of white bass comes out of the lake into the streams that feed it, crowds of eager anglers cash in on this bonanza and harvest gigantic bags of these fine-eating fish.

One of the top reservoirs in Kentucky is Lake Cumberland, with over 50,000 acres of surface water. According to a survey by fisheries biologists of the Kentucky Department of Conservation, Lake Cumberland has more bass per acre than any other bass water in the United States. But besides lunker largemouths, Cumberland also has smallmouths, whites, walleyes, bream, catfish, and chan-nel cats. Rainbows have also been stocked into Cumberland. The local hotspot for trout is below the Wolf Creek Dam. Night fishing is the most productive.

Another fine lake is Barkley, east of Kentucky Lake, with top bass and rainbows. Other good fishing lakes are Barren River, Nolin River, Malone, Beshear, Rough River, Guist Creek, Dewey, Buchorn, Bert Coombs, Mill Creek, and several other smaller lakes.

All of the big Kentucky lakes have public accesses with boat launchings, camping parks, and marinas. Some lakes even have fishing lodges or motels that cater to fishermen. Guides are available on some.

Kentucky also has fine river fishing. There are a couple of dozen trout streams with fine rainbow fishing, such as: Sulphur and Lick Fork in Simpson County; Trammel in Allen County; Big Brush in Green County; Rock and Beaver in McCreary; War Fork in Jackson; and Mountain Forks in Harlan County.

But the king of Kentucky rivers is the smallmouth bass. Nolin River is without a doubt the best smallmouth stream in the state. Salt River is the top stream for spotted bass, sometimes called "Kentucky bass". The Salt flows through the beautiful blue-grass country for about 30 miles. Besides scenery and spotted bass, it offers the angler smallmouths, largemouths, panfish, and catfish.

Another top river is the Cumberland. The turbulent waters below Wolf Creek Dam are exciting for floating and fishing. Bass, walleyes, and catfish are the Cumberland's staples.

There are other fine streams to float fish. The Red River gorge is very scenic and has good fishing. The Green River offers white water near Liberty and smooth water near Mammoth Cove. Besides bass, the Green also has muskies. Of the dozen or so other exciting rivers where it is possible to float and fish, the South, Middle, and North Forks of the Kentucky River are very productive. The Big Sandy River has fine smallmouth, largemouth, and channel-cat fishing in its waters. Tygart and Kinniconick are good bets for floating. Besides the usual run of Kentucky fish, they also have muskies.

Elkhorn Creek in central Kentucky is an outstanding smallmouth river. It is probably superior to the Nolin River, and may well be the best smallmouth stream in the nation.

All of the major streams in Kentucky have public access points where anglers may launch their canoes and boats. Canoes can also be launched by most bridges.

Where to Hunt

The dove is Kentucky's number-one game species and dove hunting is excellent with a bag approaching two-million birds. The grain belt, extending from the central to the western portion of the state, is the best. Simpson, Christian, Todd, Logan, Warren, Calloway, and Marshall Counties are the places to hunt doves. The only other upland game bird of any significance in Kentucky is quail. The same grain-growing counties that attract doves are also the top choices for bobwhites. However, the coveys are fairly widely scattered due mainly to lack of good nesting cover. The bobwhite season runs from mid-November to the end of January.

Bushytails are the number-two game species for Kentucky hunters. The moun-

46

tain region of eastern Kentucky is the main squirrel country, but hickory and walnut woods in other portions of the state always have squirrels. Cottontail hunting is best in the western portion of the state. The squirrel season in Kentucky runs from late August to the end of December with a two-week break in early November. The bunny season coincides with quail. Incidentally, Kentucky quite rightly considers the red fox a game animal and has a legal hunting season at the same time as the rabbit.

Waterfowl hunting is rather limited in Kentucky but the Ballard County Refuge in the western tip of the state across the Ohio River from Cairo, Illinois, has some very fine goose hunting. Kentucky's wild-turkey flock is limited to the larger strands of forest in the Rill country, but the flock is in excellent shape. The three-week season runs from mid-October to mid-November.

The white-tailed deer is Kentucky's only big game. Areas of good cover have a good deer population. The gun season only lasts for a few days, but for bow hunters October and December are the times to hunt the wary whitetails.

A non-resident hunting licence costs $27.50. Deer tags cost $10.50.

LOUISIANA

Louisiana Wildlife and Fisheries Commission
400 Royal Street
New Orleans, Louisiana 70130

Where to Fish

The coast of Louisiana is a world of unspoiled marshland. This is of immense benefit to wildlife. It also makes saltwater fishing more difficult because it is harder to reach. But no serious angler is thwarted by a few small difficulties! Offshore big-game fishing is not as developed as it should be, because of the lack of charter boats. But boats operate out of Port Eads, South Pass, Grand Isle, and Cameron, near the Texas border. Empire and Venice below New Orleans also have charter boats. During the peak season, charter boats in Louisiana waters are generally booked well ahead of time. Advance reservations are needed.

Billfish — blue and white marlin, sailfish, and swordfish — all can be taken in the open waters of the Gulf. Dolphin, wahoo, kingfish, Spanish mackerel, cobia, as well as some bonito and tuna are also caught. The summer months are best for billfish. Cobia fishing starts in mid-April and ends in late May, when mackerel and bluefish fishing begins. Bonito and Spanish-mackerel fishing is best in July and August.

The most abundant fish in the coastal waters of Louisiana is the spotted weakfish, usually called speckled trout. This fish is found in all the bays, inlets, and river mouths during the fall. The peak run is generally in October. Redfish runs also occur at this time. However, both species can be taken offshore around reefs in mid-summer.

47

In the fall Lake Ponchartrain at New Orleans is a popular spot for weakfish. It is easily accessible and fish can be caught around the pilings at the causeway. Lake Borgne, south of New Orleans, is also good, particularly at the south end. It is also accessible to the public.

There are no fishing piers in Louisiana, but the three-thousand oil platforms and gas flows in Louisiana waters are good and popular places to fish from. Many species of fish, including grouper, pompano, and barracuda congregate around the pilings. A map showing the positions of all the gas and oil rigs can be purchased from Tidewater Fishing Publications, P.O. Box 56, Seabrook, Texas 77586.

Louisiana has excellent tarpon fishing from May to fall, which peaks from July to September. These outstanding game fish prowl the coastal waters in large numbers.

Louisiana's freshwater fishing is known only to a few non-resident anglers. Toledo Bend Reservoir on the Louisiana-Texas line is a tremendously productive bass lake. It also produces big stringers of succulent panfish, as well as walleyes and striped bass. Angling facilities are well developed so there is no trouble with access. The shorelines are lined with ample camping facilities and there are a number of marinas. Fishing guides are available.

Bussey Brake Lake, in the northern portion of the state, is the top trophy water for largemouths. Bass of over 10 pounds have been caught here. Bream and crappie offer added action. Other fine lakes in this part of Louisiana are: Bruin, St. John, Palmyra, Cocodee, and Old River. These are old oxbow lakes formed in ancient times by the mighty Mississippi. They all have largemouths and good-sized panfish. Most of these lakes have well-developed public accesses for boats.

Southeastern Louisiana has some fine lakes as well. The Atchafalaya Basin is good for largemouths, catfish, and panfish. Ponchartrain, Theriot, and Hatch are other lakes in this area. They all have good bass and panfish angling. The bass are not overly big, but they are abundant. These lakes are hard to fish in the summer months because of vegetation. However, by December the reeds are down so that boats can pass.

Where to Hunt

Louisiana is one of the top hunting states in the nation. The hunting season opens on Labor Day with doves being the prime game. The best area for doves is in a belt closely following Highway 165 from the northeast corner of the state to the southwest corner. Squirrel (both gray and fox), marsh rabbit, and cottontail seasons open in early October. Bushytails and bunnies are found throughout the

---

Woodcock are eastern game, inhabiting moist woodlots and alder thickets. The best places to hunt them are New Brunswick, Maine, Ontario, northern Michigan, and Louisiana where the birds winter.

state in appropriate habitat. The squirrel season generally closes in mid-January and the rabbit season at the end of February.

The bobwhite season opens on Thanksgiving and runs to the end of February. The western portion of the state and Florida Parish are the best places for quail. There is plenty of good quail cover open to hunting — both privately owned piney woods and wildlife management lands.

Migratory birds find Louisiana's wetlands a real haven. Goose hunting for snow geese is excellent — white and blue-color phases — and for whitefronts. Large numbers of ducks also winter in Louisiana. The best waterfowl hunting is found on the coastal marshes. There are a number of public hunting areas plus private duck and goose clubs that charge a daily fee. There is also some fine duck hunting on the inland swamps and marshes.

Snipe, rail, and woodcock gunning is good in Louisiana and the birds are generally not hunted as much as some other game species. Rail hunting is good in the coastal marshes and excellent in the rice belt of southwest Louisiana. Snipe are found near the coastal marshes on the grassy mud flats. Woodcock are scattered throughout the state in moist habitats. Biologists estimate that 70 percent of this continent's timberdoodles winter in Louisiana.

White-tailed deer and wild turkey are both classified as big game in Louisiana. The black bear is fully protected. The best deer hunting is found in the northern part of the state. To find open land for deer hunting is not nearly the problem that it is in many other states. The deer season opens on Thanksgiving and runs to the end of February. The archery season is longer. The wild-turkey season is limited to spring from late March to mid-April. The best turkey hunting is along the Louisiana-Mississippi border.

Louisiana hunters can smile. There are over 900,000 acres of public-owned wildlife management areas open to them. Maps of all management areas are available. A non-resident all-game, all-season licence costs $25, while a five-day licence costs $5.

MAINE

Maine Department of Inland Fisheries and Game
State House
Augusta, Maine 04330

Where to Fish

When an angler thinks of Maine, he visualizes clear forest lakes and ponds with fine brook trout. That is quite true. But Maine also has good saltwater fishing, and smallmouth bass, pickerel, and white perch. On top of this, Maine is the only state that still enjoys a sea run of Atlantic salmon, the king of freshwater game fish.

Maine's top Atlantic salmon streams are: Pleasant, Denneys, Machias and East Machias, and the Narragaugus. The seasons are generally from May 1 to early fall. An attempt is being made to restore some other historic salmon rivers with the hope of re-establishing the runs.

The landlocked salmon is found in about a hundred of Maine's lakes. The landlocked salmon is a strong, leaping fighter. While angling for Atlantic salmon is traditionally a flyfishing sport, fishing for landlocked salmon is generally done by trolling lures or bait fish. Landlocked salmon can, of course, also be caught on flies. The fish are near the surface just after ice-out, so that is the time to go after them with flies. Some of the best landlocked salmon lakes are: the Fish River Chain of Lakes in northern Maine, West and East Grand, Sebec, Square, Chesuncok, Moosehead, and Sebago, just to name a few.

Maine and trout fishing go together like bacon and eggs. *The* trout in Maine is the brookie. However, rainbows have been introduced into the Kennebec River around Bingham, as well as in several other lakes, while brown trout are found in a number of streams and lakes. Occasionally they are taken by anglers trolling deep for landlocked salmon. Branch Lake near Ellsworth is a top brown-trout water.

Brook trout are found in hundreds of brooks, ponds, and lakes. An entire book could be written about Maine's brook-trout angling. The ponds and streams in the Allagash Wilderness waterway are excellent for big brookies. The Kennebago watershed is another good place. Nesowadnehunk Lake in the Baxter Park area is also a top brook-trout lake.

Togue, as lake trout are called in Maine, are also found in several of Maine's lakes. Moosehead is considered the top togue lake in the state. It produces good catches at ice-out or during the winter ice-fishing season.

Southern and eastern Maine have excellent black-bass fishing for both smallmouths and largemouths. The smallmouths are widely distributed. Top smallmouth waters are: Big Lake, Scraggley Lake, Third Machias, Wabassus, and Spendic. Belgrade Stream is considered by local experts to be the top largemouth water.

Other freshwater fish of importance are: white perch, eastern pickerel and, in a few lakes, whitefish. White perch are abundant and widely distributed. In fact, they are considered a nuisance in many lakes. Whitefish provide dry-fly action in several northern lakes. The best time to take these fine-tasting fish is in the evenings or mornings of late spring. Whitefish angling is only popular with a few devotees.

The pickerel is also widely distributed in the warmer lakes and ponds from central Maine to the seacoast. This small cousin of the pike is vastly under rated as a game fish because usually it is taken on stout bass tackle. When hooked on ultra-light spinning gear, the pickerel puts up a creditable scrap. The waters in Hancock and Washington Counties have the best pickerel fishing.

The queen of Maine's saltwater fish is the bluefin tuna. These big fish school along the entire coast. Casco Bay is the best tuna hotspot. The major portion of the tuna fleet is moored at Bailey Island. The summer months are the peak season. Striped bass are the most sought-after saltwater game fish. They can be caught along the entire coastline, but the Saco River is excellent. Orchard Beach

is another hotspot for surfcasters. Other top sports are Popham Beach, Pine Point, Georgias River, York River, and the St. Croix River between Maine and New Brunswick. June to September is the striper season in Maine.

Other marine fish such as pollock, mackerel, rock cod, flounders, and codfish are also caught by sport fishermen. Most of these are caught from docks and around pilings from boats. There are party boats that take out anglers for cod. Jigging is the usual method of taking codfish, with summer being the peak season. Boothbay Harbor is the main center for sport codfishing.

Maine is well equipped to handle tourist anglers. It fully appreciates what anglers mean to the state tourist industry. The Maine Publicity Bureau, 48 Rockefeller Plaza, New York City is the place to write for detailed information.

Where to Hunt

Ruffed grouse and white-tailed deer are Maine's chief game species. However, woodcock hunting is also good. There are also some fine duck-shooting areas in the state. Black bear are quite abundant. There are also gray squirrels and cottontails in southern Maine, but the snowshoe hare is the most important small-game mammal.

Ruffed grouse and woodcock hunting is good from central Maine to the coast. Local hotspots are south of Rangeley and south of Houlton. Northern Maine has ruffed grouse as well, but the birds are too trusting to provide good wing shooting. The grouse season runs from early October to mid-November, with the woodcock season beginning in late September.

Pheasant is the only other upland game bird found in Maine, and its range is limited from the southwestern Maine-New Hampshire border to Bar Harbor. Even here, pheasant shooting is almost a put-and-take situation.

Cottontails and squirrels are not hunted much in Maine and their range is limited to the milder areas near the coast. However, snowshoe hares are hunted fairly extensively and are found statewide. The best area for the white hares is in central Maine. The rabbit season — snowshoe and cottontail — runs from early October to the end of March. The squirrel season generally is open for the whole of October and November.

Sea-duck hunting is found along most of Maine's coast and the limits are generous. For freshwater duck species — dabblers such as blacks and teal or, divers such as scaup and ringnecks — the best place is Merrymeeting Bay. This wetland is world famous for its duck shooting. Guides and sneak boats are available on the Merrymeeting. Black ducks and other dabbling species are also found on inland beaver ponds and small marshes.

The black bear is the most abundant of the bruins, being found from Alaska east to Newfoundland and south to Florida. The most exciting way to hunt these animals is with hounds.

Deer are found statewide in Maine. Generally northern Maine has a better harvest, but this is largely because deer-hunting camps with guides operate in the vast balsam and spruce forests of northern Maine. The hunting pressure is less intense in the northern portion of the state. The deer season runs from late October to late November. Black bear are quite abundant in Maine, but elusive and hard to bag. A non-resident small-game licence costs $20.50, while big-game licences cost $42.50.

MARYLAND

Maryland Fish and Wildlife Administration
State Office Building
Annapolis, Maryland 21401

Where to Fish

Maryland may be a small state, but fishingwise it has a lot to offer. It has excellent saltwater fishing. The striped bass is an important game fish along the coast. Chesapeake Bay is as famous for its striped bass as it is for its waterfowl hunting. The rockfish action, as striped bass are locally called, begins in the spring with the first schools of smaller fish coming into the bay. Usually the best fishing is in September and October. The stripers may hang around until early December, but with the onset of winter they go back into the ocean.

There are so many local striper-fishing areas that they would take pages to cover. For example, all of the rivers (Elk, Potomac, Patuxent, Patasco, and Sassafras) and their estuaries get good runs. Many of the countless islands and points also have good fishing around them. Here are just some hotspots: Gibson Island, Poplar Island, Tilghman Island, Worton Point, Bloody Point, Hering Bay, Chesapeake Bay Bridge, and Ragged Point.

Maryland also has some outstanding offshore fishing. The white marlin is one of the top fish in the open waters. Some of the marlin grounds out of Ocean City are famous among billfish addicts. The odd blue marlin is also hooked each season.

Other offshore species regularly caught out of Maryland ports include dolphin, mackerel, bluefin tuna, and sharks. The summer months offer the best action, but in winter there is some good codfish angling offshore. Chesapeake Bay also offers a variety of fish other than striped bass. Flounders, black drum, channel bass, and spotted weakfish are all found in the Bay.

Maryland does not lack facilities for anglers. There are many marinas where boats and motors can be rented. All the tributary rivers have launching ramps. The biggest charter fleet for offshore fishing is moored at Ocean City. But Chesapeake Beach and Tilghman also have charter boats as well as party boats. For shore fishermen, the jetty in Ocean City is a popular spot. Surfcasters do well around Ocean City and Assateagueu Island. For other local hotspots, inquire at local tackle-and-bait shops. There is no shortage of motels and hotels for anglers around the key fishing areas.

Maryland's innumerable ponds have surprisingly fine bass and panfish angling, but access to many of these ponds is difficult. All the major rivers offer bass fishing along with lesser species. The Susquehanna Flats where the Susquehanna River enters the Chesapeake is a local hotspot for largemouth bass. The Potomac River has fine smallmouth fishing between Hancock and Washington. The Upper Potomac also has some walleyes.

Some of the big reservoirs have good fishing — mainly for bass and panfish. The Triadelphia Reservoir north of Washington, D.C. has both smallmouths and largemouths. April to June are the best fishing months. The Loch Raven Reservoir north of Baltimore also has big bass. In addition, it has pike, walleyes, and panfish. Being so close to a big city, it is heavily fished. Other good fishing reservoirs are Liberty, Rocky Gorge, and Pretty Boy. Electric motors only are allowed on these impoundments.

Surprisingly, Maryland has some trout streams. They are all in the western part of the state. The top ones are in the Blue Ridge Mountains. The Youghiogheney River, Hunting Creek, and Fishing Creek are probably the best streams. They are brown and rainbow waters. Deep Creek Lake also has brown trout and northern pike.

Where to Hunt

Maryland is best known for its Chesapeake Bay waterfowl gunning. Both the eastern and the mid-eastern shores in Kent, Caroline, Talbot, and Dorchester Counties are excellent for geese and ducks. Dabblers are hunted in the sheltered marshes, while divers are hunted out in the open water.

The best Canada goose hunting is in Cecil County where the birds winter. Most of the waterfowl hunting is on private land, but there are many waterfowl clubs where gunning can be had on a daily fee basis.

Other migratory birds such as snipe, rails, coots, and gallinules are also found in the Maryland wetlands, with woodcock in moist woodlands; but none are hunted a great deal. The rail gunning in Wilcomico and on the Patuxent River marshes is excellent. A few pushers still ply the trade of taking hunters out in their long, slim rail boats.

However, one migratory bird, the mourning dove, is a popular game bird. The dove is found statewide, but the best places for the doves are in farming country. The season on doves opens in mid-September, while some of the other migratory bird seasons open in early September. Duck and geese seasons open in late October and early November.

Next to the dove, the quail is Maryland's most abundant upland game bird. The better bobwhite gunning is found in the southern and central part of the state with St. Mary's, Charles, and Calvert Counties being the best. The central portion of Frederick County is also good. The ring-necked pheasant is also found in Maryland, with the central part of the state being the best ringneck range. Carrol, Frederick, and Baltimore Counties are the top choice for pheasant hunters. Both pheasant and quail seasons open in early November and run to either mid-January or the end of January respectively.

Ruffed grouse is also found in Maryland. The western part of the state is the best grouse range. The South Mountain Range, west of Frederick, is also a good bet but this area is close to population centers and gets heavy hunting pressure. Turkey is also on Maryland's hunting menu. The western counties of Garett, Washington, and Allegany are the best and all have a fall season. There is a spring season as well which includes several other counties. Of all the Maryland counties, Allegany has the best turkey flock.

Squirrels and rabbits are found statewide wherever proper habitats exist. The rabbit season opens in early November with squirrels about a month earlier. The hardwoods of the eastern shore and the western hills are the best places for squirrels but most residents hunt in the central portion of the state, closer to the big cities. The eastern shore and southern Maryland farmlands are the best areas for cottontails.

Deer is Maryland's only big game. The biggest bucks, in body weight and racks, are found along the eastern shore. The lower shore between Cambridge and Crisfield is rated as being tops. The western counties also have good deer hunting. The bucks-only season is over a month long — from late November to early January. The bow hunters have a long split season from late September to early December and they can take deer of either sex.

A non-resident hunting licence is $25 with $5.50 for deer or turkey tags.

MASSACHUSETTS

Information and Education Section
Massachusetts Fish and Game Division
Westboro, Massachusetts 01581

Where to Fish

Massachusetts is basically a mixed-creel state, offering a wide variety of marine and freshwater fish. A good bet for a mixed creel of freshwater fish is the 25,000-acre Quabbin Reservoir in western Massachusetts. This lake has rainbows, browns, brookies, and lake trout; plus largemouth and smallmouth bass, pickerel, panfish, and bullheads. No motor larger than a ten horsepower is allowed on the lake.

Two other good fishing reservoirs are the Wachusett and the Sudbury. The Wachusett's thirty-six-mile shoreline is formed of rocky shelves and ledges with deep drop-offs, making for good fishing right off shore. Bass — largemouths and smallmouths — are found in the lake, as are lake, brook, and brown trout. White and yellow perch, chain pickerel, and bullheads are also abundant. However, it

---

The striped bass is a voracious and anadromous fish, offering very exciting angling along the Atlantic Coast. It has also been stocked in many of the big reservoirs of the south and southwest.

is the smallmouth bass that attract most anglers.

Sudbury Reservoir is connected to Wachusett by the same drainage system. The Sudbury is a shallower lake than the Wachusett, so warm-water fish thrive best. Largemouth bass and pickerel grow to a good size here. Another reservoir with big bass and pickerel is the Putnamville near Danvers.

Several Massachusetts lakes have good fishing. Onota Lake near Pittsfield is a fine bass, pike, and pickerel water. Webster Lake at the town of Webster has fishing for both smallmouths and largemouths. Lake Quinsigamond between Shrewsbury and Worcester is a mixed-creel lake with bass, panfish of many species, channel cats, and several species of trout.

For those who like trout fishing in small ponds, Nicrerson State Park has four small lakes — Flax, Cliff, Little Cliff, and Higgins — which have good trout angling. Higgins also has bass.

For those who like stream fishing, Massachusetts has everything from good-sized rivers to tiny brooks. The Deerfield along the Mowhawk Trail is a fine trout stream to fly-fish. The three branches of the Westfield are a good bet for dryfly addicts. The Sguannacook between Townsend and Groton is a good nymphing river in the spring and fall. The Quinnapoxit River flowing into the Wachusett Reservoir is a good flyfishing stream in its upper reaches. The local experts say there is a sea run of brook trout at Scotron Creek, a small stream near Sandwich.

The Connecticut River itself has a fine run of shad in late May and early June. The local hotspot is below Holyoke. The Merrimack River has bass and pickerel.

Massachusetts has been a saltwater fishing center since colonial days. There is good fishing right in Boston Harbor. Fishing out of a boat anchored in Quincy Bay is always good for a few flounders. The McCorkle Fishing Pier on Castle Island also has good flounder fishing. Codfish can be caught here even in the winter months and, in the summer, pollock, mackerel, and striped bass provide the main action. Boston Harbor's islands have fine surf fishing for striped bass and, in October, the flounder are at their peak.

Another top hotspot is Plum Island at the mouth of the Merrimack River in the northeastern corner of Massachusetts. Cod and flounder provide the hottest action in April. The jetty, beach, and riverbank become lined with fishermen when these fine-eating fish come in. The small port of Newbury port has a charter fleet which takes out anglers after shoal stripers in May. But stripers, along with pollock, can be caught from the beaches as well. Later in the spring and throughout the summer, runs of big striped bass come in, along with mackerel and bluefin tuna. A 1000-pound bluefin was caught in Ipswich Bay. That is a big-game fish! In late summer, bluefish runs come in and provide a lot of action.

Cape Cod Bay is another favorite fishing area for Massachusetts anglers. The same species, from bluefin tuna to flounders, can be caught here. There are a lot of flats, shoals, and good casting beaches here to accommodate casters. Bluefish and stripers are the main quarry of shore fishermen. Boat fishermen will find boat-launching sites in all the Cape Cod towns. Charter boats are also available.

This area has many hotspots, such as the Cape Cod Canal, Race Point, Billingsgate Shoal, and many others. The Elizabeth Islands south of Cape Cod have tremendous fishing. Cuttyhunk Island, the outermost island of this archipelago, has outstanding striper fishing. There are several inns here that cater to fishermen. But the rocky ledges also have fine fishing for bluefish, bonito, fluke, and other species. There are many boat-launching facilities.

The Cape Cod Chamber of Commerce, Hyannis, Massachusetts 02601, knows what their saltwater fishing bonanza means in terms of tourist revenue. Their excellent information package for anglers is free for the asking. The Cape Cod Charter Boat Association, Box 668, West Yarmouth, Massachusetts 02673, will also send a list of its members.

Where to Hunt

Small game is the principal hunting fare in Massachusetts. Ruffed grouse are widely distributed wherever good habitat exists, but the best grouse country is the Berkshires. The season runs from early October to early January. Woodcock are also widely distributed wherever moist woodlands exist. The season is similar to that for grouse and indeed both birds are frequently hunted together.

Pheasants are found mainly in the Connecticut River Valley farmlands. The countryside around Worcester has a good reputation for pheasant shooting. The ringnecks can also be hunted on the state's thirty-five wildlife management areas. The season extends from early October to early December. Bobwhite quail are also found in Massachusetts, with open seasons on the birds in the southeastern part of the state and Cape Cod. The bobwhite season opens in early October and lasts until late November.

Massachusetts has some fine waterfowl gunning. Inland marshes and beaver ponds have wood ducks, blacks, and mallards. Also, Canada geese and black ducks are hunted on the coastal marshes. The best places are Plum Island, and Barnstable and Dennis marshes. Sea ducks are also hunted by the hardier souls and the local hotspots for eiders and scoters are the coastal areas around Plum Island, Winthrop, Monomoy, and Dusbury.

Squirrels and rabbits — cottontails, snowshoes, and jackrabbits — are the principal small-game mammals. Squirrels are not hunted much and the season is the same as for quail. The rabbit season opens in mid-October and closes in late February. Fox and bobcats are also wisely classified as game, with the winter months generally being the open season.

Deer and bear are Massachusetts's big game. Bear hunting is by special permit only, with a five-day season in late November. Deer season for shotgunners is also five days in early December, while the archers get a three-week season. The best deer-hunting areas are the Berkshires, Cape Cod, Martha's Vineyard, and the forested lands west of the Connecticut River. A non-resident hunting small-game licence costs $20.25 while a deer and bear licence costs $35.25.

The coho salmon offers outstanding sport to anglers on the west coast and to those in the Great Lakes states such as Minnesota, Wisconsin, Illinois, Indiana, and Michigan, where this one was caught.

MICHIGAN

Michigan Department of Natural Resources
Mason Building
Lansing, Michigan 48926

Where to Fish

Coho and steelhead are the glamor fish of Michigan, but the lake trout is the bread-and-butter fish for many charter-boat captains. When they cannot find coho for their clients, they can usually put them onto lakers. Chinook salmon and big brown trout are additional trophies in the Great Lakes waters.

The best coho and lake trout action is still along the Lake Michigan shoreline out of such towns as Pentwater, Ludington, Manistee, Frankfort, and South Haven. Charter boats operate out of most of these towns during the summer. The best offshore coho fishing is from August to September, but this is not an iron-clad rule.

The best lake-trout water is found in Grand Traverse and Little Traverse Bays; however, the lakeshore around Petoskey is also very productive. Black River Harbor in the Upper Peninsula is also known for its big lakers. Chinook salmon can be caught just about anywhere along the Lake Michigan coast. The Muskegon River from Lake Michigan to the dam has an excellent reputation.

Hot steelhead action comes twice — in April and May, and again in October and November. The fall run tends to have larger fish. There are many good steelhead rivers in Michigan, but some of the top ones are the Big and Little Manistee Rivers, and the Muskegon.

Michigan has fine inland trout fishing. The Au Sable River in Crawford County is almost a legendary trout stream. Rainbows and browns provide most of the action. But the northern half of the Lower Peninsula has many other fine trout streams. The more remote the stream, the better the fishing.

Michigan also has good fishing for the warm-water species. Lake St. Clair produces excellent catches of walleyes and smallmouth bass. The lake is an important recreational resource because of its position on the doorstep of Detroit. Aside from walleyes and smallmouths, St. Clair also has big muskies and a host of panfish, particularly yellow perch.

Other good walleye waters in Michigan are Lake Gogebic in the county of the same name; the Muskegon River below Newaygo Dam; and Big Bay de Noc. And with the moratorium on commercial fishing in the western end of Lake Erie, the walleyes have bounced up and sport fishermen once again are producing good stringers of these fine-flavored fish.

Pike and bass are found in many of Michigan's inland lakes. Fletcher's Floodwaters in Alpena County has big largemouths and big northerns. Mitchell's Bay on the Canadian side of Lake St. Clair is a black-bass hotspot. The Lake Michigan shore near Grindstone City is great for smallmouth. The shallows around the Hog and Garden Islands are also very good. Another top bassing ground is around Waugoshance Point at the western tip of the Lower Peninsula. Lake Erie has some fine smallmouth shoals as well.

Potagannissing Bay near Drummond Island is known for its monster-sized pike. Portage Lake in the Upper Peninsula is also a fine northern-pike water. Aside from all these fine game fish, anglers can also take home big stringers of tasty panfish. Jumbo yellow perch from the big lakes are particularly delicious.

Where to Hunt

The hunting season in Michigan begins in mid-September with the opening of the ruffed grouse season in the northern two-thirds of the state, and with squirrels over the entire state. Ruffed grouse is Michigan's chief upland game bird. Gogebic, Houghton, and Ontonogon Counties in the Upper Peninsula are a good bet. In the Lower Peninsula, Midland, Gladwin and Isabella Counties are good. Clare, Montcalm, Lake, and Mecosta Counties also have good grouse gunning. In the Upper Peninsula, grouse hunters get a bonus bird in the form of the sharp-tailed grouse, the season for which opens early in October and generally closes about three weeks later.

Woodcock is another abundant game bird in Michigan. In fact, Michigan timberdoodle gunning may be better than that of Maine. Drummond Island is the best woodcock hotspot. However, the Pigeon River watershed has many fine covers for the tricky-flying longbills.

Pheasants and quail are two of Michigan's other game birds. Both are found in the southern part (Zone 3) of the state in the better farming country. The season generally opens late in October and closes early in November. Neither bobwhites nor ringnecks are as abundant as grouse or woodcock, but there are local areas that offer good gunning for both species to hunters who know where to go, and have good dogs.

Duck hunting is also quite good in several areas of Michigan. A good flight of diving ducks — scaup, redheads, canvasbacks, and goldeneyes — come through the funnel of the Detroit River from Trenton to Lake Erie. There are also good marshes for dabbling ducks around Lake Michigan's shores. Saginaw Bay and the flats and islands in Lake St. Clair are well known hotspots. Shiawassee Flats are also excellent. This is a controlled hunting area where the number of gunners is regulated.

Squirrels and rabbits are the main small-game mammals. Cottontails and snowshoes are also found in Michigan. The snowshoe hare receives comparatively little hunting pressure. Squirrels are not hunted a great deal, except perhaps around Detroit. The best squirrel hunting is found in Lake, Newaygo, and Mason Counties. Bobcat, raccoon, and woodchuck all receive some protection in the form of hunting seasons in Michigan, particularly in the southern zones where the hunting pressure is higher.

Deer and bear are Michigan's big-game species. The bear season opens in mid-September and closes early in November. Generally, the bruins are on the increase in the Upper Peninsula. The best bear hunting is in the thick and vast brush country from Melstrand East to Raco. The area around L'Anse is also good.

The deer season for gun hunters is confined to the last two weeks in November, while archers generally have six weeks, from October 1 to November 14. The entire state of Michigan has deer, and some of the woodlots in the southern part of Michigan's farm country are known for their big bucks. The northern portion of the Lower Peninsula has the best deer population in the state.

A non-resident small-game hunting licence costs $25. A deer licence costs $40.00 and a bear licence $25.10. However, bear may be taken on the deer licence during the deer season.

MINNESOTA

Minnesota Game and Fish Division
390 Centennial Building
St. Paul, Minnesota 55101

Where to Fish

The king of the Minnesota waters is the musky. Who is his consort? It is hard to say, but probably the walleye, which is the most abundant of Minnesota's game fish. It is certainly the number-one choice of most Minnesota anglers. And Minnesota bills itself as "The Walleye State". So many of Minnesota's 15,000-plus lakes have walleyes, that it is impossible to name more than a few.

Some of the top lakes are Leech, Winnibigoshish, Millelacs, Upper Red Lake, Rainy, Vermillion, Kabetogama, and of course, Lake of the Woods. The upper Mississippi River also has walleyes, with the dams at Wabasha and Red Wing being two favorite hotspots. Other top-producing walleye lakes are Big Sand and Potato in the Park Rapids area; Cut Foot Sioux and Spider in the Grand Rapids area; and Whitefish and Gull Lakes in the Brainerd area.

The walleye's small cousin, the sauger, is also abundant. Lake Pepin has tremendous sauger fishing. Other good waters are the Rainy River watershed, the lower St. Croix River, the lower Mississippi, Lake St. Croix, and others. The same tactics that are used for walleye will take the sauger. However, for the best sport, scale your tackle down. Sauger seldom exceed 3 pounds.

Unquestionably, northern pike is Minnesota's second most-abundant game fish. The northerns are found throughout the state. There really is no top pike water. Many of the better walleye lakes also have pike. The northern pike's bigger cousin, the musky, is the glamor fish, but it is a difficult fish to catch. There are anglers who make a science of fishing for this big member of the pike family. Certainly Minnesota and Ontario must vie for the honor of having the best musky fishing. The top musky lakes in Minnesota are Leech, Cass, Winnibigoshish, Wabedo, Andrusia, and Lake of the Woods.

Bass fishing is very good in some of Minnesota's lakes. But walleyes, pike, and muskies have the bass completely overshadowed. The area around Alexandria has many good largemouth waters; while the northeastern part of the state has excellent smallmouth waters.

63

Minnesota also has good trout fishing. There are over 150 lakes with lake trout, but some of the hottest trout action is around Lake Superior. Many of the rivers flowing into the lake have tremendous steelhead runs. Some also get good runs of browns. The top steelhead rivers are Knife, Arrowhead, Kimball, Split-rock, and Gooseberry. The peak runs come in late September to November. The fish may not be as big as those in Michigan, but there is nothing wrong with a 15-pound steelhead.

Minnesota is well geared to accommodate non-resident anglers. Indeed, the tourist business is big business, particularly in the northern part of the state.

Where to Hunt

Ruffed grouse is Minnesota's favorite game bird. It is found throughout the state, but the southeast and north-central portions are the best because of the poplar forests. Northern Minnesota also has fine grouse gunning. Stands of trembling aspen are the main key to grouse abundance in the north and much of Minnesota has good habitat.

Duck hunting is also good in many areas of Minnesota, particularly in the duck-producing pothole country in the western part of the state. Mallards and blue-winged teal are the main duck species. There are a number of refuges and public hunting areas in western Minnesota open to the public. There is also good duck hunting in the St. Croix and Mississippi Valleys.

Other small-game species in the state are sharptails, woodcock, pheasants, rabbits, and squirrels. The sharp-tailed grouse is found in the northwest corner of Minnesota. The places to hunt the sharptail are poplar woodlots and overgrown pastures in farm country. Pheasant gunning is very limited in Minnesota, but at one time parts of the state had excellent pheasant populations. However, the ringnecks are making a comeback. The best pheasant hunting is in the southeastern counties. Woodcock are not hunted much, yet the woodcock shooting is quite good in areas of Minnesota from Duluth to Winona. Hungarian partridge are also found in farm country, but the coveys are widely scattered.

Squirrels are found mostly in the hardwoods of central and southern Minnesota, particularly in the timered river bottoms. Snowshoe hares are abundant in the vast forest lands, particularly in northern Minnesota, and they are underharvested. Cottontails are restricted to areas where the snow is not quite as deep in winter.

Deer, moose, and black bear are the three big-game species. The deer herd has declined because of heavy winters and deteriorating habitat, while the moose herd has increased.

The deer season is open again, with all of November as open season. However, a hunter is allowed to hunt only on three consecutive days. The reason for

---

The muskellunge is mean, savage, and cautious. A trophy musky such as this one is not easy to hook or land. Minnesota and Ontario are the best places to catch this outstanding game fish.

this is to limit the number of hunters in the bush at any one time. The Detroit Lakes area is the best spot for deer. Archers have a much longer season, beginning at the end of September.

Black bear is also legal game in Minnesota. The northeast part of the state is the best bear country. The animals are elusive and hard to hunt in the vast forests of this area. Moose are increasing in numbers in the northwest and north-central portions of the state. A limited season was held a couple of years ago.

A non-resident small-game licence costs $27.00, while non-resident deer and bear licences cost $50.25 and $25.25 respectively.

MISSISSIPPI

Mississippi Game and Fish Commission
Box 451
Jackson, Mississippi 39205

Where to Fish

Mississippi's best freshwater fishing is in the large impoundments. Some of the better-known ones are Pickwick, Sardis, Enid, Grenada, and Arkabulata, all on Interstate 55; Ross Barnett above Jackson; Okatibbee near Meridan; Bogue Homa near Laurel; Shelby near Hattiesburg; and Flint Creek near Wiggins.

All of these impoundments have fine largemouth-bass fishing plus bluegills, crappies, bream and, of course, catfish. In the Ross Barnett Reservoir, striped bass are providing added thrills. Generally the spring and early summer months are the most active, but fall is good as well. All the abovementioned reservoirs have public access for boat launching and many have marinas and camping grounds.

The oxbow lakes of the Mississippi River also have fine fishing. Some of the top-producing lakes are Eagle and Chotard near Vicksburg; Albemarle near Woodville; Rodney in Jefferson County; Washington in Washington County; and Whittington in Bolivar County. All these lakes have largemouth bass, but catfish, crappies, and bream provide the bulk of the angling. The favorite way to take catfish here is by trotlines — set lines — overnight. The best bream and crappie fishing is in the late spring after the waters begin to recede.

Mississippi has a couple of fine rivers which can be floated in a flat-bottomed boat. The Tchoutachbouff in the DeSoto National Forest is a good bet for bass and catfish. The Jordan River in Hancock County flows through some wild-swamp country. It has bass and panfish.

Mississippi's saltwater fishing is well devolped and has good access points. The brackish water of the Gulf Coast has tremendous fishing for bream and channel bass. Other fish are crappies, striped bass, spotted weakfish, flounder, crokers, and huge alligator gar. Fishing here is full of surprises.

Some of the local hotspots are the bayous, such as: De Lisle, La Croix, and Portage in the Bay of St. Louis; Mulatto, White's, Horseshoe, and Calvin near the mouth of the Lower Pearl River at Lake Borgne; in the Black Bay of Biloxi at

Bayous Fort, Bernard, and Four Jacks; plus Lakes Cates, Cedar and Big, the river mouths of the Big and Little Biloxi, and the Tchoutacabouffa.

The Pascagoula River where it enters the Gulf through myriads of swamps, bayous, and small lakes is another hotspot.

The offshore fishing out in the open waters of the Gulf begins in May for cobia and Spanish mackerel. Dolphin, bonito, and bluefish begin in June and continue on during the entire summer and into the fall. The Gulf Stream here also produces billfish, tuna, amberjack, wahoo, and red snappers.

Charter boats operate out of nearly all of the Mississippi ports, such as Bay St. Louis, Gulfport, Biloxi, Ocean Springs, and others. There is even a flying service at Columbia, Mississippi, which flies anglers to the offshore islands where small boats are waiting for them. Treemosen King has a fishing lodge. Indeed, some of the best places are the beaches on the offshore islands, such as Chandeleur, Horn, Ship, Petit Bois, North Island, and others.

There is also an abundance of inshore fishing. Weakfish, redfish, and bluefish all run in the fall. When these runs are on, they attract hordes of fishermen. Most of the ports and harbors along the coast and the main rivers have public boat-launching ramps, and there is no shortage of accommodations for visiting anglers.

Where to Hunt

Deer is Mississippi's sole big-game species with the whitetails being found all over the entire state. However, the best areas are the counties on the Mississippi River with Warren, Claiborne, Wilkinson, Jefferson, Washington, Coahoma, and Bolivar Counties being tops. Kemper and Noxubell Counties in the central part of the state, and Greene and Perry in the southeast are also very good.

The deer season is split in November and again late December-January with a bow-and-arrow season preceding the gun season. There is also a special primitive-weapons-only season. As in most states below the Mason-Dixon line, dogs can be used in some areas.

The wild-turkey season is generally limited to spring gobblers only. The season opens in late March and closes in late April. Again, the counties on the Mississippi River are the best bet.

Quail and dove are the most popular upland game birds. The mid-state area is generally best for bobwhite. The season runs from early December to late February. Dove hunting is quite good in Mississippi, particularly in the soybean-growing areas. There is good woodcock and snipe gunning in the Gulf Coast lowlands. The coastal marshes also have fine rail shooting, but none of these three birds are hunted much by the Mississippi scatter gunners.

Waterfowl hunting in Mississippi is quite good in several areas. The Mississippi and Pearl Rivers have good duck hunting in spots. The Gulf Coast has goose and ducks in the marshes. Also, the big-water reservoirs such as Sardis, Grenada, and Ross offer some fine waterfowling.

Squirrels, both gray and fox, are favorite small-game mammals. The Delta area has the unique color phase of the fox squirrel — a white-nosed black squirrel. Although the bushytails are distributed statewide, the best squirrel hunting is along the Mississippi River, the Delta, and the swamps on the lower reaches of the Pascagoula and Pearl Rivers. Rabbits — cottontails in the uplands or swamp rabbits in the swamps — are abundant in Mississippi and widely distributed. There is also fine raccoon, opossum, and bobcat hunting for houndmen.

Mississippi has fifteen wildlife management areas and two National Wildlife Refuges open to the hunting public. This amounts to over one and a half million acres of wildlife habitat. Hunters do not have the problem of where to hunt in this state. A non-resident hunting licence costs $15 for small game and $25 for all game. There are also seven and three-day licences at $20 and $6. Turkey and deer tags are $2 each.

MISSOURI

Missouri Department of Conservation
Jefferson City, Missouri 65101

Where to Fish

Fishing in Missouri is varied and good. Like the other mid-south states, the big reservoirs are the backbone of the sport. They provide the bulk of fishing; but Missouri also has some interesting river fishing, and as a bit of frosting on the cake, some fine trout streams.

Missouri shares a couple of the big reservoirs — Bull Shoals and Table Rock — with Arkansas. Both these lakes are good producers of largemouth bass. The Missouri state record for largemouths comes from Bull Shoals, while experts rate Table Rock as one of the best bass waters in the nation. Striped bass have also been planted in Table Rock. In addition, Bull Shoals has fine white-bass fishing. One local hotspot is just below the dam at Shadow Rock. The peak run is in April.

Lake of the Ozarks is the oldest big impoundment in the state. It is also one of the best known. It produces big bass, and it has good walleye fishing in its upper portion. April is the best time for the walleyes.

Two other big reservoirs — Stocton Lake and Pomme de Terre Lake — lie south of Lake of the Ozarks. Stocton is one of Missouri's newest impoundments, located about thirty miles northwest of Springfield. It has excellent walleye and bass fishing, plus northern pike which are exhibiting very fast growth. Pomme de Terre lies between Sedalia and Springfield. According to biologists of the Mis-

---

Cottontails are the number-one small-game animal on this continent, and to hunt them with a merry beagle is great sport. They are found in over 48 states, but Missouri and Texas probably have more cottontails than anyone.

souri Conservation Commission, this lake has the best walleye population in the state. Aside from walleyes and bass, the lake also has muskies.

Some of the other big reservoirs are: Thomas Hill in the northern half of the state; Wappapello north of Poplar Bluff; Montrose in Henry County; and Taneycomo south of Springfield. Thomas Hill has largemouths, walleyes, channel cats, and panfish. It also has big northerns. Wappapello is a pan-fisherman's paradise. It is considered the best crappie lake in Missouri. Montrose has good largemouth bass and panfish angling, also walleyes and channel cats. Taneycomo is one of Missouri's best trout lakes; it harbors big rainbows. Aside from this, the lake also has big largemouths.

All of the Missouri impoundments have good panfish angling for one or more species. Most of them also have good channel-cat fishing.

Missouri has a couple of dozen good trout streams. The state parks of Roaring River, Maramec Springs, and Montauk are very good, but also very popular. Other good streams are: the Current River, Dry Creek, Stone Mill Creek, the Little Piney River, and the Nianqua River.

There are a number of streams that can be float-fished in a johnboat. The Current River is one. It has smallmouth bass as well as trout. The Gasconade, Meramec, Black, Kings, and St. Francis are also good bets. Most of these are smallmouth-bass streams, but they also have walleyes, panfish, and channel cats. Some have trout. There are a number of guides who specialize in float trips.

Another fishing water in the "Show Me" State is the Osage River, famous for its gigantic blue catfish. A 117-pound blue cat was caught on a trotline in this river. The Osage River just below the Bagnell Dam is a local hotspot for big blue cats. The St. Francis and the Missouri Rivers have big flathead catfish. The Missouri also has paddlefish.

Fishing in Missouri is fairly accessible. All of the big reservoirs have public boat-launching ramps. Many also have campsites, marinas, and motels nearby. Guides are available on some. Incidentally, fishing on these impoundments is open year-around.

Where to Hunt

Missouri is another good small-game state, but it also has fine deer hunting. Quail are widely distributed with the best population in the farming areas of southern Missouri. The bobwhite season begins in mid-November and closes in mid-January. Doves are even more widely distributed and more numerous than quail. The dove season is split with an opening in early September. Pheasant is another upland game bird in the state, but its range is limited to the northwest. The wild-turkey season is in the spring; gobblers only. The southeastern part of the state is the best bet for bagging a turkey.

Waterfowl hunting is good in several areas of Missouri. Duck hunting is fairly good in some local sections of the Mississippi and Missouri Rivers. There is good snow-goose hunting in the four-county area of northwestern Missouri. The best Canada-goose hunting is found in Chariton County.

Squirrels are a popular game animal in Missouri. The best areas are the Ozark

70

Mountain forests. The season opens May 30 and closes at the end of December. There are over one and a half million acres of forest land owned by the United States Forest Service in the Ozarks. All of it is open to hunting. Rabbits are another favorite game animal of Missouri hunters. Cottontails and swamp rabbits are widely distributed throughout the state and are abundant in their proper habitat. The bunny season begins in early October and closes in mid-February.

The deer harvest has been increasing. The rifle season is about a week long in late November, but archers have two extra months — October and December. The best whitetail hunting is in the Benton and Morgan Counties of central Missouri. However, Howell, Texas, and Pulaski Counties in the south-central part of the state are also very good.

A small-game non-resident hunting licence costs $25.30 and a turkey and deer licence $30.30.

MONTANA

Montana Fish and Game Department
Helena, Montana 59601

Where to Fish

Montana is a trout-fishing state. It may well have the best stream flyfishing on the continent. There are over 4,000 miles of streams and several hundred lakes. The best trout rivers are the seven "blue ribbon" streams: Bighole, Flathead, Madison, Missouri, Rock Creek, Gallatin, and Yellowstone.

The Bighole is on the east side of the Continental Divide and flows into the Jefferson. The way to reach it is by Interstate 15 and State Highway 43. To fish it, you pretty well have to camp out. It has brook trout, rainbows, and browns. The Flathead in northwestern Montana is a good cutthroat and Dolly Varden stream. It is right in the center of the tourist district, so it gets fairly heavy fishing pressure. The time to fish it is after Labor Day when the crowds have gone. There is plenty of accommodation for fishermen close to Flathead.

Rock Creek near Missoula has to be one of the finest of streams anywhere. Access is no problem. Early fall is the best for big browns and rainbows. The Madison River is another famous trout stream. In the Geyser Basin in the Yellowstone, it can be waded. Below the Ennis Dam, the Madison flows through sheer canyon walls called the Beartrap. The Madison is a brown and rainbow water, but the upper reaches have Montana grayling and the reaches below Ennis Dam have whitefish.

East of Madison flows the Gallatin River. It is a scenic stream with the best fishing water downstream from the canyon. The river here flows slowly and has many big pools that hold browns and rainbows, as well as the odd brookie and cutthroat. Along most of the Gallatin's length there is accommodation closeby.

The Yellowstone River is a big trout stream. The best fishing waters are between Yankee Jim Canyon and Gardiner, and again between Emigrant and

Livingston. The lower reaches have rainbows, browns, and whitefish; the upper stretches also have cutthroats. The Missouri in southwestern Montana has some excellent trout fishing and, it gets less fishing pressure. The stretch between the Three Fork and the Cascade is the best bet. Besides trout, it has kokanee and some walleye. Big browns and rainbows can be caught by trolling at the Canyon Ferry Reservoir. Early fall is the most productive fishing time.

Besides these seven "blue ribbon" streams, Montana has many other streams classified as red ribbon. The fishing in these may be just as good, but access is a problem on some, and others are not as scenic. A few to remember are: Big Spring Creek, Blackfoot, Clark's Fork, Kootenai, Bitteroot, and the North and Middle Forks of the Flathead, and the Smith. There is an additional classification of "yellow ribbon" which includes hundreds of mountain rills and prairie creeks. Some of these are the favorite streams of the local people.

An angler in Montana should not overlook the big reservoirs such as Canyon Ferry and Holter near Helena for big rainbows and browns; Hungry Horse near Glacier for cutthroats and Dolly Vardens; and Bighorn near Hardin for huge trout and walleyes.

Some of the big Montana lakes have excellent fishing. Duck Lake on the Blackfoot Indian Reservation near Babb has big rainbows. Guides are available. Flathead Lake has cutthroats, Dolly Varden, lake trout, kokanee, and bass. In addition, there are about 1,500 small mountain lakes open to the backpacker and, in some cases, the horseback rider. There are outfitters who specialize in horseback camping trips to the alpine lakes.

For those who like walleyes, the Missouri River, the Nelson River, and some of the northern lakes are a good bet. Northern pike abound in Lake Ft. Peck and other north-tier lakes. The lower reaches of the big rivers — the Missouri, the Yellowstone, and the Milk — have big channel catfish.

Montana is well geared to handle non-resident anglers. There is plenty of accommodation close to most of the best waters and there are plenty of camping parks. The Montana Chamber of Commerce, Helena 59601, is a good source of fishing and travel information. The Montana Department of Fish and Game has stream classification maps and lists of guides and outfitters.

Where to Hunt

To most hunters, Montana is a big-game hunting paradise; however, Montana's bird shooting is also exceptionally good but not as well known. Deer, muleys, and whitetails are the number-one big game. About 100,000 are taken each season. Eastern Montana is the best bet for mule deer, but the watersheds of the Powder River and Missouri River are also very good. Elk have wide distribution in the more primitive parts of the state as well. The Pioneer Mountains around the Bighole River Basin, the Main Rocky Mountain Range, and the Gravelly Range of southwest Montana are prime areas for elk.

Black bear and grizzly are usually taken by hunters after elk. The best grizzly country is around the Bob Marshall Wilderness Area. Black bear are quite numerous in northwest Montana.

The pronghorn is another popular big-game species. The antelope is found mostly in the rolling grasslands. Bighorn sheep and mountain goats can also be hunted by special draw permit. Both are found in the more remote mountain ranges. Overgrazing by cattle continues to deteriorate the winter grazing lands of the bighorns. Sheep in Montana are in trouble. Moose is another of Montana's big-game species. It may also be taken by special-draw permit. Moose hunting is also confined to wilderness areas. Unfortunately, cougars in Montana are classified as predators the year around. The general big-game season opens in mid-October and ends in late November. However, there are other special seasons.

The bird-shooting menu in Montana is as variable as big game. The best ruffed and blue grouse gunning exists in the Gravelly Range, Snow Crest Mountains and Kootneai Forest. The forested foothills are primary ruffed-grouse cover, while the higher forested ridges are blue-grouse cover. The wilderness forest areas also have the Franklin's subspecies of spruce grouse.

Sage and sharp-tailed grouse, Hungarian and chukar partridge, and pheasants are also found in Montana. The best hun and pheasant hunting is in Montana's grain belt. Miles City and Fergus County are two good spots. Sharptails are also found in the grain belt, particularly in areas that are too rough to plow but close to grain fields. The sage grouse is found mainly in the rolling sage hills of the eastern and central parts of the state. Generally bird seasons start in mid-September.

Chukar hunting is poor, with coveys widely scattered in arid areas. Montana is probably too cold for these birds. Wild turkey is another of Montana's game birds, with October being the main season. The forest lands of southwest Montana are the best turkey range.

Waterfowl hunting is quite good in Montana. The grain belt has fine stubble shooting for both ducks and geese. The pothole country of eastern Montana has fine duck shooting. Other duck spots are Medicine Lake and Bowdoin Refuge. The Flathead Valley is another top waterfowling spot. It gets most of its birds from the Pacific Flyway. There is no closed season on rabbits, foxes, coyotes, or bobcats in Montana. They are all quite abundant; none are hunted very much.

The licensing system is complex. A non-resident bird licence costs $25, while a non-resident bird, elk, and two-deer licence is $151. On top of this there are special licences for antelope, goat, sheep, and grizzly ranging from $10 to $50.

NEBRASKA

Nebraska Game and Parks Commission
State Capitol Building
Lincoln, Nebraska 68509

Where to Fish

The midwest is seldom thought of as good fishing country, but many of the midwest states have fine fishing and Nebraska is no exception. The big reservoirs have contributed greatly in making the midwest good fishing country.

One of the top lakes in Nebraska is Lake C. W. McConaughy, just north of Ogala. This lake has everything from smallmouth bass to coho salmon, as well as such species as walleye, northern pike, striped bass, rainbows, brown trout, and a variety of catfish and panfish. Several fish species caught from this lake hold Nebraska state records.

There are some fine bass lakes about an hour's drive of Lincoln. They are: Bluestem near Sprague, Branched Oak near Raymond, Conestoga and Pawnee near Emerald, Wagon Train near Hickman, Yankee Hill near Denton, and two or three others. These lakes are all fairly shallow with shorelines of flooded timber where lunker largemouths hang out. All these lakes have public boat-launching ramps; Bluestem, Pawnee, Branched Oak, and Wagon Train have campgrounds. Besides largemouths, these lakes have panfish and catfish, and many have pike and walleye.

Lewis and Clarke Lake on the North Dakota line just off Interstate 81 is one of the top Missouri River lakes. It is estimated that about 750,000 pounds of fish are taken from this lake every year. The fish include walleye, sauger, white bass, crappies, channel catfish, and other species. This water is known for its paddlefish run in the spring and fall. These ancient fish are not caught by angling, but by snagging. The paddlefish hotspot is just below the dam.

The Sand Hills country of Nebraska, best known among sportsmen for its sharp-tailed grouse gunning, also has many fine lakes — over 1600 according to the Nebraska Game and Parks Commission. Some of the best lakes in the Sand Hills lie in the Valentine National Wildlife Refuge. The best lakes here are Watts, Hackberry, Dewey, Clear, Pelican, and Willow. The Sand Hills lakes have largemouth bass, pike, panfish, catfish, and brown and rainbow trout.

Another productive lake is Harlan County Reservoir near Republic. It has top walleye and white-bass fishing in the spring. Smith Lake south of Rushville is considered to be a top largemouth bass water and perhaps the best bluegill lake in the state. Rockford Lake south of Beatrice is a good mixed-bag lake for walleye, pike, bass, channel cats, and bluegills. Other fine mixed-creel lakes are Swanson south of Enders; Hayes Center Lake near Hayes Center; and Jeffrey Canyon south of Brady. The Merritt Reservoir northeast of Kennedy has some good rainbow-trout action.

Anglers driving along Interstate 80 should investigate the "Chain of Lakes" from Grand Island to Hershey. This chain consists of a group of about 50 small lakes (the biggest is approximately 50 acres) that have been stocked with a variety of fish species.

Nebraska's fishing is not confined solely to lakes and reservoirs. The state also has a number of fine fishing streams. The Calmus River in the Sand Hills is a fine float-and-fish stream, with good northern pike fishing in the spring. The Elkhorn River is another top pike water.

Most of Nebraska's trout fishing is in streams. The best trout streams are in the Panhandle area. There are about a dozen and a half good streams close to the town of Scottsbluff. A few of the best ones are: Wildhorse, Pumpkin, Red

Willow, Nine Mile, Tubb Springs, Niobrara, and White Rivers. Other good trout streams such as the Monroe, Sowbelly, and Soldier flow in the countryside around Crawford.

Most of Nebraska's lakes and streams have access points open to the public. The lakes have public boat-launching ramps.

Canada Goose

Where to Hunt

The pheasant is king in Nebraska. Indeed, this state is one of the top three for the number of ringnecks bagged. The best pheasant areas are around Alliance, Hemmingford, Broken Bow, St. Paul, and Columbus. The southern counties east of McCook also have good pheasant gunning.

The bobwhite quail is another top game bird in Nebraska. The best areas for bobwhites are around Virginia, Humboldt, Alexandria, and Odell. The season on both bobwhites and ringnecks opens in early November and closes in January.

Sharp-tailed grouse and prairie chickens are two other Nebraska game birds. Sharptails are the more numerous of the two. Both prairie grouse species are found in the Sand Hills. Areas around Rose, O'Neil, Bartlett, and Halsey are the best bets. The season runs from late September to early November. Nebraska's wild turkey flock is prospering. The season is generally confined to a couple of weeks in late October and early November. The best turkey country is in the Wildcat Hills south of Scottsbluff, the Niobrara Valley south of Valentine, and the areas around Crawford.

Waterfowl hunting is mixed, but there is some good gunning on grain stubble. The Platte River between Oshkoosh and Scottsbluff has a good waterfowling reputation. The area around Lisco is also good. Good goose hunting can be had on Lake McConaughby for Canadas and on the Tekanah Reservoir for both snow geese and Canadas. There are also several public hunting areas for waterfowl with the Plattsmouth and the Sacremento Game Areas being the best.

Cottontails and squirrels are the two small-game mammals. They are both widely distributed and neither are hunted a great deal. The season for both opens early in September.

Big game in Nebraska means deer — whitetails primarily, but also muleys. The pronghorn season is very short in late September. Whitetails are found over much of the state, with the deer management units of Upper Plate, Pine Ridge, Keya Paha, and Frenchman being the best. Mule deer are found only in the hills of western Nebraska. Deer hunting is on a draw basis if the demand for tags for any unit exceeds the supply. A non-resident small-game licence costs $25; a deer licence $30; antelope $30; and wild turkey $15.

NEVADA

Nevada Department of Fish and Game
Box 10678
Reno, Nevada 89510

Where to Fish

Nevada is best known for its nightlife — the glamor and gambling of the big cities. But it has some very fine fishing. The biggest trout in Nevada come from Lake Mojave, one of the reservoirs created on the Colorado River. Somehow the desert scenery around the lake is not one normally associated with trout fishing, but the big trout are there. The best trout water is from Willow Beach to the tailrace of the Hoover Dam.

The Mojave also has fine bass fishing. The largemouths occur in the lower portion of the lake in the warmer water. The trout are in the upper reaches. Another top bass water is Lake Mead, just on the doorstep of Las Vegas. Mead is a part of the Colorado River and Lake Mojave complex. The Mead has had its ups and downs as a bass-fishing lake, but right now it is definitely on the upswing. The bassing has never been better. Aside from lunker largemouths, the lake also has crappies, bluegills, and catfish, but these panfish play second fiddle to the rainbows. The lake has excellent trout fishing as a result of an extensive stocking program.

Nevada has a number of other trout lakes. Lake Tahoe has long been famous for its scenic beauty, but it also has excellent trout fishing. Big lake trout lurk in its cold, deep waters. The rainbow-trout fishing is very good in the spring and fall. The sweet-tasting kokanee salmon provide action in May and June.

Other big lakes in the part of Nevada around Reno are: Walker, Lahontan, and Pyramid. Cutthroat trout is the most prevalent species in Pyramid Lake and, in recent years, the fishing has been very good. Sacramento Perch are found in the lake as well. Walker Lake too, has fine cutthroat fishing, but the fish are smaller. Walker Lake is a largemouth, white bass, and crappie water.

Northeastern Nevada also has some excellent angling. Ruby Lake south of Elko is a top largemouth water. Much of the lake is a shallow marsh. Aside from harboring big bass, it is also a waterfowl refuge. Because it is shallow, it can be waded; but fishing from a boat is more popular. The Elko area has several other reservoirs — Wildhorse, Sheep Creek, and Wilson Sink. They all have rainbows; Wildhorse has kokanee as well. Sheep Creek is on an Indian reservation so a special fishing permit is needed. The entire northeastern corner of Nevada has fine fishing for anglers who are willing to hike or ride into the back country.

There are a number of rivers which also have good fishing opportunities. The complex formed by the Colorado River and Lakes Mead and Mojave has already been mentioned. Certainly the water below Davis Dam has good rainbow fishing. The Truckee River flowing from Lake Tahoe to Pyramid has good brown trout and rainbows. Access to this stream is no problem: Interstate 80 parallels it for much of its length. Actually there is no problem with access to most of

Nebraska's big fishing waters. Public boat-launching ramps are found on all of the major waters, and many places have camping parks as well.

Where to Hunt

The chukar is Nevada's glamor bird. Areas around Lovelock, Winnemucca, and Bottle Mountain are some of the better spots to hunt this fine game bird. Hungarian partridge and ringnecked pheasant are the two other imported game birds of Nevada. Both are restricted to the farming areas, particularly the grain-growing ones. The irrigated farming country in the western part of the state is best for ringnecks, while Elko County is best for huns.

Quail — mountain, Gambel's, and California — are all popular game birds and fairly abundant in the proper habitat. Generally, they are not found in as arid a habitat as the chukars. The southern portion of the state is best for Gambel's quail, while the northern part is better for California and mountain quail. Grouse — ruffed, blue, and sage — are also found in Nevada. The sage grouse is limited to the dry sage hills of north Nevada, while ruffed and blue grouse are found in the forested foothills and mountains. Good areas for blue and ruffed grouse are Ruby, Carson, and the Snake Mountain ranges. Mourning doves are very abundant and popular game birds. The best areas lie in the farming country.

The upland bird season begins early in September for doves; late September for quail, grouse, chukars, and huns. All of these species stay open for weeks except the sage grouse season which is limited to about six days. The month-long pheasant season opens in late October.

Rabbits of three species — cottontails, pygmy and white-tailed jackrabbits — are distributed throughout the state. The season on all three begins in late September.

Waterfowl hunting is limited in the state, but there is one good area north of Reno in northwest Nevada. Whistling swans can be hunted with a special permit.

Nevada has a variety of big game, including the coveted desert bighorn. Deer hunting is good in Nevada; Elko County is one top area. The northeastern portion of the state is generally good. There is a special draw for non-residents, with a tag costing $30. The bighorn sheep hunt is on a special-draw permit with a non-resident tag at $125. The mountain-lion season is open the year around but a tag is needed by both residents and non-residents. The non-resident tag costs $50. The general non-resident hunting licence costs $50, the small-game licence $25.

Elk and pronghorn are the state's two other big-game animals. Both have limited seasons open to residents only.

Rabbit

NEW HAMPSHIRE

New Hampshire Fish and Game Department
34 Bridge Street
Concord, New Hampshire 03301

Where to Fish

The streams, ponds, and lakes of New Hampshire are basically trout waters. However, the state does have some warmer waters where bass, pike, walleye, and panfish thrive.

Where are some of the top trout waters in New Hampshire? The Connecticut Lakes such as Pittsburg, First, Second, and Third have rainbows and native trout. They also have landlocked salmon. Big Diamond and Little Diamond ponds near Stewartstown have deep-bodied brook trout. The best fishing is right after ice-out. The White Mountain National Forest has some fine brook-trout fishing in several small lakes. The best ones are Mountain, Wachipauka, Three, Flat Mountain, and Big Sawyer.

The landlocked salmon are found in a number of New Hampshire lakes. The Connecticut Lakes in Coos County are a good bet. The big Ossipee Lake on the New Hampshire-Maine border is very good a week or two after ice-out. A couple of other good salmon lakes are Sunapee and Pleasant. The fish run larger than average in these two lakes. However, Lake Winnipesaukee is considered the most productive landlocked salmon lake in the state. Every year it yields fish in the eight to ten-pound class, but the average is two to three pounds. The Winnipesaukee also has big lake trout.

New Hampshire stream fishing is very good too. Nearly all the streams in the northern half of New Hampshire have trout. To get better fishing, you have to walk a distance from the road. Many of the tiny brooks and rills are seldom fished.

There is excellent rainbow fishing in the Connecticut River between Pittsburg and North Stratford. The Ashuelot River also has good rainbows above the Surry Mountain Dam. The Androscoggin River between Earl and Drummer produces many fine catches in June and then again in September. The upper reaches of the Saco around North Conway also have rainbows.

Brown trout are found in the Connecticut above North Stratford. The Blackwater has browns in the area around Webster and Wilmot. The Saco River downstream from Conway is a good brown-trout water. The locals prefer to use live hellgrammites rather than flies. Some of New Hampshire's most interesting stream fishing is for landlocked salmon in the Merrymeeting and Winnipesaukee Rivers in early spring.

Brook trout are fish of clean forest streams, and flyfishing for them is a beautiful sport. New England and eastern Canada have the best brook trout waters, with the big rivers of Quebec producing the biggest fish.

Among the warm-water fish species, New Hampshire has fine walleye fishing in the Connecticut River at Woodsville and further south at Wilder Dam. The stretches of the Contoocook are good as well. The Merrimack below Penacook also has walleyes. Good pike action can be had in Spofford Lake at Chesterfield. The chain pickerel is found over much of the southern third of the state. Just about any weedy pond will harbor these small cousins of the pike.

New Hampshire has some excellent bass fishing. Lake Wentworth near Wolfeboro may well be the best bass lake in the state. Squam Lake is good as well. Other fine bronzeback waters are Newfound Lake near Bristol and Lake Winnisquam in Plymouth. Lake Winnipesaukee produces hot smallmouth action in the summer months. Incidentally, the pickerel in this lake are above average in size.

Largemouth bass have a more restricted habitat because they require warmer water. But such lakes as Ayers in Barrington, Massasecum in Bradford, Pawtuckaway in Nottingham, Glen Lake in Goffstown, and Martin Meadow Pond in Lacoster all have largemouths. The Merrimack River around Manchester also produces fine catches of bass.

Bullheads are a favorite fish among some New Hampshire natives. They have a wide distribution in the state. White perch is probably the most important panfish. Good stringers can be caught in the Winnipesaukee River, Silver Lake near Lochmore, and Messabesic near Manchester.

New Hampshire has only a small piece of the Atlantic coastline, so it does not have the saltwater angling that some of the other New England states have. Striped bass is the most important fish, with schools of smaller fish coming in during June. Late summer and early fall produce bigger fish. Mackerel also provide action from May to August.

Public access to the better streams and lakes is no problem in New Hampshire. Some of the bigger lakes have fishing resorts on them and camping accommodation is also available. Stream fishermen will find no shortage of motels and small hotels in the smaller towns.

Where to Hunt

Ruffed grouse is the most widely distributed game bird in the state, with a two-month season in October and November. Grafton and Coos Counties are the best areas, while sections of White Mountain National Forest are fairly good. Woodcock are also abundant during the early season which coincides with that for grouse. But the timberdoodles are mostly Canadian birds heading south. Moist woodlots of the larger river valleys are the spots to look for woodcock.

Pheasant gunning in New Hampshire is a put-and-take operation. The Merrimack River watershed is the best area. The ringneck season opens in early October and closes early in November.

In New Hampshire small-game mammals mean cottontails, snowshoes, gray squirrels, and raccoons. None are hunted much except by devotees. The best cottontail hunting is in the very southern part of the state, while snowshoes tend to be best in the vast forests of the north. The rabbit and squirrel season opens early in October.

Good waterfowl gunning is available in several parts of the state. Local beaver ponds have some fine shooting for black and wood ducks. The marshes around Umbagog are local hotspots for dabbling ducks. The Great Bay and Little Bay areas of the sea coast also offer fine waterfowling. Good flights of teal come through during the early season, followed by blacks, mallards, and even Canada geese. The coastal area is good for sea ducks.

Deer and bear are New Hampshire's big-game animals. The deer season is open during the first two weeks of November. The archery season opens early in October and the primitive gun season in late October. The best deer hunting lies in Dunner, Green's, Grant, Tuftonboro, Monroe, Moultonboro, Bath, and Orford townships. The central counties of the state — Belknap, Cheshire, Rockingham, and Hillsborough — receive much lighter hunting pressure and are good bets.

The bear season begins on September 1 and ends with the closing of the deer season. Up to the start of the deer season, hounds may be used under a special permit. Coos County is the best place for bagging a bruin.

NEW JERSEY

New Jersey Division of Fish, Game, and Shellfisheries
State Labor Building
Box 1809
Trenton, New Jersey 08625

Where to Fish

New Jersey has so much good fishing water along its coast that it is hard to know where to start. The offshore fishing is mainly for bluefish, striped bass, dolphin, marlin, bonito, tuna, ground fish, and sharks. The inshore fishing is mainly for striped bass, bluefish, fluke, weakfish, flounder, and cod in winter.

Although every charter-boat captain has his favorite fishing grounds, three of the better-known ones are Berngat Ridge, Klondike Banks, and Ashbury Grounds. They all produce school tuna, white marlin, bonito, bluefish, and assorted sharks. Other top-producing grounds are: the Mud Hole opposite Sea Bright, known for big tuna and smaller school fish; the Cedars by Sandy Hook, known for its striped bass; 17 Fathom Bank, known for its bluefish and bottom fish; Roamer Shoals off Sandy Hook, known for its striped bass and bluefish; Subway Rocks, east from Long Island's East Rockway Inlet, for sea bass, and blackfish; and Shrewsbury Rocks below Sandy Hook, for bluefish.

The inshore fishing is concentrated around the big bays such as Delaware Bay, Sandy Hook, Great Egg, and Great Bay. The estuaries of the big rivers such as the Delaware and the Mullica also provide fine action during the appropriate season. The barrier islands along the New Jersey coast are very popular with surf casters.

There is no doubt that New Jersey offers prime surf fishing. When the stripers move inshore, hordes of anglers line the beaches and rocks. Almost the entire coast from Sea Bright to Delaware Bay is one long surf-casting beach. When the stripers are in, some of the local hotspots are Ashbury Park, Point Pleasant Beach, Island Beach, Seven Mile Beach, and Cape May. The beaches around Atlantic City and Ocean City are also very good.

Although stripers provide most of the action, many of these inshore areas also get good runs of bluefish, weakfish, and flukes. The action for stripers begins in April, peaking in late May. Weakfish also begin to move into the bays and estuaries in May. The bluefish come later.

All New Jersey harbors have boat-launching facilities. The marinas in many of them rent small boats and motors for inshore fishing. Charter boats are available at almost every port, and the bigger ones have party boats. On the party boats the fare includes the bait, but the angler must provide his own tackle. Some of the better-known sport fishing ports with charter and party boats are: Atlantic City, Atlantic Highlands, Ashbury Park, Belmar, Brielle, and Cape May.

The freshwater fishing in New Jersey begins in April. The northern part of the state has the best trout waters. Big Flat Brook close to the Pennsylvania border is the top trout stream in the state. It offers native brookies in the upper reaches and rainbows and browns further down. The Manasquan River in north-central New Jersey is another good trout stream. The Delaware River around Port Jarvis has some fine trout fishing.

Good bass lakes are scattered throughout the state. Such lakes as Turn Mill, Carnegie, Colliers Mills, Spruce Run, and Union offer good largemouth fishing. The Delaware River in Sussex County is a good bet for smallmouths. The Round Valley Reservoir is a fine bronzeback water as well.

Pickerel are widely distributed in New Jersey. Lakes such as Wawayanda, Greenwood, Cranberry, Union, and Swartswood all have pickerel. Also, the Cranberry Bay reservoirs in southern New Jersey have fine pickerel fishing. Some of these reservoirs also have bass.

There is a good shad run into the Delaware in mid-April and early May. The local hotspot is the stretch from Stockton to Trenton. Anglers can fish for shad and camp in the Worthington State Forest. Another interesting fishing opportunity in New Jersey is saltwater ice fishing on the Mullica River in January and February. The quarry here is jumbo white perch, frequently weighing up to three pounds.

Where to Hunt

The Garden State is basically a small-game state, with a short deer season thrown in for good measure. The pheasant is probably the most popular game bird with New Jersey scattergunners. The season starts in mid-November with the state stocking large numbers of birds in public hunting areas. Some of the better public hunting areas are Millville Tract in Cumberland County, Black River Tract in Warren County, and Flatbrook Tract in Sussex County. Quail is another New Jersey game bird for which the season opens on the same day as the pheasant season. The Peaslee Wildlife Management Area in Cumberland County and Greenwood Forest Management Area in Ocean County are good places for hunting bobwhites. Both areas are specially managed for quail. Much of southern New Jersey has bobwhites, with Cape May, Salem, Burlington, Atlantic, Ocean, and Cumberland Counties being the best. Ruffed grouse is also found in New Jersey, and the season usually opens on the same day as that for pheasant and quail. The best places to hunt ruffed grouse are Warren, Sussex, Morris, Monmouth, and Burlington Counties.

Good woodcock flights pass through New Jersey with the upper Delaware River counties of Sussex and Warren being the best in mid-October. Later in the season, the southern New Jersey counties are a better choice. Cape May and Salem are both reputed to have some very productive woodcock covers.

Other migratory game birds are rails. The top area for clapper rail is the vast tidal marsh between Cape May Point and Tuckerton, while the best sora-rail gunning is in stands of wild rice in the lower Maurice River. Wading River is another good place for the little sora rail.

Waterfowl gunning is quite good on the New Jersey marshes, but hunting pressure is a problem. Both dabblers and diving ducks are hunted. Brigantine National Wildlife Refuge, northwest of Atlantic City, is one good spot open to public hunting. Other good spots are the wildlife management areas of Egg Island, the Fortescue Tracts in Cumberland County, and the Dennisville Tract in Cape May. The state has over 50,000 acres of wetland open to public hunting.

The small game in New Jersey is squirrel and rabbit, but fox, woodchuck, and raccoon all have closed seasons during part of the year. The cottontail is the most popular game species, and is found over the entire state. However, Cape May, Morris, Unterdon, Salem, and Sussex are the best rabbit hunting counties.

White-tailed deer is New Jersey's big game, but a few black bears roam the less-settled areas of Warren and Sussex Counties. The archery deer season opens in early October and closes in early November. The gun season is open for five days in early November. Warren, Unterdon, Mercer, Ocean, Burlington, and Atlantic Counties have the best deer harvest.

A non-resident hunting licence costs $25.25, with a special woodcock stamp at $3. The Game Division publishes a handy guide (for $2) to public hunting areas.

NEW MEXICO

New Mexico Department of Game and Fish
State Capitol
Santa Fe, New Mexico 87501

Where to Fish

Trout and bass are New Mexico's top game fish. To sweeten the pot a little, New Mexico also has walleye and northern pike. And, of course, wherever there are bass, there are panfish.

A trout fisherman who likes to backpack, will find the rugged Sangre de Cristo

Mountains east of Santa Fe a trout-fishing haven. There are many excellent trout streams and quite a few trout lakes in this scenic area. Two of the best trout lakes are Lattir and Heart. Both have rainbows and cutthroats. The Rio de las Trampas in the Carson National Forest has cutthroats and rainbows too. The Santa Barbara and its many tributaries also have these species. The headwaters of the Pecos River have plentiful numbers of cutthroats.

The Wheeler Peak Wilderness Area has three excellent cutthroat lakes — Lost, Horseshoe, and Bear. Lost also has rainbows. Pecos Baldy has good rainbow fishing, with 20-inch fish. An angler seeking the unusual should go to Lake Katherine for the beautiful golden trout.

The Gila Wilderness Area on the western edge of New Mexico also has fine mountain trout lakes and streams. Iron Creek is a beautiful little stream, chock full of cutthroats. Willow and Gilleta Creeks also have trout fishing, but they get a fair amount of pressure in the summer tourist season. Snow Lake also has fine rainbows. The Gila River itself is a tremendous trout stream for native cutthroat. The Upper Middle Fork is particularly well regarded by local experts.

Other trout waters in the state are the Rio Grande from the New Mexico-Colorado line to Lynden Bridge. The best time is after spring run-off and in the fall. The Jemez River between Soda Dam and Battleship Rock is an excellent rainbow stream. The San Juan River below Navajo Dam has good rainbow and brown-trout fishing, with peak action in the fall. The North Fork of the Ruidoso River is a good bet for trout. The Cimarron River between Eagle Nest Dam and Ute Park in the scenic Cimarron Canyon is another tremendous brown-trout stream.

Stone Lake in the Jicarilla Apache Indian Reservation is a fine rainbow lake. Ice fishing is good here. The Navajo Reservoir also has rainbows, browns, kokanee salmon, and bass. Bonito Lake in the White Mountains of Lincoln County has cutthroats, rainbows, and Dolly Varden. The list of trout lakes — big and small — could go on and on. Let us now describe New Mexico's warm-water game fish. Like elsewhere in the southwest, it is the big reservoirs that provide the bulk of the bass fishing. Conchas Reservoir east of Santa Fe offers tremendous walleye fishing. The best walleye hotspots are around Rattlesnake and Green Islands. The best fishing is at night in spring. The Conchas also has excellent largemouth bass fishing with lunkers up to 10 pounds. Big crappies and channel catfish complete the roster. Another top bassing spot is Elephant Butte Reservoir on the Rio Grande in the southern part of the state. This lake is well known in the southwest for its big bass. But aside from largemouths, the lake has outstanding white-bass fishing in the spring. Crappies and catfish are also abundant.

Exotic big-game animals such as Indian black buck, sitka deer, and barbary sheep – like this fine specimen bagged in New Mexico – have been introduced in several areas of the southwest.

Anglers who like fishing for smallmouth bass will find the Rio Grande River from Arroyo Hando Bridge down to Lynden Bridge good. New Mexico's other fish include northern pike in Miami Lake near Springer and white bass in the Caball Reservoir.

Most of New Mexico's fishing is undeveloped as far as commercial fishing establishments such as lodges are concerned, but campgrounds are found almost everywhere.

Where to Hunt

New Mexico's glamorous big-game species is the prized desert bighorn. The season for this outstanding trophy is open only rarely and then only to residents. The Pecos and San Andres Mountains are two of the best sheep ranges. However, New Mexico also has an exotic sheep; the Barbary sheep from North Africa on its big-game hunting menu. Permits are by draw only and the season runs for a week or so in mid-February. The Canadian River is the best area for bagging this unusual trophy.

Deer — muleys and whitetails — are new Mexico's most popular big-game animals. The season opens early in November. The archery season is open earlier and longer. Hidalgo County is the best bet for whitetails. The best areas for mule deer are around Ruidoso and Capitan in the Lincoln National Forest and around the Guadalupes. The Mescalero-Apache Reservation has excellent deer hunting. A special tribal hunting licence is required.

Elk season opens in early September on some Indian reservations, but an early October opening is more common. Pecos wilderness is a top elk area, but some ranches around Cimarron and Chama also have good elk hunting. The Jicarilla-Apache Reservation is top elk country. A special tribal permit is needed to hunt on the reservation. Pronghorn antelope in New Mexico can be hunted on public lands by draw permit only. The pronghorns are limited to the southwestern part of the state. Some ranches also have pronghorn herds and the special draw does not apply to private land.

Javelina, black bear, and cougar are the other big-game animals. The javelina hunt, if held, is by special draw and is restricted to Hidalgo County. The black-bear season opens early in August and closes in mid-December. There is also a month-long spring bear season in April. The bruin may be hunted with hounds when no other big-game season is open. The Guadalupe, Sacramento, and Captain Mountains are the best areas for bear. The season for cougar is from late fall to late winter. The Gila National Forest has a good cougar population, but other state wilderness areas also have them.

Shotgunners will find that New Mexico has a wide variety of small game, including turkey. Most upland game-bird seasons open mid-November (except doves, grouse, and pheasant). There is both a spring and a fall season for wild turkeys, with Gila and Lincoln National Forests being the two top areas to bag a gobbler.

Three species of quail — bobwhites, scaled, and Gambel's — can be hunted. Bobwhites are found in the eastern part of New Mexico, with Roosevelt and Lea

Counties being the best bets. Gambel's quail are found only in the southwest corner of the state, and scaled quail are to be found in the southern half.

New Mexico has a three-day season on prairie chickens in early December. The best place for prairie grouse is Roosevelt County. Blue grouse are found in the forested hills, with Taos and Rio Arriva Counties being the best areas. The December ring-necked pheasant season is also a short one. The best areas are the farm fields of the Rio Grande Valley and Valencia and Socorro Counties.

Squirrels and cottontails are the small-game mammals. The tassel-eared squirrel is one of the lesser-known game species. Cottontails are very numerous, but so little hunted that there is no closed season on them. The squirrel season is open for a month in September.

Migratory birds are well represented. Both mourning and white-winged doves are popular and widely distributed. Their relative, the band-tailed pigeon, is also found in the forested hills. The season on these three species opens in early September. One of the more unusual of New Mexico's migratory birds is the lesser sandhill crane. The best area to hunt these big long-legged birds is Chavez County.

Waterfowl hunting in New Mexico is restricted to local areas. Irrigation projects in the farm country and stock ponds have duck shooting during the migration. The Rio Grande Valley is also a good area in some spots. In some places geese are hunted in stubble.

A non-resident hunting licence ranges from $10 for varmints to $100 for cougar and Barbary sheep. A bird licence costs $17.00; antelope $40.00; elk $50.00; big game including deer, bear, and turkey $50.25.

NEW YORK

New York Department of Environmental Conservation
Division of Fish and Wildlife
Albany, New York 12201

Where to Fish

Surprisingly, New York has some outstanding fishing. White marlin can be caught within sight of shore at Montauk, and brown trout can be taken on wet flies within an hour's drive of New York City. However, the best trout streams in the Empire State flow through the mountain and forest country of the north. Some of these trout streams were responsible for the development of flyfishing on this continent.

The Batten Kill, near Saratoga Springs, produces as fine a brook trout today as it did in the days of Frank Forester. This historic trout stream has 13 miles of public water. Besides brookies, it also has browns. Beaverhill and Willowemoc near Roscoe are two more fine and historic trout streams. The west bank of the Ausable near Wilmington is an excellent flyfishing river.

The St. Regis River in the very north of New York is a pristine trout water that gladdens the heart of any angler with a flyrod in his hand. A No. 5 or 6 is about right for this stream. Native brook trout still haunt the small pools, while browns lurk under banks and logs. Actually the Empire State has no shortage of brown-trout waters. The Pepacton Reservoir at Downsville has big browns. The Round-out Reservoir at Lackawack is also good for big browns.

Other trout waters in New York State are Naples Creek which flows into Lake Canandaigua and Catherine Creek which flows into Seneca Lake. They are both well known for their spring rainbow runs, but stay away on opening day and on weekends. The Fulton chain of lakes has some fine lake-trout fishing as, of course, do Seneca, Canandaigua, and the other Finger Lakes such as Cayuga and Keuka. Hemlock Lake south of Rochester has also been producing fine catches of lakers.

Muskellunge is the glamor fish in New York waters. The Thousand Islands area is probably the best big musky water anywhere. A number of musky guides operate here. This area is also known for its fine smallmouth bass fishing. Fall is the best season for muskies. Another top muskellunge water is Chautauqua Lake near Jamestown. Good pike fishing can be had in Seneca Lake, but Lake St. Lawrence may be even better. The northerns run larger there. Oneida Lake holds the honor of being the top walleye water. May and June are the best times to catch a stringer of these sweet-tasting fish. Other walleye spots are Black Lake in St. Lawrence County and the Delaware River near Narrowsburg. The walleye fishing in Lake Erie has improved recently.

New York State has some good bass fishing. For largemouths, try the Tomhannock Reservoir near Troy. This water also has smallmouths, pickerel, and panfish. The New York City reservoirs are also good. Lake Canandaigua is one of the old reliables for many Empire State largemouth anglers. The Thousand Islands area of the St. Lawrence River is tops for smallmouths. The gravelly shoals, bars, and reefs make it one big smallmouth hatchery. Another good bet for smallmouths is Lake George.

There is saltwater action the year around, but the main season is from April to October. Winter fishing is confined mostly to party boats after cod and northern whiting, with perhaps some haddock and pollock.

The ocean fishing is largely for striped bass, bonito, dolphin, albacore, tuna, swordfish, white marlin, and sharks. Party boats venture out for ling, porgies, cod, bluefish, sea bass, and the like. Inshore fishing is mainly for striped bass, blackfish, bluefish, cod, flounder, fluke, and weakfish. Porgies, snappers, and sea bass are also caught inshore. The inshore fishing can be from small boats or from jetties, piers, rocks, and beaches. Some party boats operate primarily in inshore waters.

Montauk on the South Shore is probably New York State's most famous fishing port. It has a big charter-boat fleet. This area is well known for its striped bass, bluefish, tuna, white marlin, and swordfish. Surf casters do well around Montauk Point. Hampton Bay, also on the South Shore, is a fine port for tuna, white marlin, and swordfish.

Sheepshead Bay is a popular angling spot with many New Yorkers because they can reach it by subway. It has a number of party and charter boats. Other popular fishing spots are Captree State Park, Freeport, and Coney Island with its fishing pier.

The North Shore has some fine beach fishing, but the inshore fishing from small boats is generally better. Such areas as Bayville, Cold Spring Harbor, Port Washington, and several others have fishing stations where boats can be rented. Greenport is the main fishing center, with a fleet of charter and party boats. Many of the party boats that fish in the North Shore waters sail out of City Island and Bronx River in New York City.

There are many marinas around New York City and surrounding area. Most have launching ramps for trailered boats. Many of the towns also have public-launching ramps. Although access is a problem with a few of the fishing grounds, ingenious anglers think of some way to reach them.

Where to Hunt

The white-tailed deer is the main big-game species of New York State. The deer season opens in late October and closes as late as early December depending on the area. Bow hunters have a somewhat earlier season. Generally it is bucks only, but in some areas a limited kill of antlerless deer is allowed. The Catskills and Adirondacks still attract many hunters. Delaware County in the Catskills is a good bet. Stueben and Allegany Counties are also two good deer-hunting areas. The entire area east of the Hudson River to the Connecticut border is pretty good deer country, as are many woodlots from Syracuse west to Lake Erie.

Black bear is New York's other big game. The bruins are not abundant but some are taken every year in the Adirondacks as well as the Catskills. Essex and Hamilton Counties are two of the better bear-producing counties. The bear season is approximately at the same time as the deer season.

The most important upland game birds in New York State are pheasants and ruffed grouse; but woodcock hunting is increasing in popularity. Bobwhite quail, Hungarian partridge, and wild turkey are also on the hunting menu.

Wild turkey can be hunted in both the spring and fall seasons. The fall season is from late October to mid-November while the week-long spring season is in early May. The best areas for wild turkey are in Cottaraugus, Allegany, and Steuben. The turkey flock in New York State is still increasing in numbers and becoming more widely spread under good wildlife management policies.

The bobwhite-quail season is limited to Long Island. Bobwhites are quite abundant and the season lasts through November and December, but finding a place to hunt is a problem. The huns also have a restricted habitat with coveys being found in St. Lawrence, Clinton, and Franklin Counties; but the grain stubbles of Jefferson County are the best bet for the little gray speedsters.

Ruffed grouse are widely distributed in the state but first-rate habitat is not at all plentiful. The grouse covers of the Catskills and Adirondack Mountains are the best. Woodcock are found in many covers with grouse, but the best timber-doodle gunning is found in the St. Lawrence Valley. Ring-necked pheasant can be found in most farming areas of the state but the fertile farmlands of the Lake Plain counties are the best.

Cottontails are without a doubt the most important game in New York State. More hunters hunt bunnies than birds. The cottontail is found statewide in good habitat, except perhaps the higher slopes of the Catskills and Adirondacks. Squirrel and snowshoe hare are two other small-game mammals. Southeastern New York is best for squirrels while Oneida, Essex, and Jefferson Counties are the best bets for varying hare.

Generally upland game-bird seasons open on October 1 and close in mid-November. The rabbit and squirrel season also opens on October 1, with rabbits closing at the end of February and squirrels at the end of January. Raccoons receive protection as well, with the hunting season from October to March.

Waterfowl hunting in New York State is good in several localities. A good area for both ducks and geese is the St. Lawrence Valley and eastern Lake Ontario; the Finger Lakes and the Lake Plain marshes are also good. The area from Onondaga County west to Genesse is particularly good for geese.

Long Island also has some top waterfowling areas. The south shore marshes are good for ducks and rails. Great South Bay, Moriches, and Shinnecock Bays are all good. Professional guides are available in these areas and they have the best gunning areas sowed-up for their clients.

Squirrel

NORTH CAROLINA

North Carolina Wildlife Resources Commission
P.O. Box 2919
Raleigh, North Carolina 27602

Where to Fish

There is no doubt that bass is North Carolina's top freshwater game fish. But like the other southern states, North Carolina has a variety of panfish and catfish, while the mountain counties offer fine trout fishing.

Currituck Sound is one of the best largemouth bass waters in the state but its bass are not as big as in some of the other waters. The Currituck's 40 miles create a big expanse of water where the bass are not always easy to find. Guides, boats, and motors are available in a number of communities along the Sound's shores. Lake Mattamuskeet is another fine bass lake, but it is probably better known among sportsmen for its fine waterfowl gunning. It is a swampy lake, so the best place to launch a boat is from the causeway. Besides largemouths, the lake has stripers and panfish.

It is difficult to pinpoint North Carolina's best bass water, but it may well be Lake Norman north of Charlotte. Norman belongs to the Catawba River chain, as does Lake Wylie which is also a fine bass water. Spring and fall are the best bassing times on the Norman. The lake also has striped bass, white bass, and panfish, with crappies being the most abundant. Channel cats are also found in the lake, and it has been stocked with sauger.

Fontana Lake in western North Carolina is a very fine mixed-creel lake. Like many of the Tennessee Valley Association lakes, it offers good walleye fishing. It also has smallmouths and, of course, largemouths. White bass, crappies, and bluegills offter top action along with catfish. Many of the streams running into Fontana flow from the Smoky Mountains and consequently have fine trout fishing. Rainbows can be caught in the lake near the creek mouths.

Another fine fishing water in this area is Santeetlah Lake. Largemouths, smallmouths, walleye, and even rainbow trout are the main game fish.

Other good bass waters are the Hickory and Lookout Shoals Lakes on the Catawba River. Natahala also has a fine reputation. The Piedmont Impoundments such as Tillery, Tuckertown, and High Rock are all good. I would be negligent if I did not mention Kerr Reservoir on the Virginia line. It has real lunker bass plus stripers. Lake Gaston, just below Kerr Reservoir, is a newer lake which has been producing fine stringers of bass. This lake also has pike, muskies, and pickerel. Panfish and catfish provide much action. It has striped bass as well. Another bass and panfish water in this area is Hyco Reservoir.

River fishing for bass in North Carolina can be very rewarding. Some of the best bass rivers are: Second Creek, the Little Alligator River, Scuppernong, Trent, White Oak, Chowan, and Cashie. The Roanoke River has striped bass with the peak run in early May. The Roanoke Rapids Lake has largemouths, stripers, and panfish.

The Tarheel State's coastline has a wide variety of fish on its angling menu. The offshore ocean fishing along the edge of the Gulf Stream produces blue marlin of up to 300 pounds and white marlin of up to 70 pounds, plus the occasional swordfish. There are also yellowfin, blackfin, and school tuna as well as many of the smaller species such as dolphin, wahoo, barracuda, false albacore, bonito, amberjack, and others. The marlin fishing is best in June and July, while the other fish can be caught from June to November depending on species.

Striped bass provide the fisherman with tremendous action at the Outer Banks surf, Albemarle, and Croaton Sounds, Cape Fear, and along the entire coast from Cape Hatteras to Nags Head. But *the* saltwater fish in North Carolina is the bluefish. It is available to trollers and surfcasters. The top areas are the big inlets such as Hatteras, Ocracoke, and Oregon. But such areas as Cape Point, the shoals off Cape Fear, Nags Head, and Albemarle Sound are also good.

The facilities for both saltwater and freshwater fishermen in North Carolina are generally excellent. All the big impoundments have public boat-launching ramps; marinas are found on many, as are camping parks. Most of the communities along the ocean in the big sounds and inlets have charter boats and motels and hotels. Party boats operate out of some of the bigger ports. Such places as Bogue Island, Knotts Island, Nags Head, Carolina Beach, Wilmington, and others have fishing piers. There are hundreds of marinas along the coast where boats can be launched and small boats rented. Anyone contemplating saltwater fishing in North Carolina should buy a copy of *Saltwater Sport Fishing and Boating in North Carolina.* This excellent guide is available in many marinas and bait and tackle shops along the North Carolina coast.

Where to Hunt

Doves, quail, rabbits, and squirrels are the principal small-game species in North Carolina, but the state also has ruffed grouse, wild turkey, and waterfowl. The dove season is the first to open in early September and closes in mid-January, but it is a split season with about a six-week closure in the middle. The birds are found statewide; the best gunning is in the agricultural lowlands. The limit is a generous 18 birds per day.

Quail are also found in almost every county but the eastern part of the state has the best hunting. Guilford and Mecklenburg Counties are two good spots, but the coastal plain is reputed to be just as good and has lighter hunting pressure. The quail season opens in mid-November and closes at the end of February.

The ruffed grouse is found in the hill country of North Carolina, but the birds are not hunted much. Jackson, Avery, Yancy, Mitchell, and Haywood Counties all lie in the better grouse range. The season on ruffed grouse begins in early October and closes at the end of February. The wild-turkey season in North Carolina is a spring gobbler season only. It opens in mid-April and closes early in May. The best turkey range lies west of Highway 1. North Carolina has undertaken an extensive transplanting and management program which, it is hoped, will increase dramatically the wild-turkey flock in the state.

Rabbits and squirrels are found statewide. Private lands which are closed to quail hunting are frequently open to cottontail hunting. Marsh rabbits are found in the wetlands along the Outer Banks. The rabbit season begins at the same time as quail, while the squirrel season opens in mid-October. Both seasons run into the winter months.

The best waterfowl hunting in North Carolina is found along the coast and for some miles inland. Carrituck Sound just below the Virginia boundary is one local hotspot. Lake Mattamuskeet is another good spot. This area has the best Canada Goose hunting in the state. Rails in the coastal marshes offer fine wing shooting, but are mostly overlooked. The rail season opens early in September, while the waterfowl season does not open until late November.

The white-tailed deer is North Carolina's chief big-game species, but bear and wild boar are also found in the state. Deer are found in almost every county and the herd is still increasing, but the Coastal Plain is the best deer country in North Carolina. In the western part of North Carolina the best deer hunting exists on state wildlife lands with Daniel Boone, Santeetlah, Fires Creek, Chatham, and Flat Top all being good. Generally dogs are used in the thick swamps of the Coastal Plain. Still hunting is the usual deer hunting method in the mountains.

Bear are not particularly abundant in North Carolina but are highly prized. The eastern part of the state and the hill country are the best bear range. The season lasts from mid-October to mid-November and also during the last two weeks of December. There are a number of bear refuges where the bruin is protected but these refuges are open to other game. The limit is one bear per season. They are nearly always hunted with hounds.

Wild boar is found in the rough country of western North Carolina. A hunter's best bet to bag a boar is in Graham and Swain Counties. The wild boars are a mixture of European wild boars and feral hogs. The season opens in early October and closes late in November, opening again for the last two weeks of December. Two boars per season is the limit. Usually the boars are hunted with dogs, but in the more-open areas, still hunters bag a few.

A non-resident hunting licence costs $22.00, with deer, boar, bear, and turkey tags at $1.75 each. A six-day licence costs $17.75. Hunters planning to hunt on state game management areas must have a $6.00 land-use permit as well.

NORTH DAKOTA

North Dakota Game and Fish Department
2121 Lovett Avenue
Bismark, North Dakota 58501

Where to Fish

Walleye and northern pike are North Dakota's two major game fish, but the state also has some fine trout fishing, and sauger grow to record size. Lake Sakakawea, stretching close to 200 miles behind Garrison Dam, is one of the state's top fishing waters. It offers excellent pike fishing and outstanding walleye and sauger action. Several sauger at the top of the record book come from this lake. The walleyes run up to twelve pounds; northerns to twenty.

The local hotspots for walleye on this huge lake are Beulah Bay, Charging Eagle Bay north of Halliday, Little Missouri Bay near Werner, and Van Hook Arm near New Town. The hotspots for northerns are Snake and Woolf Creeks, Van Hook Arm, and Tabocco Garden near Watford.

The Missouri River below Garrison Dam also offers fine fishing. The dam's tailrace has walleyes, northerns, channel cats, and rainbows. The river is good for channel cats, northerns, and white bass.

North Dakota has many impoundments that offer top fishing. The Oahe Reservoir south of Bismark is another of Missouri's big impoundments. Big northerns, channel cats, and big white bass offer the most action. The walleye angling is good here as well. Lake Ashtabula near Valley City has also been very good during the past few years. Northerns and walleyes are the prime attraction.

Other walleye lakes are: Lake Tschida behind Heart Butte Dam; Jim Lake near Jamestown; and Red Willow and Spiritwood Lakes about 20 miles north of Jamestown. Red Willow and Spiritwood also have rainbows.

About fifty of North Dakota's smaller impoundments such as Froelich Dam, about an hour's drive south of Bismark; Davis Dam south of Dickinson; Moon Lake near Valley City; Short Creek Dam; and many others have rainbow fishing. These impoundments are scattered throughout the state.

However, the best trout fishing is probably in the Turtle Mountains near the Canadian border. These forested hills offer different scenery from the rolling plains. Some of the better-producing trout waters are Gravel Lake, Hooker Lake, Lake Upsilon, and Lake Metigoshe. This is a major tourist area with numerous resorts and camping parks. The Metigoshe State Park has camping sites.

Most of North Dakota's impoundments have public access and boat-launching facilities, but other facilities are limited. Anglers are advised to bring their own boats. Accommodation is available in nearby towns.

Where to Hunt

Sharp-tailed grouse and ducks provide the most action for North Dakota hunters. But geese, Hungarian partridge, sage grouse, ruffed grouse, pheasants, and wild turkey are all on the shotgunning menu. The best sharptail country is in the less-settled part of western North Dakota, west of the Missouri River. Local hotspots are around Hebron and Flasher and also at Marmarth and Trotters. The Entire Slope and Billings Counties are good bets.

Hungarian partridge are found in the north-central counties of the state. The huns generally do not need as wild a country as the sharptails. Ruffed grouse are found in the forested slopes of the Pembina Hills and Turtle Mountains. The season for sharptails, ruffed grouse, and huns opens in late September and closes on December 31. Dogs are very useful for hunting all these birds, but they are particularly valuable for huns and sharptails.

Pheasant hunting in North Dakota is spotty. However, some fine ringneck gunning can be had in the southeastern part of the state. Traditionally one of the better spots has been the Oakes-Ellendale area. The area south of Bismark, particularly along creek drainage ditch banks, has also been one of the better places. Generally the pheasant season opens in mid-October and closes in early December.

Waterfowl gunning is tops in North Dakota, thanks to an excellent network of refuges and waterfowl rest areas. Some of the best goose and duck hunting on the continent is around Devil's Lake. Good hotspots in the area are Sweetwater, Alice Silver and Stump Lakes. Top areas for snow geese are Cando and Rock Lakes. Other good spots are Englevale Slough south of Valley City, Ashtabula Lake north of Valley City, and Rush Lake near Langdon. The stubbles near Sand Lake Refuge are also good. North Dakota gets a fine migration of snipe but the birds go almost unhunted. Another migratory bird that can be hunted is the lesser sandhill crane.

Deer, both whitetails and muleys, are the number-one big game, but North Dakota also has some antelope as well. The mule deer are found in the Badlands of the western part of the state. Whitetails are distributed much more widely. The river bottoms are the best whitetail cover. One of the best whitetail hotspots lies between the Missouri River and Bismark, east of the town of Killdeer. The area southwest of Willison is also good. The deer season opens in early November and closes in mid-November.

Pronghorn antelope permits are available by special draw only and are limited to residents. The season is open during the last two weeks of September. Wild turkey is hunted by special draw and is also limited to residents. Generally the season is open during the last week of November. The Missouri River bottoms are the best areas for wild turkey.

Fox and gray squirrels are two popular small-game mammals. The squirrels are largely found in the timbered river bottoms, particularly in the southeastern part of the state. The season opens in mid-September. Cottontails and jackrabbits are found throughout the state in their proper habitat, while snowshoe hares are restricted to the Pembina Hills. None of the rabbits are hunted much. Cottontails are hunted more than the other species. There is no closed season on rabbits in North Dakota. Fox and coyote hunting with predator calls is quite popular among devotees. Foxes are protected during the spring and summer months.

A non-resident small-game stamp costs $35; a deer stamp $50; and a predator stamp $15. A general hunting licence has to be purchased before the stamps. It costs, believe it or not, 50 cents!

OHIO

Division of Wildlife
Ohio Department of Natural Resources
1500 Dublin Road
Columbus, Ohio 43212

Where to Fish

One of the hottest fishing waters in Ohio is Lake Erie. This comes as a surprise to people who have heard the lake described as a "dead sea " by some of the more radical environmentalists. Lake Erie may be polluted, but it certainly is not dead. The action on Erie begins early. The winter months provide some pretty hot ice fishing for tasty yellow perch, smelt, and some walleyes around Port Clinton. When white bass and yellow perch start to run in mid to late spring, hordes of anglers line the piers and jockey around in the river mouths to cash in on the action.

But the top game fish in Lake Erie are smallmouth bass and walleyes. The prime location for both species is the Bass Islands north of Catawba Island. Here the reefs and shoals offer excellent smallmouth habitat, while the deep channels are good walleye waters. White bass provide additional sport, particularly in the spring. Car ferries sail for the islands from such ports as Clinton, Sandusky, and Catawba on daily schedules during the navigation season. Guides are available in the area.

Another top walleye water in western Lake Erie is Sandusky Bay. However, the Buckeye State has many other fine fishing waters. Leesville Lake south of Carrollton is 1000 acres of largemouth bass and crappie water. The best largemouth fishing is in the summer, while crappies bite best in the spring. Leesville Lake is one of Ohio's best musky waters as well. Other top lakes in the eastern area are Berlin Reservoir, Clendening Lake, Piedmont Lake, the Portage Lakes, plus such well known lakes as Seneca, Atwood, Wills Creek, Charles Mill, and Tappan.

Northeastern Ohio has three excellent walleye lakes — Mosquito Creek Reservoir, Berlin Reservoir, and Pymatuning. All three of these lakes also have largemouth bass plus panfish. Mosquito Creek Reservoir offers fine largemouth bass fishing along with some walleyes plus panfish, including white bass. Berlin Reservoir has smallmouth bass and walleyes along with panfish and catfish. Piedmont Lake may well be Ohio's best musky water, with a 55-pound fish taken there in 1972. The lake also has very good largemouth fishing plus crappies and catfish. The best musky fishing is in the fall when the fish are feeding actively.

The southern half of Ohio, below State Route 70, also has a number of fine lakes. Rocky Fork Lake is known for its fine musky fishing, but it produces good stringers of walleyes, largemouth bass, crappies, and catfish as well. The top musky hotspots in this area are Blinko Canyon and Catfish Hollow; while Kelly's Cove and Catfish Hollow are the best bets for largemouths and panfish.

Buckeye Lake, just 30 miles east of Columbus, gets a lot of fishing pressure, but it is a highly productive lake with fine catches of largemouth bass, along with bluegills, crappies, white bass, and yellow perch. Other top lakes here are Veto, Grant, and Vesuvius.

Knox Lake, northeast of Columbus, is good for largemouth bass. Hoover Reservoir, even closer to Columbus, has fine walleye fishing along with largemouth bass, white bass, and other panfish. Another good fishing water close to Columbus is Indian Lake. This is a mixed-creel lake offering largemouths, crappies, bluegills, yellow perch, walleyes, pike, channel cats, and bullheads.

Most of the large Ohio lakes have ample facilities for camping and other accommodation nearby. Public access and boat-launching ramps are no problem. In some locations, boats can be rented.

Where to Hunt

Ruffed grouse and cottontails are Ohio's main game, but the state also has fine squirrel hunting. Pheasants, Hungarian partridge, and bobwhite quail are three other upland-game birds. Ruffed-grouse hunting is surprisingly good in the rugged country of southeastern Ohio. The eastern and east-central parts of the state also have productive grouse covers. Generally grouse are underhunted, particularly in the southeast. (There is a fair amount of public land in that part of Ohio.) Pike, Athens, Vinton, Morgan, and Washington Counties are the best bets. The season for grouse is a long one. It opens early in October and closes at the end of February.

Bobwhite quail is Ohio's most abundant farmland game bird. The principal quail range is south of Highway 30. On the other hand, pheasant are not doing well in Ohio. The farms are just too "clean" to give the ringnecks much cover. But there are pockets in Madison, Fayette, Clark, Lucas, and Wood Counties that have some fair pheasant hunting. Lucas and Wood are the best two. Hungarian partridge are not at all plentiful but there are some coveys scattered throughout the west-central part of the state. The pheasant, quail, and hun season opens in mid-November.

Rabbits are found throughout the state, as are squirrels, but the bushytails, both fox and gray, are more numerous in southern Ohio. The season on both opens in mid-November. Cottontails are Ohio's number-one game.

Migratory bird hunting is not particularly good in Ohio. The Lake Erie marshes do have excellent gunning but they are all under lease to duck clubs and private individuals. The state-owned Magee Marsh is open to the public on a daily-permit basis. It has excellent duck hunting. Controlled goose hunting is available at Lake St. Mary's, Mosquito Lake, and Killdeer Plains. The city of Akron has some blinds available on a daily-permit basis on some of its reservoirs. Some of the small creeks have duck hunting as well. Floating by canoe is the most popular hunting method on the creeks. Opportunities for hunting other migratory birds are not much better than for ducks, but there are some good woodcock covers in northeastern Ohio near the Pennsylvania line.

Deer is Ohio's only big game. The best counties are Ashtabula, Muskingum, Morgan, Turnbull, and Williams. Big-trophy bucks also come from the woodlots of fertile farmlands. Generally the shotgun-only season opens in late November and closes early in December, while the archery season goes on into early January. There is also a special primitive-weapons season.

Wild turkeys in Ohio are hunted by draw permit only. It is a spring-gobbler season, open only for a few days in late April or early May. Raccoon is popular game with the hound-dog music fans. The raccoon and opossum season is open for November, December, and January.

A non-resident small-game licence costs $20.35, with an additional $5.35 levied for a deer or turkey-hunting permit.

OKLAHOMA

Game Division
Oklahoma Department of Wildlife Conservation
1801 North Lincoln
Oklahoma City, Oklahoma 73105

Where to Fish

There is no doubt that the big reservoirs offer the best fishing in Oklahoma. The biggest of these impoundments is the 100,000-acre Lake Eufaula just north of McAllestor. The Eufaula is a fairly shallow lake, with thousands of acres of flooded timber areas providing ideal haunts for lunker largemouths. Besides largemouths, the lake also has excellent crappie fishing plus walleyes, striped bass, and catfish.

Northeastern Oklahoma has several fine fishing lakes. Grand Lake close to

Tulsa is a hot largemouth-bass water, along with crappies, white bass and some walleyes, plus flatheads and channel catfish. The local hotspot for largemouths is Goat Island. Catfish fishermen congregate at the north end of the lake and at the spillway at the dam.

Lake Oologah on the Verdigris River is another top bass lake. The water level was raised several feet a few years ago, flooding much of the shoreline with brush and standing timber. Other top fishing waters in this area are the City of Tulsa water reservoirs, and Lakes Eucha and Spavinaw. They both offer largemouth bass, white bass, walleyes, and catfish, but crappies provide the most action.

Oklahoma has been experimenting with a number of fish that are exotic to the state. Striped bass have been introduced to Lake Keystone and have offered much exciting fishing. Northern pike have been introduced to Lakes Clayton and Arbuckle in the southeastern part of the state. However, the best northern-pike lake in Oklahoma is Etling in the panhandle. The northerns in this lake run up to fifteen or sixteen pounds.

Other top fishing lakes in Oklahoma are Tenkiller, Texoma, Foss, Broken Bow, and Pine Creek. Tenkiller's 12,000 acres offer excellent largemouth bass fishing plus spotted bass, white bass, crappies, bream, and catfish. Texoma, Foss, Broken Bow, and Pine Creek are primarily bass lakes.

However, not all of Oklahoma's fishing is confined to lakes. The Illinois River below Tenkiller Dam has fine rainbow trout fishing up to its confluence with the Arkansas River. The best way to fish the Illinois River is to float down in a boat. The only other trout stream in Oklahoma is the Blue River near Tishomingo.

Where to Hunt

Bobwhite quail and doves are Oklahoma's most hunted game birds. The bobwhite season extends from late November to early February. The northwest portion of the state has excellent bobwhite hunting. Oklahoma also has some scaled quail in the panhandle area and in the western portion of the state. The scaled quail season is the same as for bobwhites.

Mourning doves are widely distributed in the state with the best gunning being in the grain-farming areas. The dove season opens September 1 and closes at the end of October. Oklahoma may not be renowned for its pheasant hunting, nevertheless the panhandle counties do have good pockets. The month-long season begins on December 1. The irrigated fields of Texas and Cimarron Counties are the best bet for pheasants.

Prairie chickens, both greater and lesser, are abundant enough to be on the shooting menu. The grasslands of northeast Oklahoma are the main prairie-grouse range. Osage County is tops for the greater chickens, while Ellis County is tops for the lesser chickens. The prairie-chicken season is open for a few days late in October and early November.

Wild turkeys are another of Oklahoma's upland-game birds. There is both a short fall season in early November and again in early December. There is also a spring season in late April. The western half of the state is the primary turkey range. Of course, the birds are the Rio Grande race of wild turkeys. This race is perhaps the handsomest of all the wild turkeys. Ellis County is the top hotspot but the brushy and wooded stream courses throughout the northwest are good places to hunt turkeys as well.

Waterfowl hunting is mostly confined to the large reservoirs, but the Arkansas and Verdigris Rivers also offer fine duck gunning. Geese, particularly Canadas, can be hunted north of Enid in the south. The area around Tishomingo Refuge is also good. Lake Oologah in northwest Oklahoma is another good spot. The waterfowling is confined almost solely to birds migrating south to Mexico for the winter.

White-tailed deer is the number-one big game. The Ozark Mountain counties have the biggest deer herds, but the bucks from Nowata and Rogers Counties in the panhandle are bigger. The firearms deer season is usually a week in late November while the archery season opens in mid-October. There is also a special primitive-weapons (muzzle-loading guns) season. Pronghorn antelope and elk are also found in Oklahoma but they are not numerous enough for a regular open season. Occasionally short special-permit hunts are held on both species for residents only.

Squirrels, cottontails, and jackrabbits are abundant in their proper habitats. The rabbit season opens in early October and closes in early March. Squirrel season for both gray and fox squirrels opens in mid-May and closes in late December. The Ozark Mountains are a top area for bushytails.

A non-resident hunting licence costs $15.00, a deer tag $25.00, a turkey tag $3.00.

OREGON

Oregon Game Commission
P.O. Box 3503
Portland, Oregon 97208

Where to Fish

Oregon's many rivers, lakes, and coastline offer so much good fishing water that an entire book could be devoted to it. The fish range from black bass, trout and salmon, to many saltwater species. The steelhead is probably the most sought-after fish in Oregon, but coho and chinook salmon must rank a close second. Other salmonids include cutthroats, browns, lake trout, kokanee, and even Atlantic salmon.

There are 22 coastal streams with runs of steelheads, chinook, coho, and sea-run cutthroats. It would be difficult to name the best one, but the Rogue River ranks very high. The river has fine runs of coho, chinook, and steelhead, providing almost year-around fishing. The upper reaches have resident rainbows.

Other major rivers are the Columbia, Umpqua, Coos, and Coquille. They all have salmon and steelhead. Generally the steelhead run in the winter months, but the lower Deschutes River and the Rogue River both have a summer run of

The coastal streams of Oregon, Washington, and British Columbia still have the best steelhead trout fishing, but there is also top steelhead action in a number of streams in Michigan, Minnesota, Wisconsin, and Ontario.

steelhead, with August and September being the best times. The Willamette River has been restored and cleaned up, and once again it is getting fine salmon and steelhead.

The mountain country of the Cascades and Wallowas offer hundreds of lakes for anglers who are willing to hike in. Flyfishing purists will find the Atlantic salmon a real challenge in Hosmer Lake. The fishing here is for sport only; all fish must be released. Good rainbow-trout fishing can be had in several of the large lakes such as Klamath, Waldo, and Diamond. Klamath has a reputation for big rainbows. The lake's waters are rather shallow and very fertile. Diamond Lake produces tremendous catches. Other interesting lakes are Odell and Crescent, both of which have lake trout and kokanee. Many of the reservoirs on the Willamette watershed also offer fine rainbow-trout action. Fly fishermen will find sections of such streams as the Donner, Williamson, Blitzen, Grande Ronde, and Wood excellent waters for rainbows and browns.

But trout and salmon are not the only fish in Oregon's lakes and rivers. Smallmouths offer fine and largely overlooked angling on the Snake River. The big impoundments in western Oregon's "desert" country, such as Malheur, Gerber, and Owyhee, have largemouths and panfish. The biggest largemouths in Oregon come from Siltcoos Lake near Florence. The closeby Tahkenitch Lake has fine bass fishing as well. Both lakes also have steelhead, coho, and cutthroat trout.

Striped bass run in several of Oregon's big rivers. The best runs are in Coquille, Coos, Umpaqua, and Yaquina. Big sturgeon offer unique sport in many of the coastal rivers, with Umpaqua, Smith, and Columbia being the best. Tremendous shad runs come up the Rogue, Coos, Coquille, and Columbia Rivers. These shad runs have been getting stronger during the past few years.

The Oregon coast produces some saltwater action. Salmon fishing is excellent during the summer months. Coos and Tillamook Bays are local hotspots. The offshore area outside Depoe Bay is also excellent. This is where a big commercial salmon fleet operates. Other top areas for salmon are Cape Kiwanda, Nehalem Bay, and Winchester Bay. Many of these areas produce steelhead and sea-run cutthroats as well. The salmon can be either coho or chinook, depending on the season.

Many of the small coves and bays have good fishing for bottom fish such as ling cod, rockfish, flounders, snappers, and the like. Big halibut are found in some locations as well. Many of these fish can be caught from shore, off rocks, jetties, and docks.

The albacore schools off Oregon's shores offer as yet a largely untapped sportfishing bonanza. Already some of the more adventurous fishermen are going out after these tuna. Many bays with coastal streams and rivers get good striped-bass runs.

Charter boats are available in most of Oregon's coastal communities. The main charter-boat ports are Salmon Harbor in Winchester Bay; Hammond, Warrenton, and Astoria at the mouth of the Columbia River; Newport in Depoe Bay; and Charleston Bay in Coos Bay.

Where to Hunt

Oregon is one of the top hunting states in the nation. Mule and black-tailed deer are the chief big-game mammals but antelope, elk, bighorn sheep, and cougar are all open to at least limited hunting. Black bear are numerous and small game is found in great variety, with some species being very abundant.

The deer season begins early in October and closes in late October or in some zones early November. Principally mule deer are found east of the Cascade Mountains with northeast Oregon being the best bet, particularly for hunters who are willing to pack-in to the mountains. The Blue Mountains, Wallowas, and the Oregon Plateau in the central part of the state are also good. Black-tailed deer are found west of the Cascades right to the coastal valleys. The Rogue River Basin, the Coast Range, and the west slope of the Cascades are top areas for blacktails. In several zones, blacktails of either sex may be taken.

Oregon has both the Roosevelt race of elk and the Rocky Mountain race of elk. The Roosevelt-elk season is open for about two weeks in mid-November for bulls only. The Rocky-Mountain-elk season generally runs the first two weeks of November, with antlerless animals allowed in some zones. The best area for the Roosevelt elk is the Coast Range with Clatstop County being the local hotspot. The best area for Rocky Mountain elk is in northeastern Oregon with the Wallowa Mountains being the best bet.

Bighorn sheep are limited to residents only and the permits are by special draw. The week-long season is in late September. Hart and Steen Mountains are the two top areas. Pronghorns are also available to residents only by special-draw permit. The plains of southeastern Oregon are the main pronghorn range. The season is open for only a few days in mid-August. Cougar permits are available to residents by special draw only. The big cats are found in the major wilderness areas of the state. The season lasts for all of December.

Black bear are widespread throughout the less-settled parts of the state. The Coastal Range is the top area for bear. The season is from September 1 to December 31, and again from mid-April to mid-May.

Oregon has some exceptionally fine waterfowl gunning. The Willamette Valley is a flyway for both ducks and geese. Waterfowl also migrate through Harney Basin in eastern Oregon. Both areas have excellent gunning. The coastal estuaries are a good bet late in the season. The waterfowl season opens in early October and closes in early January, depending on the area.

Doves and band-tailed pigeons are two other important migratory birds. The Coast Range and the interior valleys are best for bandtails, while the farming areas are best for doves. The season for these two birds is usually the month of September.

California and mountain quail, Hungarian and chukar partridge, blue, ruffed, and sage grouse, pheasants, and wild turkey can all be hunted in Oregon. California quail are found in the drier valleys of eastern Oregon; chukars are also in this part of the state. Generally these birds are found in the very dry canyons and hillsides. Mountain quail are also found in the hills of eastern Oregon and in the Coastal Range. Huns are limited to the grain-growing farmlands of northeast Oregon.

Ruffed grouse and blue grouse are widely distributed, with the Coast Range having some of the better ruffed grouse covers, and the Wallowa Mountains having some of the best blue-grouse cover in the state. Sage grouse are limited to the sagebrush plains of southeast Oregon. The seasons on all these upland-game birds open in early October, with the sage grouse season open only for a few days. Blue and ruffed grouse seasons are open for a month; the others much longer.

Pheasants in Oregon are mostly found in the northeastern part of the state. The birds are spotty, but Umatillia, Baker, and Union Counties have good pockets of pheasants. The irrigated farmlands in the Snake River Valley are very good. The pheasant season opens in mid-October and closes in mid-November.

Rabbits — cottontails, snowshoes, and jackrabbits — are also found in Oregon. They are not hunted much and have no closed season. The sagebrush country of northeast Oregon at times literally teems with cottontails and jackrabbits. Squirrel season for the very attractive silver-gray squirrel is generally open for the entire month of September. The top squirrel hunting is in southwestern Oregon.

A non-resident hunting licence costs $50, with a deer tag costing $15, and an elk tag $35.

PENNSYLVANIA

Pennsylvania Fish Commission
P.O. Box 1673
Harrisburg, Pennsylvania 17120

Pennsylvania Game Commission
P.O. Box 1567
Harrisburg, Pennsylvania 17120

Where to Fish

Pennsylvania has some superb trout fishing for the fly-fisherman. The limestone streams in the Pennsylvania valleys have insect hatches which delight the flyrodder. Some of the top limestone streams in the state are: Falling Spring Creek in Franklin County; Yellow Breeches Creek in Cumberland County; Honey and Kishacoquillas Creeks in Mifflin County; Spring Creek in Centre County; and Penns Creek in Centre and Union Counties.

Generally the mountain streams run through freestone. They are not very fertile or productive, but they still offer fine fishing. And since many of them are not easily accessible, they do not get much fishing pressure. Some of the top mountain streams are: Tionesta Creek in Warren and Forest Counties; Kettle Creek in Potter and Cameron Counties; Pine Creek in Potter County; Fishing Creek in Columbia County; Mehoopany Creek in Wyoming County; and Big Buskill in Monroe County.

Although trout streams are the backbone of Pennsylvania's trout fishery, there

are several lakes with fine trout fishing. Upper Woods Pond, and Wallenpaudack and Harveys Lakes, all in Poconos, are the state's top trout lakes. Upper Woods Pond and Harveys Lake have rainbows, lakers, and kokanee salmon, while Wallenpaupack has lunker browns.

Pennsylvania has excellent fishing for a number of warmwater game fish. The larger rivers such as the Delaware, the Susquehanna, the Allegheny, and the Juniata offer smallmouth bass, walleyes, panfish, and catfish. The Delaware also gets a trer,endous shad run in May and June. Certainly some of the best smallmouth-bass fishing in the United States is found in the Upper Allegheny, the Juniata, and the North Branch of the Susquehanna. The Upper Allegheny, the Juniata, and Susquehanna also have excellent walleye fishing. Other top walleye waters are Kinzue Reservoir, Lakes Wallenpaupack and Pymatuning, and the Delaware River.

The lower reaches of the Susquehanna from Harrisburg down, and the Allegheny River from Kittaning downstream, also have muskies. However, Tionesta Reservoir, Pymatuning Bay, and Presque Isle Bay on Lake Erie probably have even better muskellunge fishing. Certainly the fish there are larger.

Aside from the muskies, the Susquehanna and the Juniata are noted for their big channel cats. The tributary streams of these two rivers, plus the Delaware, have chain pickerel. Such species as largemouth bass, crappies, and bluegills are found in numerous lakes and man-made reservoirs throughout the state.

The Pennsylvania Fish Commission has an excellent booklet called *Fisherman's Guide to Pennsylvania Waters and Access Areas*. It is available free upon request.

Where to Hunt

Despite its dense population, Pennsylvania has fine hunting. White-tailed deer is the major big-game species. The hill country across Pennsylvania's northern counties has an excellent deer herd, but big deer are found in the woodlots of the farming counties. The firearms deer season opens in late November and closes in early December. The last couple of days are open for any deer. Bow hunters can start in late September and get another chance to notch their broadheads for a couple of weeks in mid-winter.

Black bear is a highly prized big-game animal in Pennsylvania with a two-day season in late November. The best bear hunting is in Cameron, Elk, Clinton, Tioga, and Sulivan Counties.

Pennsylvania has surprisingly good wild-turkey hunting. These big-game birds are most abundant in the high timbered hardwoods. Good turkey range is generally poor deer range because the birds prefer mature forests with plenty of

---

The white-tailed deer is our most abundant and most cosmopolitan big-game animal. Over 25,000 whitetails are killed annually by cars in the state of Pennsylvania alone.

mast. Such forests have very little browse for deer. The turkey season begins in late October to late November. Also there are two weeks of gobbler hunting in mid-May. Forest, Pike, Monroe, and Carborn Counties are good bets for a turkey hunt.

Grouse hunting in Pennsylvania is best in the southwest counties and in the Sasquehanna River drainage. The grouse season can open as early as late October and close as late as mid-January, depending on the region. Bobwhite quail is another indigenous Pennsylvania game bird. The south-central counties right to the Maryland boundary are the best spots for bobwhites. Pheasants are another farmland game bird. The best ringneck hunting is found south of Blue Mountain and east of Adams County. The pheasant and quail season opens in late October and closes in late November.

Woodcock and mourning doves are two important game birds in Pennsylvania. Doves are most plentiful in the farming country but they are distributed throughout the state. The dove hunting is found in the area from Allentown to Harrisburg and Gettysburg. On the other hand, the best woodcock covers are found in the northern part of the state wherever there are good pockets of alder, aspen, and hawthorn. The dove season opens early September and closes mid-November, while the timberdoodle season opens mid-October and closes mid-December.

Pennsylvania's waterfowl gunning is concentrated in the marshes of Mercer, Crawford, and Erie Counties. The lower Sasquehanna River below Harrisburg is another good area.

Although squirrels and cottontails are found throughout the state, the hunting is spotty. The best squirrel hunting is found in the oak forests of central and south-central Pennsylvania. Snowshoe hares are found in the forests of the northeast portion of the state.

A non-resident hunting licence costs $40.25, with deer tags for antlerless deer at $1.15.

RHODE ISLAND

Rhode Island Department of Natural Resources
Veterans' Memorial Building
Providence, Rhode Island 02903

Where to Fish

Anglers in the small state of Rhode Island are basically saltwater oriented. The state's 400-mile coastline offers superb year-around fishing. But it also has some fine trout fishing, plus under-exploited bass, pickerel, and panfish angling.

The heavy action begins towards the end of April, when the school stripers move into Rhode Island waters. The school stripers are small fish in the 4 or 5-pound class. Right behind them come the trophy-sized lunkers, up to 30 pounds or more. These stay in local waters until November.

As if outstanding striper fishing were not enough, Rhode Island waters also get superb bluefish action. The bluefish come in around mid-May and stay until the end of October. Bluefish action sometimes rivals striper action. The stripers and bluefish can be caught by surfcasting or from boats. Some of the local hotspots are Brenton Reef, Sakonnet Point, and Beaver Tail. The Charleston Breachway, a rock-lined channel, is another hotspot for stripers.

Other inshore fish provide good angling in Rhode Island's salt water. Weakfish have been making fine runs into Narraganset Bay in recent years. Nearly all of the inlets are good, but some of the best ones are East Greenwich Bay, Nayatt Point, Pine Hill Cove, and Green River. Pollock provide fine fishing from spring to fall, as do black sea bass, kingfish, and tautog. Flounder can be taken from early spring to late fall. Cod, at the mouth of the Narraganset or around the Block Islands, can be taken the year around.

Rhode Island's offshore fishing is excellent as well. Tuna begin in June, but the peak action is in mid-summer. Both school tuna and the big heavyweights are taken. White marlin also provide fine trolling action through the summer, along with bonito and some dolphin. The odd swordfish is boated as well. Sharks are also present.

Rhode Island has only one major trout stream and that is Wood River in the Arcadia State Management Area. Brook trout, rainbows, and browns are all found here. The Wood River is a fine flyfishing stream. The only other trout water worth noting is Wallum Lake on the Massachusetts line. It has browns and brook trout. Brickyard Pond near Barrington also has rainbows and browns.

Some of the top lakes in Rhode Island are Deep Pond in Charlestown, Worden's Pond in South Kingstown, and Bowdish Reservoir in Glocester. They offer bass, pickerel, panfish, and catfish. Worden's Pond also has northern pike.

Woonasqutucket Reservoir in Smithfield and Pascoag Reservoir in Burrillville both offer fine bass fishing, along with other species. Indian Lake near South Kingston is a shallow lake of some 200 acres. It has fine bass fishing for both smallmouths and largemouths, plus pickerel and panfish. Another important fishing water is the Palmer River, which gets a fine run of shad in mid-spring.

All the major streams and lakes in Rhode Island have some public access. Boat-launching facilities exist on some. Saltwater access is also no problem. Numerous marinas offer boat-launching ramps as well as boats for rent. There are a number of public fishing areas. The best one for stripers and bluefish is Ocean Drive Public Fishing Area in Newport. Charter boats are available at Little Compton, Galilee, and other ports.

Where to Hunt

This tiny, densely populated state offers surprisingly good small-game hunting. The dove season comes first, opening in late September. The farmlands near the towns of North Smithfield and Little Compton, and the countryside between Narranganset Bay to Black Island Sount are good bets for doves.

Pheasant, quail, and ruffed grouse are Rhode Island's three other game birds. Ruffed-grouse hunting is best near the Massachusetts line. The Great Swamp

Management Area is a good bet. This portion of Rhode Island is also the best area for woodcock. Bobwhites are most plentiful in southern Rhode Island. The best ringneck pheasant hunting is found in southern Rhode Island, particularly in the truck gardens and other fertile farmlands.

One would expect that Rhode Island would have good waterfowl gunning and it has; but unfortunately, the best marshes are privately owned. There is some fine open-water shooting, particularly for sea ducks in late season but also for blacks and mallards in season. Narraganset Bay has good shooting for diving ducks, particularly bluebills.

Squirrels, cottontails, and snowshoe hares are all hunted in Rhode Island. Cottontails far outrank the other two game animals in hunting importance. The bunnies are found almost statewide. Snowshoe hares are limited to the bigger forests and swamps. Arcadia, Indian Cedar Swamp, and Great Swamp Tracts are good bets for the varying hare.

White-tailed deer is the only big game in the state. There is a week-long shotguns-only season in late October and a couple of days again in late November. The archery season opens three weeks before the shotgun season. The northern counties tend to be the best for bagging a deer.

A non-resident hunting licence costs $10.25, with a deer licence being $20.00.

SOUTH CAROLINA

South Carolina Wildlife Resources Department
1015 Main Street
Columbia, South Carolina 29202

Where to Fish

South Carolina's 280 miles of coastline offer fine saltwater action for inshore small-game fish, plus the big stuff offshore. The state's rivers and lakes also boast top bass and panfish angling.

South Carolina shares a couple of big impoundments with Georgia. These are the Hartwell and Clark Hill Reservoirs. The Hartwell Reservoir has over 60,000 acres of fine fishing water. Largemouth bass is the main game fish here, plus crappies, bream, and catfish. Walleyes are found in the lake too. The Tugaloo and Seneca Rivers, which empty into this reservoir, also have fine bass fishing.

Clark Hill Reservoir, on the Savannah River north of Augusta, Georgia, has an area of over 78,000 acres. It is also a top bass water, and offers excellent white-bass fishing, plus striped bass and a hybrid of the white and striped bass, along with crappies and catfish.

The Santee-Cooper Lakes, also known as Lakes Marion and Moultrie, are two other highly productive fishing waters. Landlocked striped bass offer hot action here. But the lakes, and particularly Moultrie, are also known for lunker largemouths and the general run of panfish.

Other excellent fishing waters are Wateree Reservoir, Lake Murray, and Lake

Greenwood. Wateree, north of Columbia, has excellent white-bass fishing in the late spring when the whites are on their spawning run. It also has largemouths. Lake Murray, just west of Columbia, and Lake Greenwood, near the town of that name, are excellent bass lakes. In both lakes the largemouth fishing is best in the spring and fall.

All of South Carolina's reservoirs have ample public access and boat-launching facilities. Many of the lakes have campgrounds on their shores. Clark Hill alone has over twenty campgrounds.

Many of South Carolina's rivers have excellent fishing. Rainbow trout and browns are stocked in Savannah below the Hartwell Dam for about a 12-mile stretch. The lower reaches of the Savannah have good shad and striper action in the spring. The reaches above Clark Hill Reservoir get a white-bass run in the spring. Largemouth bass, panfish, and catfish are found over almost the entire length of the river.

Other top rivers are Wateree, Pee Dee, and the Edisto. They all have black bass, bream, bluegills, and catfish. They also get stripers in the early spring, and Wateree has a white-bass run.

The best trout streams in the Palmetto State are in the mountain country of northwestern South Carolina. These streams offer surprisingly good fishing for browns, rainbows, and even brookies. The top streams are Big Eastatoe, the three forks of the Saluda River, the Chattooga River, the Keowee River, the Whitewater River, and perhaps four or five others. The best fishing is in the more remote stretches.

South Carolina's coastline has some fine habitat for a number of fish species. Bluefish offer fine sport for surfcasters and boat fishermen in the many bays and inlets during the summer and fall months. The local hotspots are islands at the mouth of Winyah Bay. Striped bass are found in a number of the inland reservoirs, but the coastal rivers and their bays also get hot action. The top ones are Black, Edisto, Santee, Combahee, Savannah, and a couple of others. The waters around Winyah Bay, Sullivans Island, St. Helena Sound, and Port Royal Sound also are excellent and less heavily fished.

Weakfish provide action in the inlets and bays around rocks and reefs, and in the creeks. Other inshore fish such as channel bass, whiting, black sea bass, flounder, sheepshead, pompano, and cobia provide fine sport as well. Whiting, flounder, black sea bass, and sheepshead can be caught the year around. Pompano are mainly summer fish and channel bass are spring-and-fall fish.

Tarpon fishing is best from July to September. Some of the top tarpon grounds are Charleston Harbor, Winyah Bay, and Edisto Island.

Offshore big-game fishing is best in summer. Sailfish, white marlin, and the big blue marlin are caught on the edges of the Gulf Stream. Dolphin, bonito, amberjacks, groupers, and snappers are also available. Dolphin are caught mainly on the edges of the Gulf Stream, while snappers and groupers have a wide distribution around reefs and wrecks.

Charter boats are available in a number of harbors. Charleston, Little River,

Georgetown, and Myrtle Beach all have charter fleets. Some also have party boats. Many of the other small coastal towns have charter boats as well. Boat-launching facilities and marinas are scattered over the entire South Carolina coast. There is no shortage of these in the main fishing ports.

Fishing piers exist in the Little River, Ocean Drive Beach, Garden City, Pawleys Island, Sullivans Island, Edisto Island, and several other places. There is no shortage of accommodation here. Hotels and motels are scattered over much of the coast. Some of the top fishing areas also have campgrounds and trailer courts.

Where to Hunt

The Palmetto State has an abundance of small game but the main problem is to find a place to hunt. Most of the better quail covers and dove fields are privately owned and zealously guarded. Unless you know the local people, getting permission to hunt is not easy. Both quail and doves are found almost statewide, with the mountain areas being poor and the farmlands being very good. The quail season opens in late November and generally closes at the end of February. The dove season is one of the first hunting seasons to open in early September. It is a split season, with final closing in mid-January.

Ruffed grouse are found in the mountainous regions of the state. The birds are not hunted a great deal. The season opens in late November and closes at the end of February. Rabbits and squirrels are the backbone of South Carolina's small-game hunting. Both are found throughout the state. The cottontail season opens in late November and closes in mid-February. The bushytail season opens in mid-September and also closes in mid-February.

Wild-turkey hunting is quite good in South Carolina. Piedmont is the best area, but there are other good pockets of turkey woods elsewhere in the state. The spring gobbler season runs from mid-March to the end of April.

Waterfowl hunting in South Carolina is limited to the public hunting areas near the Santee National Wildlife Refuge. Mallards, pintails, black, and wood ducks are the main game, with some Canada goose. There is also some duck hunting on the main rivers. Black, Edisto, and Little Pee-Dee are the best bets. Rail and marsh-hen shooting is available on part of Cape Romain National Wildlife Refuge. Woodcock migrate through South Carolina's low country but they are not hunted much.

Deer is South Carolina's only big-game species. The Piedmont area is one of the best spots for deer, but some of the swamps in the low country are also excellent. Again, access can be a problem.

The game department maintains over a million acres of wildlife management areas for quail, squirrels, rabbits, wild turkey, and deer. These management areas are open to public hunting. Frequently they have special seasons. The state also has about 50 dove fields for public hunting. Also, the South Carolina Forestry Commission maintains lands for public hunting.

A non-resident hunting licence costs $22.50 with a three-day licence $12.25. A special permit costing $4.25 is needed to hunt on game management areas.

SOUTH DAKOTA

South Dakota Department of Game, Fish, and Parks
State Office Building
Pierre, South Dakota 57501

Where to Fish

South Dakota has several major fishing areas. The glacier lakes of the north-eastern part of the state are one. The four lakes — Oahe, Sharpe, Francis Case, and Lewis and Clark — on the Missouri River are another. The trout streams and lakes in the Black Hills are the third.

The rolling hills along U.S. 81 have many fine, cool, and clear lakes as a result of the last ice age. These lakes offer some fine walleye and northern-pike fishing, plus crappies, bluegills, white bass, and other panfish. It is difficult to name all of the lakes in this area, but some of the better ones are Long, Kampeska, Clear, Nicholson, King's, and Plican, all near Watertown. The area around Brookings also has a number of fine lakes such as Whitewood, Thompson, Preston, St. John, and a couple of others. The Sisseton area has good fishing waters in Lakes Roy, Buffalo, Enemy Swim, and Waubay.

All of the Missouri River lakes offer excellent fishing for walleyes, sauger, northern pike, white bass, channel cats, and paddle fish. The southernmost lake in the group is Lewis and Clark, which South Dakota shares with Nebraska. Lewis and Clark is the smallest lake of the four, only 35-miles long. The top areas to fish here are Snatch Creek, Charley Creek, and Sand Creek.

The next lake up the Missouri is Francis Case, formed by the Fort Randall Dam. This lake is 110 miles long and over 100 feet deep in many places. It has hundreds of small coves and bays which offer fine fishing for the boat fisherman. Some of the fishing hotspots are the tailwaters below the dam, Bull Creek, and Whetstone Creek.

Lake Sharpe, above Big Bed Dam, may have the best fishing of the four Missouri lakes. It is 80 miles long and its water level tends to be stable. Lake Sharpe has a tremendous crappie population in its upper portion, but the lake is best known for its big northerns. Pike in the 15-pound class are common, while 18-pound fish, which qualify for the South Dakota "Proud Angler Club", are not rare. The record northern for the state, a 35-pound fish, came from this lake.

Some of the local hotspots are Medicine Creek, Soldier Creek, and Cedar Creek. The mouths of all of the tributary streams are good for crappies in the spring.

Lake Oahe is the biggest of the "Great Lakes". It stretches for some 250 miles up the Missouri River. The Oahe is a top white bass and walleye water. Also, Kokanee salmon and lake trout have been introduced into this lake to utilize the lower strata of cold water. One of the top walleye hotspots is the tailwater at the dam. But other good fishing areas are Fairbank Creek, Mission Creek, Plum Creek, and Bloody Run Creek.

All of these "Great Lakes" have ample public access, public boat-launching

facilities, and campgrounds. For more information on fishing and public access areas, write to the Great Lakes Association, Pierre, South Dakota 57501.

The Black Hills of South Dakota offer the angler many fine brooks, gurgling among stately pines and scenic lakes nestled in valleys. The streams offer excellent flyfishing for browns, rainbows, and brookies. The best known are Spearfish, Spring, Grace Coolidge Creek, and Rapid. Some of the top lakes are Cox Lake, Pactola Reservoir, Sheridan, Cold Brook and Major Lake, plus Stockade, Deerfield Center, Horse Thief, Legion, and Sylvan Lakes. The last five are in Custer State Park. The entire area has plenty of campgrounds for trout fishermen. The Angostura Reservoir, just south of the Black Hills National Forest, is an excellent walleye water with panfish on the side.

The prairie country of west-central South Dakota may seem dry at first glance, yet it is dotted with hundreds of small-stock ponds that offer excellent largemouth bass fishing. These reservoirs may range from a mere few acres up to 250 acres, but the bass are in the 6 or 7-pound class in some of them. Most of these ponds are on private ranch land, but courteous fishermen can get permission to fish many of them. Many of these ponds can be fished from shore, but a boat is handy on the larger ones.

Where to Hunt

The ring-necked pheasant is the number-one game in this state. The bird is found in almost every county, but the best pheasant hunting is east of the Missouri River in the central part of the state. The season opens in mid-October and closes late in November, and again opens in early December for an additional three weeks.

South Dakota has fine prairie-grouse hunting, both for sharptails and prairie chickens. The best prairie-grouse range is in the grasslands of the Missouri River. The counties along the Missouri River, plus Meade, Jackson, and Haakon are the best. The prairie-grouse season opens in mid-September and generally closes at the end of November.

Sage grouse are also on the game list. The season is short, a few days in late August and early September. The range of these big birds is very limited. The sage brush plains of Harding and Butte Counties are the best bets. Hungarian partridge are also found in the state. In some areas the season opens as early as mid-September. The grain-growing northern counties are the best for huns. The mourning dove can also be hunted in South Dakota. It is widely distributed and little hunted. Usually the season is open for the first two weeks in September. Wild-turkey hunting is limited to the last week in October. The spring season is a month long, beginning in early April.

The mountain goat is a unique big-game animal, dwelling in the craggy peaks of the western mountains. Alaska, British Columbia, the Yukon, the Northwest Territories, and a number of western states including South Dakota, have seasons.

Small game — cottontails, fox and gray squirrels — are abundant in good habitats over most of the state. The best squirrel hunting is in the wooded river bottoms. Neither cottontails nor squirrels are hunted much and there is no closed season.

Waterfowl hunting in South Dakota is quite good. The northeastern portion of the state has good gunning for diving ducks and snow geese, while the reservoirs along the Missouri River are best for mallards and Canada geese. Good flights of snipe pass through South Dakota, but the birds are rarely hunted. The lesser sandhill crane is also a legal game bird in the state.

Deer, mainly whitetails but also some muleys, are the number-one big game in South Dakota. The famous Black Hills have fine whitetail hunting. Generally the firearm seasons open in November. They seldom stay open longer than a week, depending on areas. The prairie country west of the Missouri River has a fine deer herd and the hunter-success ratio is higher than in the Black Hills. Because of this, the seasons there are shorter, depending on specific areas. Both mule deer and white-tailed deer are found here, but the whitetails are more common. In some years hunters may take a whitetail of either sex or a buck mule deer. Archery seasons for deer are much more generous than gun seasons.

South Dakota also has pronghorn antelope and mountain goats on its big-game list. They can be hunted only on a special-draw permit, and only by residents. The rolling plains of northwest South Dakota are the best areas for pronghorns.

A general hunting licence costs $1, but stamps must be purchased for specific game. A non-resident upland-game stamp costs $25; waterfowl $30; predators $5; wild turkey $5; and deer $35.

TENNESSEE

Tennessee Game and Fish Commission
P.O. Box 40747
Ellington Agricultural Center
Nashville, Tennessee 37204

Where to Fish

Tennessee, the home of country music, is a fine fishing state. The foundation of Tennessee's good fishing is the lakes of the Tennessee Valley Association — the TVA. The state has over 20 large, man-made lakes with a total of more than half a million acres of fishing water.

Walleyes make the tastiest shore lunches ever. The hottest walleye waters extend from Manitoba south to Minnesota and east to central Quebec, but the world-record fish comes from Tennessee.

The largemouth bass is Tennessee's top game fish, but walleye and striped bass are a close second. The ferocious muskellunge is the glamor fish of the Tennessee waters, but big brown trout also lurk in some Tennessee rivers. Largemouths are found over nearly all of the state. Some of the top largemouth bass lakes are Ocoee, Hales Bar, Watts Bar, Fort Loudon, Pickwick, Davy Crockett, Daniel Boone, Watauga, Old Hickory, Reelfoot, Chickamauga, and several others. Dale Hollow is also excellent, but it is better known as a small-mouth water.

In many of Tennessee's waters, the walleye and sauger fishing is just short of sensational. For example, the tailwaters below Pickwick Dam produce thousands of sauger every winter. Norris Lake has top walleye fishing plus largemouths, smallmouths, and whites. The best walleye lake may well be Center Hill. The world-record walleye came from Old Hickory, right on the doorstep of the Grand Old Opry. However, most of the TVA lakes have walleye and sauger.

There are striped bass in a number of Tennessee lakes. They are voracious fish, ready to strike a lure at almost any time. The top places for stripers are Norris, Percy Priest, Watts Bar, and Kentucky Lakes, Stones River below Old Hickory Dam, and Holston River below Cherokee Lake. Some of these lakes also have a hybird bass, a cross between a striper and a white bass.

Tennessee's muskellunge fishing is restricted to a few lakes and rivers. Norris Lake holds the state record of 33 pounds, but Wood's Reservoir is another top musky lake. The Caney and South Forks of the Cumberland River, the Emory River, and several streams of the Tennessee River also produce good muskies every year.

Smallmouth-bass fishing is found in a number of Tennessee waters. Dale Hollow smallmouths are very famous. They are plentiful and big. The world-record smallmouth of 11 pounds 15 ounces came from here. Watts Bar has top smallmouths too. Piney River is an excellent smallmouth stream. The Hiwasee River is also known for its battling smallmouths. The best crappie lake in the state is, without a doubt, Kentucky Lake.

Trout in Tennessee can be very good. The tailwater below Dale Hollow has produced a brown trout of 26 pounds, 2 ounces, while the Dale Hollow Reservoir itself has very good rainbow-trout fishing. Some of the streams in the hills of Tennessee still have native brook trout, but most of Tennessee's trout fishing comes from stocked rainbows, browns, and brookies. Several of the state's wildlife management areas have top trout fishing in their waters. They are Tellico, Andrew Johnson, Ocoee, Kettlefoot, and Laurel Fork. The Tellico River has yielded a brook trout weighing 11 pounds.

Most of Tennessee's lakes and rivers also have fine panfish and catfish angling. Channel cats are found in many of the rivers. The Tellico River is known for its big blue catfish.

Most of the top fishing waters in Tennessee have abundant public access with boat-launching ramps. Certainly the big TVA lakes are well serviced. Campgrounds exist on all of them. The big problem among Tennessee fishermen is deciding where to fish, not how to get access to the fishing.

116

Where to Hunt

Basically Tennessee is a small-game state with some fine deer hunting and a little boar hunting thrown in to sweeten the bag. The squirrel season is first to open in late August. The bushytails are found statewide in all the mast-bearing hardwoods, but the timbered shores of Lake Kentucky and the Anderson-Tully Wildlife Management Area are two local hotspots. The squirrel season traditionally closes on January 1.

The mourning-dove season is the next to open on September 1, and the first lap closes at the end of September. It opens again in October and December for two or three-week periods. The best dove gunning is found in the farm country. The ruffed-grouse season is next to open in mid-October. The grouse are found in the wooded hill country. Cumberland Plateau and the Cherokee National Forest both have fine grouse hunting is some years. The grouse season is a long one, generally closing at the end of February.

The quail and rabbit season opens early in November and closes in mid-February. The best quail counties are Fayette, Hardeman, McNairy, Hardin, Wayne, Lawrence, Giles, and Lincoln. The best cottontail hunting is found in Wilson, Williamson, Smith, Overton, and Jackson Counties. There is some fine swamp-rabbit hunting in the lowlands along the Mississippi River and the flooded lowlands around Lake Kentucky.

There is no closed season on fox and woodchuck, but the racoon, opossum, and bobcat season opens in mid-October and closes at the end of January.

Waterfowl hunting in Tennessee is mostly confined to the Mississippi Valley. The valley is one of the continent's chief flyways. There are a number of marshes and flooded bottomlands with fine duck gunning, but many of these are owned or leased by duck clubs. Reelfoot Lake is one of the top hotspots. Woodcock migrate through Tennessee but they are not hunted much.

Deer hunting in Tennessee is quite good. The deer herd is still increasing. The best deer hunting is west from Nashville on both sides of Lake Kentucky. The counties of Cheatham, Stewart, Hickman, Humphreys, and Perry east of Kentucky Lake are good bets, as are the counties of Henry, Benton, Carroll, and Henderson on the west side of the lake. Deer season opens November 17 and closes January 1.

Wild turkey and wild boar are two other prized game species in the state. Turkeys can be hunted only in a short spring season. Shelby County is the best area. Usually the wild boar season is open for a week in December. Cumberland, Scott, Overton, Pickett, Fentress, and Morgan Counties all have wild boar. The Catoosa Wildlife Management Area is one local hotspot for boar.

Non-resident hunting licences are very reasonable. An all-game licence costs $25 with tags for boar, deer, and wild turkey at $5 each; while a state waterfowl stamp costs $15. A special $6 permit is needed to hunt in wildlife management areas. There is also a three-day non-resident small-game licence for $6.

TEXAS

Texas Parks and Wildlife Commission
John H. Reagan Building
Austin, Texas 78701

Where to Fish

Texas now brags that it is one of the best fishing states in the nation. This boast is quite true. Top fishing can be had along the entire coast of the Gulf, and many of the big impoundments are producing wrist-wrenching bigmouth bass action.

The hottest bass fishing in Texas, and perhaps in the entire United States, is in the Toledo Bend and Sam Rayburn reservoirs. Frequently bass-fishing experts rate these two lakes among the top five bass lakes in the United States. Toledo Bend Lake is on the Sabine River on the Louisiana line, while all of Sam Rayburn is in Texas. The fish in Sam Rayburn run a little larger than those of Toledo Bend, but that is because Sam Rayburn Lake is a little older. The fish have had a bit more time to grow. Besides largemouths, both lakes are full of hungry panfish.

Another lake in this area is Livingston. This 90,000-acre lake is a bit smaller than Sam Rayburn and only half the size of Toledo Bend; it is also the newest, having been developed in 1968. But already Livingston Lake is producing bass in the 5 and 6-pound class, plus tremendous catches of jumbo white bass as well as stringers of crappies, bream, and catfish.

There are several other fine but smaller reservoirs in this part of Texas. Lake Texarkana on the Texas-Arkansas line is one. Lake o' the Pines near Jefferson is another. Lake Murvaul in Panola County produces largemouth bass in the 6-pound class. All these impoundments also yield good catches of panfish and catfish. In fact, panfish are more sought after than bass by the local fishermen. That should come as no surprise. After all, they are more abundant, more available, and better eating.

Central Texas has several fine fishing lakes on the Colorado River. They are called Highland Lakes by Texans. Lake Buchannan is the biggest of these and the best known for its outstanding white-bass fishing. The best largemouth water in this area is probably Lake Lyndon B. Johnson. Lake Bastrop, also in this area, has good bass fishing. There are other fishing lakes in this part of central Texas such as Cavalleras, Stillhouse Hollow, Belton, Brady, Hubbard Creek, and a few more. The Dallas area has one fine bass water in Lake Texoma on the Oklahoma-Texas line. This lake has outstanding white bass, as well as crappies, catfish and, of course, largemouth bass.

One of the newest Texas reservoirs is Lake Amistad on the Texas-Mexico border. Formed by the Rio Grande, this lake is nestled among the arid foothills of the Davis Mountains. Despite the fact that it is very new, Amistad — which incidentally means friendship in Spanish — is already producing bumper catches of largemouth bass. This lake may one day rival Sam Rayburn and Toledo Bend. Besides bigmouths, Amistad also has white bass and catfish. Downstream from

Lake Amistad is Falcon Lake. It too has largemouths, white bass, crappies, and catfish.

Public access is no problem on any of the big Texas reservoirs. Boat-launching ramps are available on all of them. Many have excellent camping facilities and, near most of them, other accommodation is available. Guides are available on the big lakes such as Sam Rayburn, Toledo Bend, and Livingston. Facilities are not as well developed on Amistad or Falcon, but they are developing. These two lakes are excellent for anglers who like to rough it a bit.

The number-one fish along the Texas coast is the spotted weakfish, locally called the speckled trout. The reason for its popularity is simple. It is available along the entire coastline. It can be caught from docks, jetties, from surf, in small bays and inlets, in creek mouths and, from boats or by wading.

The channel bass, locally called the redfish, is number two in the popularity contest. It is not as widely distributed as the weakfish, but fall fishing in the surf is excellent.

Offshore fishermen find the Texas salt water good for a number of species. Offshore fishing for such fish as king mackerel, Spanish mackerel, cobia, jack crevelle, dolphin, wahoo, blackfin tuna, sailfish, white marlin, and some blue marlin is best during the summer and early fall months. But party boats take red snappers, grouper, and giant warsaw the year around on deep reefs offshore. Many fish, such as jack crevelle, Spanish mackerel, cobia, and others can be taken inshore from small boats during the peak summer season.

All the major ports such as Galveston, Freeport, and Port O'Connor, have charter boats and party boats. Party boats also operate out of Texas City, Kemath, Seabrook, La Porte, Baytown, and others. Many of the smaller communities around Corpus Christi also have charter and party boats. There is no shortage of marinas along the Gulf Coast in Texas. There are boat liveries and public boat-launching ramps in most communities.

Where to Hunt

The Lone Star State has a tremendous variety and abundance of game. The only problem is the lack of public land. This does not mean that finding a place to hunt is difficult, but it does mean that the hunter has to pay a hunting fee to the landowner. Deer hunting is outstanding in Texas. Edwards Plateau is the best whitetail area in the state, but the entire hill country of Texas is very good. There are plenty of ranches where a hunter with a "day lease" will find bagging a deer quite easy if he is not too particular about the sex or trophy.

The more trophy-conscious hunter will find the ranches with "no deer no pay" a better bet. Bagging a trophy whitetail of eight points or more will cost the hunter about $150. The best trophy deer in Texas are found in the low-brush country running from Laredo to Del Rio. The deer are not as numerous but they are big. Generally hunters are allowed three white-tailed deer per season, one of which must be a doe. There are a few wildlife management areas scattered throughout Texas that have deer hunting, but only residents can hunt on them.

119

Mule deer in Texas are found west of the Pecos River. Ranchlands around Big Bend National Park are a good bet for muleys. Ranches around Marathon and Alpine have "no deer no pay" hunting. The Texas mule deer are not as big as those in some of the western states. The mule-deer season opens in late November and closes in mid-December, while the whitetail season opens a week or two earlier and closes two or three weeks later in most counties.

The other big game in Texas is black bear, with bear hunting being generally poor, and restricted to the more remote areas. A short elk season is also on the books. It is by special permit and only for residents. A pronghorn season is open for a week in early October. The hunting is also by the permit system. The Permian Basin and the Texas Panhandle are the best areas for antelope.

Javelina is fairly abundant in Texas, with a season from early September to the end of January, depending on the area. South Texas is the main javelina range with Val Verde, Terell, and Pecos Counties being the best for bagging this little desert pig.

There is also a week-long season on Aoudad sheep. Hunting is by special permit only in the Palu Duro Canyon. Texas has a tremendous variety of exotic big-game species open to hunting. Many of the ranches such as the famous Y O Ranch have trophy-fee hunting for such game as blackbuck, mouflon sheep, fallow and sitka deer, roebuck, and even some African antelope.

Bird shooting is exceptionally good in Texas. In abundance and in distribution the number-one game bird is the mourning dove. The bird is found over the entire state. Southern Texas has the best dove hunting, with local hotspots being in the Rio Grande Valley. Areas around Pearsall, Crystal City, and Hondo have tremendous mourning-dove concentrations. The mourning dove season is a long one, beginning on September 1 and ending in late January. The season for white-winged dove is limited to a few days in September.

Quail are almost as widely spread as the dove. Again, south Texas is the best quail country. The ranchlands in the Permian Basin and the cactus and brush country southwest of San Antonio are two top bobwhite areas. In the drier areas, the scaled quail or "blues" take over. West of the Pecos River only "blues" are found. Generally the quail season opens on December 1 and closes in mid-February.

Ring-necked pheasant, wild turkey, and prairie chicken are open to some hunting. Pheasants have a two-week season in mid-December. The best area is the northwest panhandle. The prairie chicken season is restricted to a few days in late October. Prairie grouse are found in Collingsworth, Donley, Lipscomb, Ochiltree, Wheeler, Roberts, Cochran, Hockley, Terry, and Yoakum Counties. The turkey season is open for a week in late April and from November 1 to January 1. The best turkey range is the hill country called the "Divide" by the locals. The town of Kerrville is in the center of the best turkey hunting area.

Squirrel season in Texas is open from May 1 to July 31 and again from October 1 to January 15. The best bushytail hunting is in the east and central parts of the state. There are no closed seasons on cottontails or jackrabbits, both of which are abundant in good habitats. The rabbits get very little hunting pressure.

Texas has some outstanding waterfowl hunting. Large water reservoirs close to the Louisiana line have fine waterfowl shooting and are open to the public. The best known is Toledo Bend for mallards, teal, and gadwall. The rice fields and saltwater flats of south Texas have good goose and pintail hunting. The coastal flats around Port O'Connor and Port Arkansas have fine goose hunting. The top waterfowling spot is probably Eagle Lake. The town calls itself the "Goose Capital of the World". The hunting here is for snow geese, whitefronts, and lesser Canadas, as well as pintails, widgeon, and mallards. Guided hunts can be arranged for about $25 a day out of Eagle Lake.

A non-resident hunting licence costs $37.50, while a five-day migratory bird licence costs $10.25.

UTAH

Utah Division of Fish and Game
1596 W. N. Temple
Salt Lake City, Utah 84116

Where to Fish

Like the other mountain states, Utah is basically a trout-fishing state. But there is some fine bass fishing as well. The Uintas Mountains offer some very fine trout streams for the angler. Those willing to hike in get the best fishing. The Pravo River is one of the best-known streams here. It yields good catches of brookies and cutthroats, as well as some lunker browns. Another good stream is the Weber. Both it and the Pravo have grayling in their upper reaches. Two other good streams are the Uinta and Whiterocks. The best stretches are on the Ute Indian Reservation near Roosevelt. The Ute Indian Fish and Game Department, Fort Duchesne, Utah, is a good source of information on local fishing packages.

There are a number of fine lakes in the Uintas where good catches of brookies, cutthroats, and even golden trout can be made. The Uintas have over 1000 lakes and about a dozen major trout streams.

The Beaver Mountains offer a number of fine trout waters. The top stream here is the Beaver River. This stream flows through some of the most scenic country anywhere. But there are other streams besides the Beaver. Puffer Lake is the most popular lake, mainly because of the fishing lodge, but again there are a number of other fine trout lakes.

Boulder Mountain, a very scenic plateau covered with pine and poplar, offers tremendous trout fishing. This area is in the Dixie National Forest. This is a very wild piece of real estate, ideal for backpackers and horseback campers. Again, this area offers many miles of relatively unfished streams and many fine mountain lakes such as Kolob and Navajo. Forest Service maps show all streams and lakes.

Generally the trout in the mountain streams and lakes do not run very big, but there have been exceptions. Utah's largest brook trout, a 7½-pound fish, came from the Boulder Mountains, while brown trout of 13 pounds have been taken from the Uintas River. But these are exceptions. For trophy trout, the angler should fish the bigger rivers or some of the bigger lakes and reservoirs.

Fish Lake in Sevier County has lake trout up to 20 pounds and brown trout almost as large. Small rainbows are very abundant. Bear Lake on the Idaho line also has lake trout. In addition, it has cutthroats of a good size, and in mid-winter ciscos (a freshwater herring) run into feeder streams.

Another top lake for trophy trout is Strawberry Reservoir about 80 miles southeast of Salt Lake City. It is known for its good-sized cutthroats of over 5 pounds. A giant cutthroat of 26 pounds once came from this lake. Big brookies and fair-sized rainbows lurk here as well.

For those who like to fish in rivers, the Green is hard to beat. It has rainbows, cutthroats, and browns. The most popular stretch is from the dam at Flaming Gorge Reservoir to Little Hole. But stay away from here on opening day. The stretches down into Brown's Park are a better bet.

The Fremont River near Loa is a fine flyfishing stream. The stretches along the highway get a fair amount of fishing pressure, but there are areas when an angler can hike to get to seldom-fished waters. Browns and rainbows both occur in this stream. Usually the bigger trout come from the stretch around Grover. Certainly the previously mentioned Whiterocks River has to rate as one of the finest dryfly streams anywhere and, because it is on Indian Reservation land, it does not get as much fishing pressure.

Other top trout streams are the Cache Valley creeks in northern Utah. The Logan River there has big browns. The Blacksmith Fork is also very good.

No report on Utah's fishing would be complete without a rundown on Lake Powell on the Colorado River. The waters from this huge reservoir back up from Arizona. The lake has excellent largemouth fishing, with fish running up to 5 or 6 pounds. Jumbo crappies of up to 3 pounds are caught by the stringerfull on their spawning beds in spring. Powell also has big rainbows, up to 10 pounds. The best trout fishing is in the colder water near the dam. Bass are found in every cove, but the big arms are the top producers. Aside from tremendous fishing, the lake is renowned for its fantastic scenery. There are a number of jumping-off points to the lake. Two of them are Bullfrog and Hall's Crossing in Utah. These places have boat-launching sites.

Public access to most of Utah's lakes and streams is generally no problem. Guides with packhorse strings are available in the small ranching communities near all of the major wilderness areas. Camping parks exist close to, or on all of, the major rivers and lakes, including Powell. The Utah Travel Council, State Capitol Grounds, Salt Lake City 84116, is a good source of fishing information.

Where to Hunt

Utah is one of the top hunting states in the nation. Mule deer are the only big-game species open to non-residents, but residents can hunt (by special permit) elk, moose, pronghorn, desert bighorn and, even at times, buffalo. The 16-day mule-deer season opens in mid-October and closes in early November. The only exceptions are Indian reservations which have earlier seasons by special tribal-council permits.

The top deer country in Utah is probably West Tauaput Plateau and the Book Cliffs along the Colorado line. This is rugged country with few roads. Other good areas are the Blue Mountains from Monticello to Lake Powell, La Sal Mountains near Moab, the area around Circilevill and Escalante, and the Green River. There are other top areas such as Fish Lake National Forest, the Uinta Mountains, and the Deep Creek Mountains. In Utah deer are found just about everywhere, but generally the further away one goes from the roads, the better the hunting and the bigger the rocks.

Antelope hunting is confined largely to the desert country of western Utah. Daggett County is good. Most of the remote mountain ranges have elk, while moose hunting is confined to the north slope of the Uinta Mountains. Buffalo may be hunted in Garfield County. The desert bighorn season is in San Juan County. The seasons for these big-game species vary from mid-August for the antelope, to mid-October for elk. All hunting permits go to residents by special draw. Cougar is another of Utah's big game. The season is from early November to mid-April. The big cats are most numerous in the remote wilderness areas.

Small-game mammals are squirrels, snowshoe hares, jackrabbits, and cotton-tails. No closed season exists on the first three, but the cottontail season opens late in September and closes early in March.

Utah has a tremendous variety of upland game birds. Ruffed grouse and blue grouse are found in the forested hillsides in the northern part of the state. The sage grouse season is open for a few days in late September. The sage brush hills of Rich, Garfield, and Duchesne Counties are the best bets.

The best Gambel's quail hunting is in Washington County; while the best California quail hunting is in Morgan, Davis, Utah, Uintah, and Duchesne Counties. California quail are not particularly abundant in Utah. Wild-turkey hunting is best in Kane, Garfield, and San Juan Counties. Ring-necked pheasants and Hungarian partridge are found in the farming areas. The best hun shooting is in Box Elder, Rich, and Cashe Counties. The best pheasant hunting is on the irrigated farmlands. Chukar partridge is Utah's most numberous and most widely distributed game bird. The eastern portion of the state is somewhat better than the western.

The lakes of central and southern Utah are good duck-shooting spots. Clear Lake, Powel Slough, and Utah Lake are three well-known hotspots. The big marshes such as Farmington Bay, Turpin Marsh, Howard Slough, and Bear River Bay on Great Salt Lake are all good for pintail, mallards, teal, and some-times Canada geese. Indeed, much of the eastern shore of Great Salt Lake has good wildfowling close to Salt Lake City, Brigham City, and Ogden. One of the best hotspots is Book Cliffs. The dove is another of Utah's game birds and, in some of the farming areas, the shooting is excellent.

Most of the upland game-bird seasons open in late September and, in the case of huns and chukars, run as late as mid-January. The pheasant season opens in early November and closes in early December.

VERMONT

Vermont Fish and Game Department
Montpelier, Vermont 05602

Where to Fish

Trout fishing is a way of life in Vermont. The Battenkill River is one of the most important trout streams in North America from the standpoint of flyfishing history. It is still a good stream from Manchester to the New York border. Other fine trout streams are the Black and Barton Rivers in Orleans County, the Trout River in Montgomery, the Nulhegan in Essex, the upper Connecticut from Brunswick to Canaan, and the Willoughby at Orleans for rainbows during the spawning run.

The Dog River from Roxbury to Montpelier, the White River below Hancock, the Mar River in Waitsfield, Otter Creek upstream from Danby, and the New Haven and Middlebury Rivers are good as well. Other fine streams are the Lamoille and Missisquoi upstream from Enosburg Falls. The Winooski has trout and bass. Three species of trout — brookies, browns, and rainbows — are found in Vermont streams.

There are many lakes in Vermont that have fine trout fishing. In the northeastern part of the state, there are: Harvey's, Willoughby, Seymour, Echo, Crystal, Maidstone, Averills, and Memphremagog, to name a few. Most of these lakes offer lake trout, rainbows, browns, and landlocked salmon. The Vermont Fish and Game Department is conducting major restorations for salmon in several of these lakes and the program is already producing results. Other trout waters are: Bourn Pond in Sunderland, Little Rocky Pond in Wallingford, Martin's Pond in Peacham, Job's Pond in Newark, Colton Pond in Sherburne, and Brewer Pond in Holland. These are all brook-trout lakes.

Several of the bigger reservoirs, such as Somerset, Harriman's, and Chittenden in Pittsburg are the top trout waters in southern Vermont. They are noted for big browns. Lakes Fairlee and Dunmore have rainbows, but Dunmore also has lakers.

One of Vermont's brook-trout fishing bonanzas lies in the back country beaver ponds on tiny brooks. Much of this fishing is underexploited. Those who do not mind hiking to get a catch of native squaretails, should explore the many beaver ponds in central and northern Vermont.

Lake Champlain is the biggest warm-water lake in the state. Fishingwise, it is very important. It produces fine catches of walleye and bass. It even has muskellunge and, of course, northern pike. Missisquoi Bay is a hotspot for muskies in the fall and for walleyes in the spring. Perch are the most abundant fish in the lake. The northern half of the lake is best for warm-water species. The cold water of Lake Champlain also has lake trout, rainbows, and landlocked salmon. Lakers are stocked annually.

Lake Memphremagog on the Vermont-Quebec border also has fine walleye fishing, but the best warm-water fishing is found in the southern part of the state. Previously mentioned Lakes Dunmore and Fairlee have good bass fishing. Lakes Bomosee and Hortonia in Rutland County are also good.

Some of the trout rivers such as the Winooski, Missisquoi, and Otter have good spring runs of walleye in their lower reaches, while Winooski is known for its good bronzeback action.

Usually public access to the better fishing waters is no problem, but some of the streams do flow through private land. Northern Vermont is very tourist-oriented, so there is no shortage of accommodation.

Where to Hunt

Vermont is one of the best hunting states in New England. One reason for this is the diversity of habitats. The white-tailed deer is the chief big-game species. Whitetails are numerous in Vermont, and indeed overpopulation is a fact in many of the winter deeryards. There is no doubt that there will be a population crash caused by winter starvation in the not-too-distant future. Winter kills already have occurred in some of the major deeryards. The Vermont Game Department has been advocating a season on antlerless deer, but opposition by hunters has prevented it.

The best deer hunting is in the south and central portions of the state. Top counties are Windsor, Rutland, Windham, Orange, and Washington. However, bigger deer come from Essex, Orleans, Lamoille, and Caledonia Counties. The deer season opens in early November and runs for about two weeks. A two-week archery season precedes it.

Black bear is highly prized as big game in Vermont. The Green Mountain range is good bruin country. Essex County is a good bet. Generally the bear season runs from September 1 to November 30.

Ruffed grouse and woodcock are the two main game birds in Vermont. Both are distributed statewide, but the ''partridge'' hunting is best in the northern part of the state. Usually the grouse and woodcock season opens in late September and closes in late November. Pheasant hunting in Vermont is strictly on a put-and-take basis. The winters are just too cold and the snowfall too heavy for ringnecks to survive. The farmlands of southern Vermont are the main pheasant country.

Cottontails and snowshoe hares are important game. They occur over most of the state. The farming country has better cottontail gunning, while the hares are more abundant in the forests of northern Vermont. The raccoon is also a game animal, with a season from August 1 to December 31. The rabbit and hare season runs from late September until the end of February. Gray squirrels are hunted in Vermont but not as much as cottontails. The beechnut and oak groves of southern Vermont and in the Champlain Valley are the main squirrel range.

Vermont has some fine wildfowling. Lake Champlain marshes and bays provide most of the action. Dabbling ducks, as well as divers, are hunted on the lake. The mouths of major rivers such as Missisquoi, Lamoille, Otter, and Dead Creeks are good bets. Lakes Bomoseen and Memphremagog are also good. The eastern shore of the Connecticut River has some good duck-hunting spots. Inland creeks and rivers can provide a fair amount of action for blacks and woodies when floated in canoes. About the only Canada goose shooting in the state is in the fields of Grand Isle County during the migration.

An all-game non-resident hunting licence costs $30.50, while a small-game licence costs $10.50. A non-resident archery licence costs $5.00.

VIRGINIA

Virginia Commission of Game and Inland Fisheries
P.O. Box 11104
Richmond, Virginia 23230

Where to Fish

Virginia is another good fishing state that one seldom hears about. But Virginia's excellent saltwater fishing facilities have been expanding at a rapid rate, while its fresh water continues to produce fine catches.

The striped bass is the most important game fish in Virginia's salt water. Good striper action can be had from March or early April to as late as December. Generally there are several peak periods, such as June and again September. Usually the earlier fish are small schoolies, with bigger fish of up to 50 pounds coming in later.

The stripers can be caught from boats, from shore, or from marine installations including bridges over the big rivers. There are so many places where stripers can be caught that naming them all is almost impossible. All the rivers such as the James, Rappahannock, and York produce stripers at their mouths on their lower stretches. The eastern shore around Saxis, Tangier Sound, Cape Charles, Gloucester Point, Bluefish Rock, the Barrier Islands, the Chesapeake Bridge-Tunnel, and a couple of dozen other spots are all good.

Weakfish provide fine action from April to October. Some of the brackish waters are the most productive. Again, some of the rivers are good bets, as is the Chesapeake Bay Bridge-Tunnel. The inlets on the eastern shore are also good.

Fluke inhabit the same waters as weakfish, and at about the same time. They run a good size — up to 10 or 12 pounds. Channel bass come in during the spring and fall. Virginia Beach gets a good fall run, while the Barrie Islands and eastern shore marshes get good spring runs.

The only other important inshore fish is the tarpon. The shallows of the eastern shore get sporadic runs of big tarpon during the summer. The peak is generally in July. The offshore fishery is also the best in the summer months. The first pelagic fish to come in are the big bluefish in May, but their peak run is in late June or early July. The blues are followed by dolphin, wahoo, amberjack, king mackerel, and false albacore, plus yellowfin and school bluefin tuna. The billfish — blue and white marlin and sails — also come in during the summer.

Charter and party boats operate out of all the coastal communities, such as Irvington, Kinsale, Quinby, Rudee Inlet, Lewisetta, Norfolk, Virginia Beach, and several others. There are many marinas and small boat liveries in these towns as well. The main fishing areas also have free public-boat launching ramps, but at many of the marinas you have to pay.

The communities of Virginia Beach, Norfolk, Hampton, and White Stone also have fishing piers. Accommodation, including camping, is no problem in this area. Two useful publications are *Saltwater Sport Fishing in Virginia* and the *Virginia Accommodations Directory*. Both are available free of charge from the Virginia Travel Service, State Office Building, Richmond 23219.

The freshwater fishing is also excellent, but receives more pressure than the saltwater fishery. Virginia has some outstanding smallmouth bass fishing. The Rappahannock River above Fredericksburg, the upper reaches of the James River, the North and South Forks of the Shenandoah, and the main trunk in the Shenandoah National Park all have top bronzeback fishing. These rivers can be fished from shore, but a float trip may be even more productive.

The Kerr and Gaston Reservoirs on the Virginia-North Carolina border are both fine producers of largemouth bass. Kerr also has landlocked stripers. Both yield stringers of tasty crappies in the spring. Other good largemouth waters are the Chickahominy Reservoir and River. Pickerel and crappies are also found in these waters, and the river below Walker's Dam has stripers. The Philpott Reservoir near Martinsville has been producing fine bigmouths, despite its small size (600 acres). Black Bay on Virginia's eastern shore is good largemouth water. This is a shallow, marshy expanse of water of some 25,000 acres. White perch, crappies, pickerel, and catfish are the other fish species here.

Smith Mountain Lake near Roanoke is a top mixed-creel water. Its 20,000 acres harbor smallmouths, largemouths, landlocked striped bass, several species of panfish, catfish, plus walleyes, northern pike, and muskellunge.

Again, public access is no problem in Virginia's top lakes and rivers. Public boat-launching ramps are found on all of them, and car-toppers may be launched at bridges that cross the rivers. Marinas on some of the bigger reservoirs have small boats for rent. Accommodation, including camping and trailer facilities, is available close to most of these waters.

Two useful publications for anyone planning a fishing trip to Virginia are *Let's Go Freshwater Fishing in Virginia* and *Boating Access to Virginia Waters*. Both are available without charge from the Commission of Game and Inland Fisheries, Box 11104, Richmond 23230.

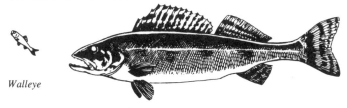

Walleye

127

Where to Hunt

Virginia is basically a small-game hunting state with some deer and a little bear hunting as a side dish. The small-game season for quail, grouse, wild turkey, pheasants, and rabbits opens in mid-November. The seasons for these species vary in length, with the quail season staying open the longest (until mid-February). Dove and squirrel seasons open earlier. The split dove season starts in early October and comes to a close in early January with a six-week closure in between, during November and early December. East of Blue Ridge the squirrel season opens as early as October 1.

Although doves are distributed statewide, the best gunning is in the soybean and grain fields of the Virginia farm country. Doves are the most hunted game birds in the state. The best bobwhite hunting is in central and southern Piedmont. The entire southeast section of Virginia has fairly good quail shooting. The farmlands in the valleys of western Virginia also have bobwhites.

Ruffed grouse are found in the hill country. The foothills of the Blue Ridge Mountains are the best bet. Squirrels are found statewide, with grays predominating. The hardwood ridges of the hill country are the best. Fox squirrels are found in the farm woodlots of the valleys. Cottontails are also found statewide in the proper habitats.

The best wild-turkey hunting is in the Piedmont area. But the northwest portion of the state has some fair turkey flocks. Pheasant hunting in Virginia is not particularly good. The season is only open for a few days in mid-November.

Waterfowl hunting in Virginia is limited. The eastern shore and Black Bay are two good spots. Most of the best waterfowling on the Tidewater is tied up by duck clubs and private individuals, but some hunting is open to the public. The hunting in the open water is mostly for diving ducks. The James River, west of Richmond, and the two forks of the Shenandoah River have good shooting for dabbling ducks for hunters who are willing to float down.

Both snipe and woodcock migrate through the state via the Atlantic Flyway. The Tidewater has good snipe hunting in the bogs and mud flats, but access is a problem. Some of the woodlots in eastern Virginia have good flights of timber-doodles. The only trick is to time the flight well.

Deer season in Virginia opens in mid-November and closes early in December west of the Blue Ridge, and early January east of the Ridge. Piedmont and Tidewater have fine deer hunting but the land is controlled by hunt clubs. The Blue Ridge Mountains have good deer country, with George Washington and Jefferson National Forests being good bets. Hill and Pickett Military Camps and Quantico Marine Corps Camp are also open to deer hunting by the public. Many of the lumber companies open their forests to public deer hunting.

Black bear are pretty well restricted to the Blue Ridge. Specialized bear hunts are held in the national forests. The annual harvest is about 300 bruins. The black-bear season opens early in November and closes late in December.

A non-resident hunting licence costs $15.75, while turkey, deer, and bear licences are $20.00.

WASHINGTON

Washington Department of Fisheries
115 General Administration Building
Olympia, Washington 98501

Washington Department of Game
600 North Capitol Way
Olympia, Washington 98501

Where to Fish

Fishing in Washington is divided into salt and freshwater sport. The saltwater sport-fishing scene is dominated by salmon, while trout (steelhead and rainbows) provide most of the freshwater fishing action. One thing is certain. Both salt and fresh water offer year-around sport for Washington anglers.

The top salmon action begins in June and ends in September, when big king or chinook salmon and coho salmon come to the offshore waters. The top offshore areas lie off such places as Westport, Ilwaco, La Push, Neah Bay, and Port Angeles. This is open-water fishing with long runs out, requiring maritime knowhow. Charter boats are available at Westport, Ilwaco, and Port Angeles.

The coho and chinook also invade the more sheltered waters of Puget Sound and the channels between the San Juan Islands, as well as Sekiu Strait east of Neah Bay. When the salmon are in, they are within good range of small craft. Fishermen flock to such places as Roche Harbor on San Juan Island, Deception Pass, Mutiny Bay, Shilshole Bay, and Elliott Bay at Seattle, Point Defiance at Tacoma, and Johnson Point near Olympia. Charter boats and rental boats are available in all of these places.

The winter salmon fishing is for immature chinooks, usually called black-mouths by the local anglers. Winter fishing is only now coming into its own. Down garments and small gas heaters have contributed greatly to making winter fishing feasible. But it is still a cold, rugged sport.

The blackmouths come close to shore, so they are within easy range of small boats, They can even be caught right in the protected harbor of Port Angeles and such sheltered areas as Elliott and Shilshole Bays in Seattle, and Puget Sound from Whidbey Island south. The Strait of Juan de Fuca, Neah Bay, and Sekiu Strait all have blackmouths in winter.

Other marine fish are only now beginning to get the attention they deserve. The various bottom fish, such as rockfish, sole, flounder, and ling cod are all available. Giant halibut of up to 200 pounds can be caught in such areas as Port Angeles and Crescent Beach. Occasionally charter boats go out after these fine-flavored fish. Surf perch attract flocks of anglers when they are running along jetties and beaches from Columbia to Kalaloch and around Westport. Albacore are also getting attention in the offshore areas.

Saltwater anglers are turning to sea-run cutthroats. These trout stay in the shallow water of the coastal areas. They can be caught from boats or by wading and casting from beaches. Saltwater flyrodders find these trout very challenging. Puget Sound is the top area for these sea cutthroats.

Saltwater fishing in Washington comes under the jurisdiction of the State Department of Fisheries. Inquiries should be directed to that department.

129

Freshwater fishing in Washington is spread over several thousand lakes, plus hundreds of streams, several dozen of which are major rivers. Only the highlights can be touched upon here. The Olympic Peninsula offers some of the finest steelhead fishing anywhere. The top streams here are Elwha, Hoh, Queets, Clearwater, and Quinault. The Quillayute system of Calawah, Bogachiel, and Sol Duc is also tops.

Southwestern Washington also has some top steelhead streams such as Toutle, Tilton, Kalama, Lewis, Naselle, Elochoman, and a couple of others. Cowlitz is another top stream which gets spring chinook. The most heavily fished steelhead rivers are the Green and Puyallup because they are near heavy population centers. These two rivers, along with the famous Skagit, are the top steelhead producers. Other fine steelhead streams are the Stillaguamish and the Snohomish, along with its tributaries, the Skykomish and Pilchuck.

The winter months are the best for steelhead. However, the Snare and the Grande Ronde in southeastern Washington are known for their summer runs of steelhead which start in August and peak in October and November.

The Yakima River has some outstanding trout fishing. In its upper reaches, up in the tributaries, it has brook trout and cutthroats; its lower reaches have browns, rainbows, and whitefish. The lower Yakima has steelhead. Lake Keechelus, the headwater of the Yakima, has cutthroats, rainbows, and Dolly Varden.

Ross Lake in the Skagit River is one of Washington's biggest lakes. It offers rainbows, cutthroats, brook trout, and big Dolly Varden. Other lakes are Jameson, Alta, Spectacle, Wapato, and Wannacut in central Washington. The Twin Lakes on the Colville Indian Reservation offer top trout fishing. For the backpacker, Washington's mountain country offers a real bonanza of small alpine lakes that are seldom fished.

For those who want warm-water fish species, Silver Lake in Cowlitz County is hard to beat for bass. It also has crappies and catfish. The lower stretches of the Yakima River produce fine smallmouth bass, while the irrigation lagoons have bigmouths.

The pothole lakes below O'Sullivan Dam also have top bass fishing. This irrigation project has produced over 50 small lakes. O'Sullivan Lake itself also has bass and crappies in its shallow bays and coves. This is probably the best bass water in Washington. Big rainbow trout lurk in the cold water layers of this lake.

Public access to Washington's freshwater fishing is no problem. Freshwater fishing falls under the jurisdiction of the Department of Game. Inquiries should be directed to that agency.

Where to Hunt

Washington is one of the top ten hunting states. It has a wide variety of small and big game. The shotgunning season opens September 1 with dove and band-tailed pigeon hunting. The best dove gunning is in the Yakima and Ikanogan

Valleys. The Wenatchee area is also good. Bandtails are found in the forested hillsides. The low-lying mountain passes offer the best gunning.

The ruffed and blue grouse season opens next in early September. The birds are widely distributed throughout the forested areas of the state. Chukar and Hungarian partridge seasons open in mid-September. The best hunting for these birds is in eastern Washington. For chukars, the arid cheat-grass hills along the Smoke River are good. Asotin and Whitman Counties are excellent. Other good areas are Ellensburg Canyon and Yakima Valley Hills. The huns are also found in this part of the state but the best hun gunning is in the grain-growing country. Huns do not like the dry hills.

The next bird season to open, generally in mid-October, is for sharptails, sage grouse, quail, and wild turkey. Sharptails are found in the rolling grasslands near brushy ravines and wooded hillsides. The Okanogan Valley is the top area for sharptails. Sage grouse are limited to the remnants of the vast sagebrush plains. Douglas County is a good bet for these big birds. Both sharptails and sage grouse seasons are open for only a week or so.

California, mountain, and bobwhite quail are all found in Washington, but the quail hunting is not particularly good. There is no top area for bobwhites. The coveys are scarce and scattered. Mountain quail have a fairly wide distribution, with Asotin County being the best bet. California quail are probably a bit more numerous than the other two species. Pockets of Yakima County have good gunning for these birds.

The best wild-turkey hunting in Washington is in Klickitat County. Besides the fall season of two weeks, there is also a nine-day season in early May. Ring-necked pheasant hunting is restricted to the farmlands of the more sheltered valleys. The Columbia Basin and Yakima Valley are the two hotspots.

Cottontails, snowshoe hares, and jackrabbits are all found in Washington. None are hunted much. The Columbia Basin is a good area for jacks, while the forested areas of Okanogan County are good for snowshoes. The best cottontail country is Yakima County. There is no closed season on jackrabbits. Generally the seasons on all small game are generous; up to the end of March for rabbits, and early January for some species of birds. Rockchuck, raccoon, and bobcat all have designated seasons.

Washington has excellent waterfowl hunting. The pot-hole and grainfield country of the Columbia Basin is the top waterfowling area for mallards, pintails, widgeon, and some Canadas. The coastal marshes and bays also offer some fine waterfowling. Skagit Delta is another top spot.

Deer is the number-one big game in Washington. Whitetails, blacktails, and mule deer are all found in the state. Although the general deer season opens in mid-October and closes in mid-November, in some localities there is a special early season and winter-deer season, depending on specific deer populations. Some areas allow deer of either sex during the last few days of the season.

The northern high Cascades have an early buck season for mule deer. Okanogan and Chelan Counties are the best bets for mule deer during the regular season. The northeastern part of Washington is the main whitetail range, with Stevens County being the best bet for bagging a buck. The forested areas of the western slopes are the main blacktail range. Lewis County is a top-notch area.

Elk, both Roosevelt and Rocky Mountain races, are also important big game in Washington. Generally the elk season is open for two weeks in mid-November. The best elk areas are the Blue Mountains of southeastern Washington, the region between Ellensburg and Wenatchee, and the Olympic Peninsula.

Mountain goats and bighorn sheep are the glamor animals of Washington. A few special-draw permits are available in most years for bighorns. These are restricted to residents only. The mountain-goat season opens in mid-September and generally runs until the end of October. The best areas are the very high slopes of the North Cascades. Goat permits are also drawn, but the number of permits can be as high as a thousand. A few permits are open to non-residents.

Cougar and black bear are other Washington big-game species. The length of the season varies, particularly on black bear, because in some counties the bruin is classified as a varmint. Grays Harbor is good bear country, while the area around Olympic Park is good for mountain lions. Both animals are widely distributed throughout the wilderness areas of the state.

A non-resident hunting licence for small game and deer costs $50. Supplementary tags for elk and goats are $35. Tags for black bear, turkey, and upland game birds are $2.00.

WEST VIRGINIA

West Virgina Department of Natural Resources
Division of Fish and Game
1800 Washington Street East
Charleston, West Virginia 25305

Where to Fish

Smallmouth bass offer some superb fishing in many West Virginia rivers. The top three rivers are Greenbrier, South Branch, and New. The Greenbrier in southeastern West Virginia flows through some very pretty country. It flows through Pocahontas, Greenbrier, and Summers Counties, and joins the New River at Hinton. In its upper reaches, the Greenbrier has fine trout fishing for rainbows, browns, and brookies. The biggest bass come from stretches in Greenbrier County, but the stretches in Pocahontas County have more fish. Other fish in the lower stretches are walleyes and rock bass.

The New River in the southern portion of the state is also a scenic stream. The stream has many falls, rapids, and pools. Smallmouth bass are most abundant in the lower reaches. The biggest bass come from below Sandstone Falls. Walleyes and channel cats are two other fish species available to the angler and, even muskies lurk in the quiet stretches. The South Branch produces fine bronzebacks in Hardy County and in the famous Horseshoe Bend area in Hampshire County.

Other top smallmouth streams are the Potomac River, with the South Branch being particularly good. The Little Kanawha River, along with its many tributaries such as the Leading, Saltlick, and Cedar Creeks, are also productive.

All these rivers can be waded or fished from shore. They can also be float-fished in many stretches. Several towns on the New River have guides with boats.

Some of the big reservoirs in West Virginia also offer fine fishing. The top three for bass are: Sutton in Braxton County, Summersville in Nicholas County, and Bluestone in Hinton County. Bluestone has big bronzebacks as well as largemouths. It also has walleyes and several species of panfish and catfish. Summersville has had excellent smallmouth and walleye fishing in recent years, but probably the best walleye fishing is in the tailwaters of the Sutton Reservoir.

The glamor fish of West Virginia waters is the musky. The Elk River through Braxton and Clay Counties harbors big muskies in some of the large pools. The river also has smallmouths and largemouths. The Little Kanawha River is another top musky water, as is Middle Island Creek. Both also have bass.

The best trout fishing in West Virginia is in the Monongahela National Forest. There are several fine trout streams there. The Cranberry, Williams, and Shavers Rivers are probably the best. Other good trout waters are: the Back Fork of the Elk River, the Lost River, the Capacon River, and the Blackwater River in Canaan Valley. The Blackwater's tributaries are also good.

All these trout waters are in prime vacation areas. They all have accommodation and camping facilities near them. Both Capacon and Canaan State Parks are well geared for vacationers. Access is generally no problem on the other West Virginia waters — West Virginia is tourist-minded.

Where to Hunt

White-tailed deer have become a very important part of West Virginia's hunting scene. The deer herd is still increasing and whitetails are found in every county. One of the top deer-hunting areas is the Eastern Panhandle. However Grant, Pendleton, Randolph, Pocahontas, Preston, Mineral, Tucker, and Greenbrier Counties are all good.

There are a few public-hunting areas in these counties. George Washington and the Monongahela National Forests are open to public hunting. The Potomac Wildlife Management Unit near Franklin is a local hotspot for deer.

Bear is a highly prized big-game species in West Virginia. The bear hunting is not particularly good, but some bears are taken in the forested mountain country during the short split season in early November and mid-December.

West Virginia also has a good wild-turkey flock. There is both a spring season from late April to mid-May and a fall season from mid-October to mid-November. Pocahontas, Hampshire, and Hardy Counties are top turkey-hunting areas. Pendalton, Grant, and Randolph Counties are also good. Shenandoah, Warrensville, Potomac, Rimel, Neola, and Cranberry Wildlife Management Units have good turkey hunting and are open to the public.

Bobwhite quail, ring-necked pheasant, ruffed grouse, and mourning dove are all found in West Virginia. Pheasant hunting is poor and largely confined to the Northern Panhandle between Ohio and Pennsylvania. Bobwhite-quail hunting is quite good in local pockets of farmlands in the Eastern Panhandle. Ruffed grouse are found mainly in the northwest portion of the state. The grouse hunting is not outstanding, but some pockets of cover in Ritchie, Tyler, Jackson, Roane, Calhoun, and Doddridge do provide some grouse gunning.

Woodcock also migrate through the state. Woodlots in the Canaan Valley get good flights in late October. The mourning dove is the most important game bird in the state. The doves are found statewide, but farming areas have the best gunning.

Seasons for the upland game birds vary. Doves open on September 1. It is a split season with three open periods, the last closing in mid-January. Grouse and woodcock open in mid-October, while the bobwhite and pheasant season opens in early November. Grouse and quail stay open the longest; until the end of February.

Waterfowl hunting in West Virginia is limited. About the only really good spot is at the McClintic Wildlife Station in Mason County. Both geese and ducks can be hunted there.

Many West Virginia hunters view squirrels and rabbits as their bread-and-butter game. Squirrel and rabbit hunting is popular. Both bushytails and cottontails are found statewide. Squirrels are more numerous in the counties with vast mast-bearing forests, while cottontails are mainly found in farmlands and scrublands. Snowshoe hares are also found in the state. The white hares are restricted to the high mountain forests of Tucker, Randolph, Grant, and Pendelton Counties. The rabbit season opens early in November and closes at the end of February. Squirrel season opens in mid-October and closes early in January. The raccoon season runs from mid-October to late January. A non-resident hunting licence costs $30.00.

WISCONSIN

Division of Fish and Game
Wisconsin Department of Natural Resources
Box 450
Madison, Wisconsin 53701

Where to Fish

It is difficult to name the single most important fish species in Wisconsin. The state has several important game fish. Walleye, bass, northern pike, muskellunge, and steelhead all rank at the top, but brook trout, coho, and lake trout are also important.

A decade ago, the Great Lakes of Superior and Michigan drew hardly any attention from Wisconsin anglers. The coho, chinook, and lake trout changed all that. All along the coast of Lake Michigan from Racine to Door Counties, anglers take coho, chinook up to 35 pounds, and lake trout. They also land steelhead and big browns. The local hotspots for browns are small bays such as Cave Point, North Bay, Bailey's Harbor, and Rowley's Bay, all in the Door Peninsula.

The waters of Lake Superior are also producing fine salmon fishing, and the lake-trout fishing today is probably as good as it was in the years before the blood-sucking lamprey invaded the upper Great Lakes and devastated the laker populations. Lake Superior also has some excellent brown-trout fishing; indeed the U.S. record of 29 pounds 9 ounces came from Superior. Nearly all of the rivers flowing into Superior have good steelhead runs. The Bois Brule is probably the best.

Other good trout streams are the Big Souix and White Rivers in Bayfield County and the Wolf River in Langlade County. The Waupaca River system also offers trout — browns and rainbows — in its lower reaches, and brook trout up in its headwaters. There are many small trout streams in such counties as Waupach, Waushara, Adams, and Portage.

Walleye fishing in Wisconsin is excellent. The best walleye action is in the northern half of the state. Some of the top walleye waters are Nelson Lake in Sawyer County, Lake Winnebago in Winnebago County, and Lac Vieux Desert in Vilas County. The Mississippi River is a top walleye water, but it also has excellent smallmouth fishing.

One of the most popular walleye waters is the Wisconsin River, below the dam at Prairie du Sac. The river stays open throughout most of the winter and, there is a closed season on walleyes there. Other good walleye waters are the Willow Flowage, Castle Rock Lake, and Butternut Lake. The Wolf and Fox Rivers in the Winnebago drainage system have good spawning runs of walleyes. Lakes Poygan, Puckway, and Butte des Morts in central Wisconsin have good walleye fishing, while in southern Wisconsin, Fox and Beaver Lakes have walleyes, as has Lake Geneva almost on Milwaukee's doorstep.

Wisconsin's muskellunge fishing is also centered in the northern half of the state. Lac Vieux Desert and North Twin Lake are top musky producers. Lake Chippewa is another. Lac Court Oreilles and Grindstone Lake also have fine musky fishing, along with northern pike. Other musky waters are Lakes Squirrel, Trout, and Arbor Vitae. The musky's cousin, the northern pike, is found in all of the major waters of Wisconsin. In some of the better walleye lakes, northern pike also enter the fray.

Smallmouth bass are widely distributed across the state. The St. Croix River is a well-known smallmouth stream. So is the Mississippi. The Wolf River in its lower reaches has an abundance of bronzebacks. The Cedar River in Dunn County is good as well. Many of the small rocky bays of the Door Peninsula offer hot bronzeback battles in the summer months. Largemouths are found in Lake Geneva and Lake Yellowstone. Panfish are found statewide. The Wolf River gets a fine run of white bass.

Northern Wisconsin is tourist country, so access to fishing is no problem.

Indeed, even in southern Wisconsin access is no problem. Accommodation, including camping, is available near all the major fishing waters. Charter boats are available in some of the major salmon and lake-trout areas on the Great Lakes.

Where to Hunt

Ruffed grouse is Wisconsin's number-one upland game bird. The northern third of the state is the main grouse range. Old logging roads and young poplar stands on old forest-fire burns are the best places to hunt. The Newwood and Wolf River areas are good bets. So are areas around Necedah, Babcock, Wisconsin Rapids, and Plainfield. The coulee country of western Wisconsin also has some fine partridge covers.

Sharptails and Hungarian partridge are also found in Wisconsin. The huns are mainly in the farm country of eastern Wisconsin, while sharptails are found in the northwest portion of the state. Woodcock migrate through the state and the river bottoms along the Wolf and Black Rivers have some fine timberdoodle covers.

Pheasant hunting in Wisconsin is confined largely to the southeast. Farmlands around Racine, Kenosha, Watertown, Whitewater, and Brandon are good spots. The state stocks birds to bolster the natural pheasant population. Many of the birds are stocked on public hunting areas. There are jackrabbits, cottontails, and snowshoe hares in Wisconsin. The white hares are found mostly in the vast forests of northern Wisconsin. Jackrabbits are found in the open lands of western Wisconsin, while cottontails live on the farmlands in the southern half of the state. Gray and fox squirrels have a range similar to the cottontail.

Woodcock is the first small game to open in mid-September, followed two weeks later by all the other species, except huns and pheasants, which open in late October. Sharptail season is the first to close in late October, with rabbits and squirrels the last at the end of January. There is no closed season on snowshoe hares. Bobcat and fox both have open seasons from early October to January 31.

Wisconsin has some fine waterfowl hunting. The Horicon Marsh area is famous for its Canada goose hunting. The area from Lake Pepin to the Iowa line has some fine duck hunting. The bottomlands and marshes along the Mississippi River also offer fine duck gunning. It reaches its peak when the northern ducks from Canada come through.

White-tailed deer hunting has remained quite good, with a stable harvest of around 100,000 animals. Buffalo County in west-central Wisconsin is a top whitetail producer. However, some of the other northern counties such as Waupaca, Shawano, Portage, Wood, Jackson, Marinette, Vilas, Ashland, and Forest are also very good. Another interesting place to hunt deer is the rugged Apostle Islands in Lake Wisconsin.

The black bear is highly prized and Wisconsin is probably the top bear state in the Great Lakes area. The best bear hunting is in the northern counties with their vast forests. Areas around the towns of Iron Belt, Crandon, and Argonne are good.

The deer and black-bear season opens in mid-November and closes late in November. In recent years there has been a special, early-fall bear season allowing the use of hounds. The archery season for bear and deer opens in mid-September.

The non-resident deer-hunting licence costs $35.50. A combination deer, bear and small-game licence costs $50.50, and a small-game and bear licence costs $25.50, as does the archery licence.

WYOMING

Wyoming Fish and Game Commission
P.O. Box 1589
Cheyenne, Wyoming 82001

Where to Fish

Trout are the main fishing fare in Wyoming, but such warm-water species as walleyes and even channel catfish are also on the menu. The high country of Wyoming offers outstanding trout fishing. For example, the Bridger Wilderness and indeed, the entire Bridger National Forest, has hundreds of trout lakes and small streams. Most of these fine trout waters require packing in, either by "shanks' mare" or on a real mare in a mountain-pony string. Yellowstone National Park has many fine fishing waters, but many of them are subjected to more fishing pressure than the waters of the wilderness areas outside. Yellowstone is a popular place for tourists. Also, some areas of the park are closed to fishing because of the grizzly bear hazard.

The Green River is the best known trout stream in Wyoming. It offers fine rainbows and browns. The river's entire length can be fished, including the reservoirs at Flaming Gorge and Fontenelle. Some of the favorite sections are from Pinedale to La Barge and below Fontenelle Reservoir. The lower reaches are best fished from a boat. There are a number of river guides with boats for float fishermen. Two other very worthwhile waters in this area are the Black Fork and the Hams Fork Rivers. They both have fine rainbows.

Other good trout streams in Wyoming are the upper North Platte, the Salt River, the south fork of the Snake, the Laramie River, and the Shoshone River. The upper North Platte flows from Colorado, and the best fishing for browns and rainbows is from the Colorado line to Saratoga. The North Platte's tributaries — the French and Encampment Rivers — also have fine trout angling. The Big and Little Laramie Rivers, east of North Platte, have some fine rainbows and browns. However, being close to the town of Laramie and not far from Cheyenne, they get heavily fished.

The Salt River is not a big stream, and is frequently fished by anglers who fish the nearby Snake. The stretches around Alton are the most productive. Besides browns, the Salt also has cutthroats and whitefish. The Snake's tributaries (the Gros Ventre and the Hogback) can also provide hot trout action.

The south fork of the Snake River is one of the most scenic streams anywhere. It is popular with floaters. The stretches of the river downstream of Wilson Bridge have some excellent holding water for trout. The Shoshone River is not fished as much as some of the other streams. Many anglers pass it by as they head for Yellowstone. But the Shoshone has some fine cutts, rainbows, and browns. The stretch to fish is from the park boundary to the town of Cody.

Up in the Big Horn County, there are several fine trout streams: Shell Creek, Tensleep Creek, Piney Creek, Clear Creek, and the Tongue River. The upper reaches of all these streams get little pressure and are good bets.

Not all of Wyoming's fishing is confined to streams. Two lakes, the Flaming Gorge Reservoir and the Fontenelle Reservoir, have already been mentioned. The rainbow fishing in Flaming Gorge can be tremendous. Jackson Lake is a top water for rainbows and big lake trout. Incidentally, lakers are called mackinaw trout by the locals in all the mountain states.

For something different, Lily Lake in the Big Horn has fine summer fishing for grayling. Another good grayling water is Beartooth Lake close to the Montana border. Other top trout lakes are the Buffalo Bill Reservoir near Cody and the Woodruff Narrows Reservoir near Kemmerer. Both are good for cutthroats. The Wind River Range near Pinedale has several fine trout lakes. The top ones are Fremont, Half Moon, and New Fork. Rainbows and lake trout are caught here. Meadow Lake, also in this area, has grayling.

The nearby Wind River Indian Reservation has excellent angling. An angler who wants something exotic can try Alpine Lake on the reservation lands for golden trout. The Boysen Reservoir has rainbows and browns, as well as what is probably the best walleye fishing in Wyoming. Fishing on the Indian Reservation requires a special permit.

Another excellent walleye hotspot is the Keyhole Reservoir in northeastern Wyoming.

There is usually no problem in getting access to the better fishing waters in Wyoming. Some of the good stretches of the top streams flow through private ranch lands, but even these can be fished with permission or float-fished from a boat. Nearly all of the jumping-off communities for the better fishing waters have guides, either for float trips or with pony strings for pack-in trips to fish wilderness lakes in such areas as the Big Horn Mountains, the Beartooth Mountains and of course, the Bridger Wilderness.

Where to Hunt

For hunters, Wyoming is synonymous with big game; but the state also has fine upland game-bird and waterfowl gunning. The first big game to open is bighorn sheep — in some areas the season opens as early as August 15. Sheep licences are sold on a draw basis, with twenty-five percent of the licences reserved for non-residents. The biggest heads come from the Wind River Mountains and the mountain country around Yellowstone National Park.

Mountain goat, grizzly, antelope, deer, elk, moose, and black-bear seasons open in early September. A few mountain-goat licences are also issued by draw. The Beartooth Mountains are the best goat country. Antelope hunting in Wyoming is the best in North America. The hunter success rate is high — over ninety-five percent. The best antelope country is in the south-central part of the state, but pronghorns are present over most of Wyoming's plains country.

Mule deer is Wyoming's bread-and-butter big game. In recent years the number of non-resident deer licences has been limited to 50,000. Mule deer are widely distributed in the state, but Sublette, Lincoln, and Carbon Counties are the best bet for big heads. White-tailed deer hunting in the northeast portion of Wyoming is excellent, but generally non-residents prefer a mule-deer trophy.

Elk is Wyoming's big attraction. Non-resident elk licences can be had on a draw-only basis. The wilderness areas of Cody, Jackson, and Pinedale are top areas for bull elk. There are a number of good outfitters who take hunters into these areas by horse pack-train. Such a hunt is an exhilarating experience.

Generally grizzly and black bear are taken on an elk or deer hunt. But baiting is a more certain way of bagging a bear. Areas around Yellowstone National Park are the best bet for both grizzly and black bear. Moose hunting is also by special-draw permit. Wyoming's best moose range is in the northwest portion of the state. The Green and Gros Ventre River drainages are two top moose-hunting areas. Lately, moose have been increasing in numbers.

The sage grouse is the first game-bird season to open — in late August. The season varies, but generally it stays open for two weeks. The rolling sagebrush hills are the only areas where this large grouse can be hunted. The season for blue and ruffed grouse opens in early September. The forested hillsides are the places to look for these grouse. The forest grouse are usually taken by local residents or by hunters after big game.

The season for chukars opens at the same time as the grouse season. The best area is Big Horn Basin. Chukar hunting there is excellent. The Hungarian partridge season opens along with chukars. However, the huns are found in the grain-growing farmlands. The hun shooting can be very good for hunters with good dogs.

Wild turkey and pheasant seasons open in early November. The farms in Goshen, Fremont, Sheridan, and Johnson Counties are good pheasant country. Wild turkey permits are available by special draw. The Black Hills are the best bet for gobblers.

Rabbits are found statewide, with snowshoe hares in the forested mountains, jackrabbits on the plains, and cottontails in habitats ranging from brushy ravines and hillsides, to plains, to the sagebrush country. Big Horn Basin is a top cottontail area.

Waterfowling in Wyoming is largely confined to the major river systems, but some of the cattle ponds get good flights during migration. There is also some stubble shooting for both ducks and geese in the grain-growing areas. Waterfowl hunters are mainly residents who know the local hotspots. Generally non-residents have their sights set on big game.

For big-game hunting, a non-resident must be accompanied by a guide. The non-resident hunting licence costs are: wild turkey $25, black bear $30, deer $50, antelope $50, moose $125, sheep, goat, and grizzly $150 each. Archery licences are only $5 per species. A non-resident small-game licence costs $10.

Canada

Canada has long been known as an outstanding fishing and hunting country. Indeed, some parts of Canada have the finest fishing and hunting on this continent. Fishing and hunting licences are issued by each province, but hunters intending to hunt migratory birds also require a Federal Migratory Bird Permit which costs $2.00 and can be purchased in any post office. Non-resident hunters will encounter no severe problems in bringing rifles, shotguns, or hunting dogs into Canada under the following conditions:

Firearms — A visitor does not require any permit to possess rifles or shotguns in Canada. However, he must provide the Canadian customs with a full description, including the serial numbers of the guns he is bringing into Canada, so that they may be readily cleared upon return. Two hundred rounds of ammunition per person are admitted duty free. Non-resident marksmen competing in matches organized by Canadian shooting associations are allowed 500 rounds, duty free.

Fully automatic firearms, pistols, and revolvers may not be brought into Canada. However, participants in bona fide handgun marksmanship competitions may apply to the Collector of Customs and Excise for permission to bring handguns into Canada temporarily.

Dogs — Dogs from the United States must be accompanied by a certificate signed by a licensed veterinarian certifying that the dog has been vaccinated against rabies during the preceeding twelve months. The vaccination certificate must also carry a legible and adequate description of the dog and date of vaccination. The vaccination certificate should be initialled by the inspecting official at the customs port of entry and returned to the owner.

Non-resident fishermen can also bring in boats, motors, campers, and tent trailers without any problem. However, these may be registered by Canada customs officials to ensure that they are taken out of Canada when the tourist leaves.

The Canadian Government Office of Tourism publishes a useful booklet on everything a tourist should know, entitled *So You're Going to Canada*. It is available free of charge by writing to them at 150 Kent Street, Ottawa, Canada K1A 0H6 or, from the Canadian Government Offices of Tourism in Boston, Buffalo, Chicago, Cincinnati, Cleveland, Detroit, Los Angeles, Minneapolis, New York, Philadelphia, Pittsburg, San Francisco, Seattle, or Washington, D.C.

ALBERTA

Fish and Game Division
Alberta Department of Lands and Forests
Natural Resources Building
Edmonton, Alberta

Where to Fish

Alberta's fishing has a split personality. The mountain country and the streams that originate there are trout waters; the north is perhaps better knows for its pike and walleye, but it also has some top lake-trout lakes plus good fishing for brook trout and even grayling.

The best trout streams in southern Alberta are the Oldman and Castle Rivers, not far from the town of Pincher Creek. Both are full of native rainbows and cutts. Another fine water is the Bow River for a couple of dozen miles downstream from Calgary. This stream regularly produces rainbow trout in the five to six-pound class. An angler who wants to fish what may be the finest cutthroat water in North America, should wade the Ram River watershed. The beautiful stream, the Clearwater River, is a flyfisherman's dream.

For brown-trout fishing, Shunda Creek is hard to beat. This stream is a good flyfishing water. Other good trout streams are the Jackfish and the Mikkna Rivers, both tributaries of the Peace.

Trout fishing in Alberta is not restricted to streams. The northern part of the province contains a great many lakes with excellent lake-trout fishing. The province's record lake trout, a giant of 52 pounds, came from Cold Lake in northeastern Alberta. Other good lakes are Swan, Grist, Wentzel, Peerless, and Namur, the last of which also has big northerns.

Brook trout are found in many of the northern lakes. Three excellent lakes for trophy brook trout in the 5 or 6-pound class are Muskiki, Elbow, and Fairfax. All of the lakes in Banff and Jasper National Parks have fine trout fishing. The species include cutthroats, rainbows, Dolly Varden, brook trout, brown trout, and Rocky Mountain whitefish. Fishing bulletins are issued regularly at the information centers in the parks. For scenic beauty and fine trout fishing, the Amethyst Lakes in Jasper are hard to beat. The Astoria River is also a fine fishing water, as are Maligne Lake and Twintree Lake in the northern part of the park.

Some other good trout lakes in Alberta are: Carson Lake in the Swan Hills; Christina Lake east of Pelican Hills; and Beauvais Lake near Pincher Creek. The province also has an extensive rainbow-trout stocking program in the potholes of the prairie country. Many of these small waters are open to public fishing. The growth rate for trout in these fertile ponds is extremely rapid.

The most popular fish in Alberta is the walleye, at least among the local fishermen, but non-residents probably prefer northern pike. Both species are very widely distributed. They are found in nearly all the lowland watersheds. The best walleye and pike fishing is found in the northern half of the province. It

142

is difficult to name the top walleye waters, but the Athabaska River and the Pembina River must rate high. Their associated lakes are full of walleyes. Other good rivers are the Red Deer and the South Saskatchewan.

Someone after trophy pike should try Seibert Lake, east of the village of Lac La Biche. Fish in the 20-pound class come out of this lake regularly. Other good lakes are Gardiner, Andrew, and the previously mentioned Namur.

Most of the best fishing in northern Alberta is a fly-in proposition and most of the top waters have fishing lodges on them. To fish the remote lakes and streams in the large national parks, an angler has to hike in or pack in with horses. Outfitters with mountain horse-strings operate in both Banff and Jasper.

Where to Hunt

Big game is the main attraction for resident and non-resident hunters. However, some non-residents are also discovering that Alberta has fine bird shooting. Pheasant hunting on the irrigated farmlands of the Taber-Lethbridge area is very good in some years. Sharptail hunting along the Saskatchewan boundary is also good. The shelterbelts produce some good ruffed grouse gunning, but the Rocky Mountain foothill country is even better. Blue grouse are found on the higher slopes but only visiting big-game hunters and local residents hunt them.

Hungarian-partridge hunting in the grain stubbles of southeastern Alberta can also be very good. And the far north has both willow and rock ptarmigan, with spruce and ruffed grouse in the forests. Again, only moose hunters take some of these birds for the pot.

Waterfowl hunting is exceptionally good, particularly in the prairie country of eastern Alberta. The ducks are hunted over stubbles as well as on sloughs. Goose hunting is also carried on in stubbles. It helps to have a good spread of goose decoys and to know how to call. The area around St. Paul is a well-known waterfowl hotspot.

The upland game bird and waterfowl seasons generally open in early September, but some zones open a little later. The pheasant season opens in early October. The week-long sage-grouse season opens in mid-October. The sagebrush plains of southeastern Alberta are the range of this big grouse. Most bird seasons close in early December.

Moose and deer are Alberta's most abundant big-game species. Both mule deer and whitetails are found in the province. The best whitetail racks come from areas around Wainwright and Hardisty; while top mule-deer racks come from Milk River Ridge. However, muleys are widely distributed throughout the Rocky Mountain foothills.

Alberta has some of the finest moose hunting on the continent. Big racks come from the vast area around Lesser Slave Lake in the north, but all the major forest lands of Alberta have moose. Elk is also found in the forested slopes of the Rockies of Alberta. Elk hunting may not be as good as in British Columbia, but hunters who pack into the hills with horses do well.

Bighorn sheep and grizzly are Alberta's most highly coveted trophies. The remote mountain country has both species. The best grizzly hunting is around Jasper and Banff Parks. Mountain caribou is fairly abundant on the Alpine tundras of the Rockies. A caribou hunt also means a pack-train trip into the high slopes. The success rate for caribou hunters is high. Good heads for both bighorn sheep and caribou can come from just about anywhere where the animals are found.

Black bear are abundant over much of the mountainous and forested regions of the province. On the other hand, cougar are found mostly in the foothill country. The other two big-game species are pronghorn antelopes and mountain goats. Mountain-goat licences are available by special draw only, while pronghorn seasons are open in some years. Both species are restricted to residents.

Big-game seasons vary according to the different zones, but some seasons begin in late August, particularly in the north or at high elevations. The grizzly season is open from April 1 to May 31 only. A black-bear season is open at the same time.

Non-resident hunters must be accompanied by a licenced guide. All hunters must purchase a $3.00 Wildlife Certificate. Non-resident licence costs are: birds, $50; black bear, $25; deer, $50; cougar, $75; moose, elk, caribou, $100 each; bighorn sheep and grizzly, $200 each.

BRITISH COLUMBIA

Fish and Wildlife Branch
British Columbia Department of Recreation and Conservation
Parliament Buildings
Victoria, British Columbia

Where to Fish

This land of towering mountains, vast forests, and many rivers is the best fishing country in the world, certainly for trout and salmon. It is impossible to do justice to British Columbia's fishing in one brief chapter. A whole book — no, several books — would be needed to cover the subject. Mike Cramond has written several, published by Mitchell Press in Vancouver.

Steelhead, chinook, and coho are the three main sportfish in British Columbia, but the rainbow trout, or, Kamloops as it is called locally, cutthroats, and Dolly Varden are also important in inland waters. Fishing is a year-around sport in this big province.

Chinook salmon is the glory fish here. Fish up to 90 pounds have been caught on a hook and line. Anything over 30 pounds (trophy class) is called tyee by sportsmen; fish under 30 pounds are called kings. Chinook can be caught in rivers or by trolling in salt water.

Saltwater salmon fishing is a year-around proposition. Chinooks are caught from winter to fall, and coho provide action from May to October. August and September are the best months to catch a big tyee. Chinooks can be caught almost along the entire British Columbia coast, including of course, Vancouver

Island and the Queen Charlotte Islands. Some of the chinook hotspots lie close to the mouths of the Bella Coola, Powell, Skeena, Kispio, and Kitsumkalum Rivers, Howe Sound, Phillips Arm, and in the channels between the Queen Charlottes. The waters around Saltspring, Galiano, and Gabriola are also very good. On Vancouver Island, good places are Long Beach, off Port Alberni, and around such rivers as the Comox and the legendary Campbell.

Chinooks run into about 150 of British Columbia's rivers, so river fishing is not at all difficult. Some of the previously mentioned rivers are excellent. A 92-pounder was once caught in the Skeena. The rivers of the Queen Charlottes provide hot action. The Fraser River gets a run of jacks, precocious chinooks of 2 to 3 pounds. These are excellent fish for flyrodders.

Coho salmon provide tremendous fishing. They are more abundant than chinooks. Nearly all of the previously mentioned waters have fine coho fishing. Other top coho waters are: Cowichan Bay, Oyster Bay, Duncan Bay, Comox, and Nanaimo, all on Vancouver Island. The Queen Charlottes are excellent. Copper Bay on Moresby Island is good. Then there are all the major river systems, such as the Skeena with its tributaries of Kispiox, Morice, Kitwanga, and a host of other rivers. All are good.

Steelhead also run into nearly all the major rivers, plus dozens of minor ones. Again the tributaries of the Skeena come close to being tops, with the Kispiox ranking with the best. But the Morice, Telkwa, and Cooper are excellent as well. The Veder River in the lower mainland of British Columbia is close to big population centers and gets fished heavily, but it still produces top fishing during the winter and early spring months. On the other hand, the rivers of Queen Charlotte Islands get very light pressure. The islands lie off the beaten path.

Vancouver Island has several top steelhead streams. Cowichan is probably the best, but the Campbell is better known, largely because of the enchanting fishing stories of Roderick Haig-Brown. The Nimpkish River is another fine steelhead stream on the island.

British Columbia's inland fishing is mainly for the Kamloops race of rainbow trout, plus other trout such as cutthroats and Dolly Varden. Sea-run cutthroats are also popular sportfish. All the Vancouver Island streams have coastal cutts, while lakes such as Buttle, Sproat, Cowichan, and Campbell have inland cutts. The East Kootenay waters have top cutthroat fishing for the brightly colored Yellowstone race.

Dolly Varden can also be sea-run or resident. The Columbia River system in the upper reaches is top Dolly Varden water. Some of the tributaries of the Skeena also have these fine game fish. The Thompson River, including North Thompson, is excellent. But the Kamloops is unquestionably the king of British Columbia's inland waters. The lakes and streams of the Kootenay Range, and the Okanagan Valley are probably the best areas to take this fish. The Kamloops is also found on some of the lakes in Vancouver Island, as well as throughout most of the streams and lakes of the mainland interior.

The brook trout and brown trout have both been introduced to British Columbia. Brookies are found in some of the Kootenay streams and Vancouver Island

Chinook salmon goes under several names – King when it is under 30 pounds, and tyee when it is over 30 pounds. Trolling in the coastal waters of Oregon, Washington, British Columbia, and the upper Great Lakes is a good way to catch a chinook.

lakes; the best brown fishing is in the Cowichan system. Lake trout are found in many lakes of northern and central British Columbia. Adams, Babine, Morrison, and several others are probably the best.

Other interesting fish are the grayling, most abundant in the tributaries of the Peace and Yukon Rivers. Rocky Mountain whitefish are also found in all of the major river systems of the mainland. Kokanee salmon are found in a number of lakes, both on Vancouver Island and the mainland. They are an important game fish in Kootenay Lake.

British Columbia also has such warm-water fish as smallmouth bass, walleyes, and yellow perch, but they are completely overshadowed by the trout and salmon.

The only other important game fish is the pink salmon or humpback, which provides additional action for trollers in inshore areas. These delicious salmon come in only every two years. Their runs are unpredictable.

British Columbia's salt water has outstanding but, as yet untapped, potential for other sportfishing. Ground fish are abundant in many areas, including huge halibut and tuna offshore.

There is no problem with accommodation for non-resident anglers in British Columbia. The hardest thing for an angler is to decide where to go. Charter boats for salmon are available in all the major fishing ports such as Vancouver, Victoria, Prince Rupert, Campbell River, Nanaimo, and several others. The Provincial Tourist Bureau, Victoria, British Columbia (or its Vancouver office) is a good source of fishing information.

Kokanee Salmon

Where to Hunt

British Columbia has the greatest variety of game on the North American continent. The ecological reason for this is the diversity of habitats, varying from subarctic tundra to sagebrush desert. As one would expect in mountain country, sheep are British Columbia's most prized big-game species. The mountains of northern British Columbia have the snow-white Dall sheep and the Stone sheep. The Dall sheep range is restricted to the very northwest corner of British Columbia, but the Stone sheep range goes much farther south. Both are generally referred to as "thinhorns". The mountains of southern and central British Columbia have the prized bighorns. The encroachment of agriculture and civilization has reduced the bighorn herds to a shadow of what they used to be; fortunately the thinhorn sheep ranges are too remote to be overgrazed by domestic cattle and sheep.

Mountain goats and grizzlies are found the entire length of British Columbia, with the grizzlies also being found along the coastal salmon streams and the lush interior valleys. The goats generally stick to the high rocky crags. The alpine tundras also have mountain caribou which are found over nearly the entire length of the mountain range. They are much more numerous in the northern regions.

The forested hills have deer, elk, and moose. The elk are not found in the northern portions of British Columbia, while moose are more numerous in the northern two-thirds of the province. The forested slopes of the Kootenays are top elk country. Mule deer are most numerous east of the Coastal Range. The blacktails are found on the western side of the Coastal Range. Black-tailed deer are principally found in the coastal rain forests, the best area being the Queen Charlotte Islands. The whitetail range blends with the mule deer in parts of southern British Columbia. The East and West Kootenays are a good bet for trophy whitetail bucks.

Cougars are more numerous in the southern half of the province, with Vancouver Island probably having the densest mountain-lion population on the continent. Black bears are found province-wide but they are most numerous along the remote coastal salmon streams. Habitats of many British Columbia big-game species overlap.

The big-game season opens on August 1 for all three sheep species; while the caribou and goat seasons open in mid-August; and deer, elk, moose, grizzly, and black bear in early September. Most big-game seasons close in mid or late December. Cougar and wolverine seasons stay open to the end of March. All seasons vary according to specific areas.

Bird hunting in British Columbia is also varied. A hunter will find everything from California quail to willow ptarmigan. Blue grouse is the most important game bird in the province and is found province-wide on the forested hillsides. Ruffed grouse is principally found in the lower slopes and valleys in areas that have fewer coniferous trees. The Franklin's race of spruce grouse is found in the evergreen forests of the more remote areas. Ptarmigan are found in the northern mountains far above the tree line, while sharptails are found in the Peace River prairies and sage grouse in the sagebrush desert of southeastern British Columbia.

Hungarian partridge are found in the farms of the interior valleys, while chukar partridge are quite numerous in many of the arid canyons and hilly slopes of the southern British Columbia interior. California quail are principally centered in the more sheltered valleys, the Okanagan Valley perhaps being the best. Ring-necked pheasant hunting is mostly confined to the farmlands of the Delta. But here, urban sprawl is destroying much of the best habitat. Bandtailed pigeons are gunned in the forested mountain passes, while doves predominate in the farming areas.

The seasons for ptarmigan, sharptail, blue, ruffed, and spruce grouse begin in early September. So do the bandtail and dove seasons. Hungarian and chukar partridge open in mid-September; pheasant and quail in early October. The quail and pheasant season closes in late November, but most of the others do not close until mid-December or even later.

Waterfowl hunting is very good in many areas of British Columbia. The valleys between the three major mountain ranges — Coast, Cascade, and Rocky Mountains — are all used as flyway by waterfowl. The coastal marshes and estuaries also have fine waterfowling, particularly in southern British Columbia. There is exceptionally fine brant gunning and some good Canada goose shooting along the coast.

Non-resident hunters after big game must be accompanied by a licenced guide. The British Columbia licensing system is unique. The non-resident hunting licence is $75, with licences for black bear, $40; deer, $50; wolf, $75; moose, caribou, elk, cougar, mountain goat, $100 each; mountain sheep, $250; grizzly bear, $300.

MANITOBA

Tourist Branch
Manitoba Department of Tourism, Recreation, and Cultural Affairs
408 Norquay Building
Winnipeg, Manitoba

Where to Fish

Northern pike are Manitoba's most abundant game fish, and they grow huge in some of Manitoba's lakes. The provincial record is 41 pounds, but any fish over 18 pounds is considered a trophy and will get you into the Manitoba Master Anglers Awards. Over 500 such trophy pike make the list every year. Some of the top producers of big northerns have been such well-known waters as Kississing Lake, God's Lake, and Cormorant Lake, but the current hotspots are lakes around The Pas and Flin Flon — the Cranberry Lakes, Athapapuskow Lake, Reed Lake, and Red Lake. However, northerns are distributed almost province-wide from the southern bays of Lakes Winnipeg and Manitoba, right up to the Churchill River.

The walleye is probably as widely distributed in Manitoba as the northern. These fish are unbelievably abundant in some of the small northern lakes. The Saskatchewan River around The Pas is an excellent walleye water in the spring. The southern rivers such as the Assiniboine also have good walleye runs in the spring.

Since there are over 100,000 lakes in Manitoba with walleyes in the majority of them, it is difficult to pick the best ones. Such lakes as Sasaginnigak and Dogskin are rated high by local experts. Other good lakes are God's, Cormorant, and St. Martin's. Another top walleye water is the Narrows at Lake Manitoba. A lot of big walleyes have come from this spot. The Narrows are also in the center of some of Manitoba's best waterfowl gunning.

The waters of Island Lake River and God's Lake have become legendary among anglers seeking trophy brook trout. Only the rivers of Labrador produce bigger brookies consistently. But brook trout are also found in many of the smaller lakes and streams in the northeastern part of the province.

Manitoba is not top rainbow-trout country, but Riding Mountain National Park has rainbows in several of its lakes, the best being Lakes Katherine and William. On the other hand, lake trout are Manitoba's forte. In the far north, such fly-in lakes as South Knife, Nejanilini, and Neultin regularly produce lunkers in the 25-pound class. God's Lake is good as well. Clear Lake, near The Pas, is excellent right after ice-out. Athapapuskow Lake still yields many eating-sized lakers, but it is unlikely that another 63-pounder will be pulled out again.

The southeastern corner of Manitoba has many lakes brimming with battling bronzebacks. Falcon, Crowduck, and Eaglenest Lakes are some of the top ones, but other lakes in the scenic Whiteshell Provincial Park also have smallmouths. The Winnipeg River is another fine smallmouth water in Manitoba.

Manitoba is very tourist-minded. In the north fishing lodges abound. Many of them are totally isolated on fly-in lakes. There are many campgrounds, and camping is allowed in many areas on public land. More adventurous anglers will find that excellent fishing can be had on canoe-camping trips in the wilderness areas. Maps of canoe routes are available from the Manitoba Tourist Branch.

Where to Hunt

Waterfowl are Manitoba's big hunting attraction. Manitoba's pothole country is the big duck factory of North America. The best duck hunting in the province is found in the sloughs and potholes from Minnesota to the Saskatchewan River during the early season. The Saskatchewan and Carrot River country west of The Pas is also good, particularly for mallards. The marshes around both sides of Lake Manitoba are also very good. The Lake Winnipegosis and Waterhen marshes have outstanding duck gunning, particularly for diving ducks. The canvasback is king here. Manitoba's Delta Marshes are world famous for their duck hunting, but there is increasing evidence that they are being overhunted, and reduced seasons and bag limits will probably come into effect soon. Outstanding goose hunting is found in several areas of Manitoba. The Cree Indian fly-in camps at Cape Tatnam and the Kaska River on Hudson Bay have excellent Canada-goose hunting, with some snows and whitefronts. The port of Churchill is the jumping-off point for these camps.

Top goose hunting can also be had on the grain stubbles along the Saskatchewan River east of The Pas. The big birds stop here on their migration south. The areas around Dog Lake, Whitewater Lake, and Shoal Lakes near Winnipeg are good as well. The grain stubbles of the Interlake country, the area between Lake Manitoba and Lake Winnipeg, also have fine goose and duck hunting.

The two main upland game birds are sharptails and ruffed grouse. The Interlake country is tops for both. The town of Ashern Holds is the site of the International One-Box Sharptail Hunt in which select VIP's are invited to com-

---

Northern pike are the leopards of the northern lakes and rivers. The lakes of northern Minnesota, Manitoba, and Saskatchewan have the best pike fishing, but some of the big impoundments of the mid-west also produce fine northerns.

pete. But there is fine sharptail hunting in the entire Interlake area. There is fine ruffed grouse and sharptail gunning on the west side of Lake Manitoba, along Highway 50. The area just north of Lake Winnipegosis is also a good bird-hunting spot. The areas around Langruth and Amaranth and around Melita and Broomhill have good sharptail gunning.

Ptarmigan and Hungarian partridge are two of Manitoba's other game birds. In some years the ptarmigan are numerous in the north. The huns are scattered throughout the wheat fields of southern Manitoba. Except for local pockets, they are not very numerous, particularly when compared to the sharptails. Spruce grouse are found in the vast forests of the north, but the fool hens are not a highly regarded game bird. Snipe are found in many Manitoba wetlands but they are not hunted very much. The lesser sandhill crane is also on the shooting menu during the first two weeks in September.

Generally the grouse and ptarmigan season opens in early September, the hun season in mid-September. The waterfowl season also opens in early September. The grouse and ptarmigan seasons close at the end of February, while the waterfowl closes in early December.

The white-tailed deer or "jumpers" as they are locally called, are abundant in Manitoba. Some areas allow the resident three deer per season. Whitetail hunting in the southwest portion of the province is probably the easiest anywhere. The deer are found in small woodlots and shelterbelts and can be driven out even by two or three men.

Areas further north have more deer, but hunting in the bigger forests is harder. The Interlake region probably has the highest deer population and is the best bet for non-residents.

The vast forests north of The Pas have outstanding moose hunting. The area from Canberry Portage to Wobowden along the Grassy River lakes chain is a local hotspot. The north Interlake region is also good, particularly west of Highway 6.

Woodland caribou is Manitoba's other big game. The caribou range through the far north, and hunting them is generally a fly-in proposition. Top caribou country is the area east of Norway House.

Black bear is widely distributed in the province. The best areas to bag a black bear are around the Riding Mountain National Park and the northeast part of Duck Mountain Provincial Forest around Cowan and Garland. Elk in Manitoba can be hunted by residents only. The best elk country is around Riding Mountain National Park.

The bear season begins in early September, while deer, moose, and caribou seasons open in mid-September. The exact opening dates and length of seasons depend on the area.

The non-resident hunting-licence costs are: game birds, $35; deer, $40; moose, $100; caribou, $100; black bear, $15. Canadian non-residents pay a little less for licences on some species. Every hunter must purchase a wildlife certificate for $2.25 before he can obtain the game licences.

NEW BRUNSWICK

New Brunswick Travel Bureau
P.O. Box 1030
Fredericton, New Brunswick

Where to Fish

The name "New Brunswick" is enough to conjure up the image of quiet mornings on serene pools of the Restigouche or the Miramichi and, that fabled fish, the Atlantic salmon.

The salmon season in New Brunswick begins on April 15 for spring salmon — "black salmon". The rivers are high then, and fishing is done from a boat. By mid-May the waters have receded and the rivers can be waded. The season continues to late September. The Atlantic salmon do not run into all the rivers at the same time. The Miramichi — along with all its tributaries such as the South, Southwest, and Northwest Miramichi Rivers and the Cains River — gets good salmon runs from June to September. But such headwater streams as the Alma, Jacquet, Bartibog, and Big Salmon are better in September and October. The Restigouche and the Upsalquitch Rivers are best in June, July, and August.

All these rivers get good runs of grilse as well, precocious Atlantic salmon, around 3 to 5 pounds. The peak runs for grilse come in July and again in September. Sea-run brook trout also ascend the rivers in June and July, and offer additional sport for the angler.

Native brook trout are found in countless New Brunswick brooks. The trout are small, rarely over a foot long. The serious angler views these small trout as fish fit only for boys, but they are delightful in the frying pan. Many of New Brunswick's lakes also have brookies. The brookies run bigger in the lakes. Some of the better brook-trout lakes are Magaguadavic in York County, McDougall and Antinouri in Restigouche County, and Caron in Madawaska County. Incidentally, brook trout in Canada are generally called "speckled trout" and sometimes "squaretails", while lake trout are called "togue".

Lake trout are found in some New Brunswick lakes. Baker Lake in Madawaska County is good. It also has squaretails. Other togue lakes are Victoria, Long, Glazer, and Shancock. The Shancock also has landlocked Atlantic salmon, called ouaniniche in eastern Canada. Palfre and Magaguadavic are two other ouaniniche lakes. Smallmouth bass share the Magaguadavic with the landlocks. However, bass are not fished much in New Brunswick. There are other bass lakes in the province, particularly along the New Brunswick-Maine border.

Saltwater fishing is excellent along New Brunswick's east coat. The main quarry are cod, hake, pollock, and mackerel. Many of these fish can be caught right off harbor installations and from shore. The angling for these species is done as much for the pot as for the sport. Striped bass also run into New Brunswick waters, with the St. John River getting good runs from May to October. The bigger fish come later in the summer, but they never reach the size

that they do further south along the Atlantic coast. However, 30-pound stripers are common enough. A couple of local hotspots are Hartz Island and the Reversing Falls on the St. John River.

New Brunswick is a tourist province and non-resident anglers are welcome. All the major salmon rivers have fishing camps with guides, while other accommodation including camping is available in or near all communities. The coastal towns and villages all have local fishermen with dories who will take out tourists to handline a mess of cod fish or pollock. Tourist Information Services, Box 1030, Fredericton, is a good source of information on guides, charter boats, and accommodation. Incidentally, the only way a fishermen can legally kill a salmon in New Brunswick is with a flyrod, which is only fitting for such an elegant fish.

Where to Hunt

To upland game-bird hunters, woodcock and New Brunswick are synonymous. New Brunswick has the best timberdoodle hunting on the continent. The top woodcock-hunting counties are Kent, Charlotte, Albert, West Morland, Kings, Queens, York, Victoria, and Northumberland. Grouse hunting can also be excellent in New Brunswick and indeed, grouse are frequently found in the same covers as woodcock. The top timberdoodle counties are also good grouse counties. The only other game bird found in significant numbers in New Brunswick is the spruce grouse. The spruce grouse is found only in evergreen habitats in the very remote areas of the province.

New Brunswick also has some fine waterfowl gunning. The black duck is the important game bird in New Brunswick marshes. But sea-duck hunting is very popular as well. The coastal tide flats and marshes of Gloucester, Kent, and Albert Counties have good duck hunting. The St. John River watershed has good duck gunning, particularly in Kings, Queens, and Sunbury Counties. Charlotte County along the Bay of Fundy also has good duck hunting. Canada geese provide fine waterfowl hunting. The marshes of Albert County are a favorite resting place, as is Grand Lake. The coastal areas of Gloucester and Kent Counties have fine goose shooting as well.

The snowshoe hare is the principal small-game mammal in New Brunswick. It is found in forests and woodlots all over the province. Bobcat, fox, and raccoon also have game status with open seasons.

The woodcock season opens in late September followed by the grouse, duck, bobcat, raccoon, and fox seasons in early October. The grouse, fox, and raccoon seasons generally close late in November, but the seasons for other game stay open for a month longer. Sea ducks stay open until the end of February.

The Atlantic salmon is considered by many fly fishermen to be the finest game fish on the continent. The rivers of Quebec, New Brunswick, and Newfoundland are the best bet for catching a salmon.

White-tailed deer, black bear, and moose are all found in New Brunswick forests. Moose hunting is restricted to residents only. Whitetail hunting is very good in New Brunswick. The best counties are Madawaska, Victoria, Charlotte, Kings, and Queens. Grand Manan Island also has good deer hunting. The main moose range is the central and southern portion of the province. Licences are available by special draw only. Black bear are found in the forested areas over much of New Brunswick; but Victoria, Carleton, and Northumberland are the top counties.

Deer seasons vary from area to area, with some areas opening in early October and closing in late November. The bear season is open at the same time as deer, with an additional spring season from mid-April to late June. Generally, the moose season is open for five days in late September.

Non-resident hunters must have a guide for hunting in New Brunswick. One guide per two hunters is acceptable for small game. The non-resident small-game licence costs $10; deer (including bear) $35.50; while a spring bear licence costs $10.

NEWFOUNDLAND AND LABRADOR

Newfoundland Tourist Development Office
Confederation Building
St. John's, Newfoundland

Where to Fish

Newfoundland and Labrador, particularly the latter, are two more of Canada's fabulous fishing frontiers. The lakes and rivers of Labrador have already become legendary for their huge brook trout, and there are a dozen or more rivers that get good salmon runs. Some of the top brook-trout waters are Lakes Marie and Minonipi, and the Minipi River. The Eagle River may well be the top salmon stream. Other Labrador game fish are arctic char, landlocked salmon, and northern pike. Char are found in dozens of rivers, while lake trout and landlocked salmon inhabit many of the inland lakes. The Kaniapiskau River offers fine fishing for landlocked salmon. The Churchill River watershed provides top fishing for brook trout, lake trout, and northerns.

The fishing in Labrador is largely a fly-in proposition. Goose Bay is the jumping-off point for the fishing lodges in the interior. There are a number of fine fishing lodges on Labrador's top fishing waters. More are opening up, particularly in the north. Anglers are only scratching the surface of Labrador's fine arctic char and salmon fishing, but this does not seem to be the case for trophy brook trout.

Newfoundland also offers excellent fishing. What is particularly attractive about Newfoundland angling is that it can be had even with a moderate financial investment. An angler can drive to many of the top streams. And no guide is needed, even for salmon, if the angler does not go more that a quarter of a mile from the road. To fish the more remote pools, a guide is needed.

Excellent salmon fishing is found close ot the provincial capital of St. John's on such rivers as the Colinet, Placentia, Trepassey, and the Salmonier. These streams get a fair amount of pressure, but they bear up surprisingly well. However, for the non-resident angler the more remote streams are a better bet. The better northern streams are the Southwest and Northwest Gander Rivers and the main Gander itself. On the western side, the Highland, Fox Island, New Branch, and the South Branch are all top producers.

The Humber River and the Upper Humber just south of the Long Range Mountains of the Northern Peninsula yield many big salmon every year. These two rivers may well be the most productive salmon streams in Newfoundland.

The Northern Peninsula itself offers some fabulous salmon fishing in a dozen or more streams right along Highway 73. Most of these streams have only grilse, precocious salmon that have ascended the rivers prematurely, but big fish can be taken in some of the bigger streams. The best salmon fishing in Newfoundland begins in July, with some rivers peaking in August. Salmon are a flyfishing-only proposition.

Other top game fish in Newfoundland's fresh waters are brook trout and landlocked salmon or ouaniniche. Brookies are found in countless streams, brooks, and ponds all over the province. Getting a few pan-sized brook trout for breakfast is no problem in most parts of Newfoundland. For trophy brook trout, the bigger lakes and rivers are best. Some of the better ones are the Indian Bay watershed in the northeast near Gander, the Round and Long Ponds watershed north of Bay D'Espoir, and the Granite Lake area, also nearby.

Brook Trout

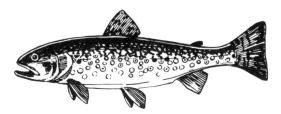

Lake trout and pike are found in the inland lakes, while arctic char run into the northern streams. Two other trout in Newfoundland are the rainbow and the brown. Rainbows are found in several streams and lakes, with Gallows Cove and Brock's Head watersheds being the best. Brown trout occur in Chance Cove south of St. John's in the Avalon Peninsula. The browns are sea-run. Witless Bay south of St. John's has yielded a 27-pound 10-ounce fish.

Newfoundland's salt water offers some of the best tuna fishing anywhere. St. John's is in the center of this big-game fishery. Conception Bay is one of the best tuna grounds in Newfoundland. Some of the smaller bays also produce tuna.

There is no problem with fishing access in Newfoundland, but accommodation may be a problem in the more remote areas. However, there are fishing lodges on the better waters. Camping may be necessary on some. For more information, write to the Tourist Development Office, Elizabeth Towers, St. John's, Newfoundland, and ask for a free copy of *The Newfoundland Fishing Guide*.

Where to Hunt

Moose and caribou are the big attractions on Newfoundland and Labrador's hunting scene. The woodland caribou is the premium trophy here, and the caribou herds on both the island and mainland are increasing. The top caribou hunting areas in Newfoundland are La Poile, Buchan's Plateau, Grey River, and Middle Ridge. In Labrador, Wabush is the top area, with the town being the main jumping-off point for the hunting camps. The non- resident hunter success rate is high — 94 percent.

Moose is the most abundant big game in Newfoundland, and the island offers some of the best moose hunting on the continent. The animals were introduced to the island, and the non-resident success rate is high — over 90 percent. The best hunting areas are the western portions of the island, Long Range Mountains, and the region south of the Trans-Canada Highway. Top Pond, Victoria Lake, and Granite Lake are the top local hotspots. Black bear are scattered throughout the island and some lucky caribou and moose hunters also bag a bruin. The jumping-off points for moose hunters are Gander and Deer Lake.

Small-game hunting in Newfoundland rarely attracts non-resident hunters. Ruffed grouse were introduced to the island and are increasing annually. The best areas are around the Salmonier River and just northwest of Gander. Of course, grouse are also found in Labrador. Willow-ptarmigan hunting during the peak cycle is outstanding in Newfoundland. Willow ptarmigan are the North American race of the famous Scottish red grouse and, when hunted over pointing dogs, offer some outstanding wing shooting. The ptarmigan are found in "barrens" — the muskeg country of Newfoundland — and are distributed province-wide. Three hotspots are the Trepasse, St. Shott's, and Terrenceville areas. The rock ptarmigan is also found on the rocky hills, particularly in the north. Newfoundlanders call them "rock partridge".

The snowshoe hare is an important game species on the island and chasing snowshoes with big beagles is a popular sport. Some of the more remote areas of northern Newfoundland also have the big Arctic hare.

Newfoundland and Labrador have some fine waterfowl hunting. Black ducks are the important birds in the interior waters. Newfoundland has many wetlands and marshes. The coastal waters have fine sea-duck hunting which the hardy Newfoundlanders pursue with vigor. Canada geese also migrate over Newfoundland and are gunned in local areas.

The caribou, moose, and bear seasons open in early September, while waterfowl and upland-game seasons open in mid-September. Moose and bear seasons close in mid-November with caribou in late October.

Non-resident hunting licences for caribou cost $175; moose, $125; bear, $15; game birds, $5; rabbits, $5. The Newfoundland Tourist Development Office publishes a *Hunting Guide* which is available free of charge.

NORTHWEST TERRITORIES

Travel Arctic
Yellowknife, Northwest Territories

Where to Fish

This vast piece of real estate stretches from about the sixtieth parallel right up into the high Arctic. Its huge lakes and long rivers offer fantastic fishing for lake trout, arctic char, and grayling. Brook trout, walleye, and northern pike complete the picture. The inconnu or sheafish, a giant and savage member of the whitefish family, inhabits the Mackenzie River and Great Slave Lake.

The brook trout and walleye are found in the more southerly watersheds of the Northwest Territories, while pike are much more widely spread. But none of these species is as important as the lake trout, the char, or the grayling.

The great lakes of Great Slave and Great Bear have become world famous for their outstanding lake-trout fishing. The top five world-record lake trout came from these waters. Both lakes have a number of fly-in fishing lodges on their shores. Several of these lodges offer complete packages, including round-trip transportation by chartered jet from such cities as Edmonton, Alberta, or even Minneapolis.

But the gem of the Northwest Territories lakes is Colville, north of Great Bear. It offers outstanding lake-trout angling plus grayling in the tributary streams and, of course, pike in the shallow bays. Hardly anyone bothers with the pike. The Colville Lake Lodge, the only camp on the lake, stands right on the edge of a Hareskin Indian village clustered around the mission station. These Indians still live traditional lives by trapping and hunting. They act as guides during the July-August fishing season. All this gives the lodge a unique atmosphere. The angler has an opportunity to see a life style that will soon vanish.

Arctic char are found in all of the rivers. The Tree River has become legendary for its big fish. But the streams of Chantney Inlet, Bathurst Inlet, and the Arctic islands including Baffin and some of the islands in Hudson Bay, all have good char fishing. The Coppermine River sometimes rivals the Tree. The arctic grayling is found in many of the streams and brooks that flow through the tundra. It is widely distributed and offers top sport on a light flyrod with tiny black flies.

Great Bear Lake, the east arm of Great Slave, and the Tree River require anglers to use only barbless hooks on their lures to ensure that released fish will survive. These vast northern waters are not very fertile; the fish grow slowly, and trophy trout could be decimated if proper conservation practices were not followed. Hence the rule of barbless hooks.

Travel Arctic, Government of the Northwest Territories, Yellowknife, offers a good information brochure for the angler.

Where to Hunt

The Northwest Territories are North America's last frontier. In fact, when it comes to hunting, the Northwest Territories are the closest thing to virgin country on this continent.

Big game is the magnet that draws hunters to the Territories. However, at times small game are also abundant. Ruffed, spruce, blue, and sharp-tailed grouse are all found in the Territories, as are ptarmigan. Both ducks and geese nest on the many wetlands of this vast land, and indeed the Mackenzie Delta is one of the most important nesting grounds for ducks on this continent. The waterfowl migrate down the Mackenzie Valley in great profusion. The snowshoe and the big Arctic hares are the two small-game mammal species. The snowshoes are forest dwellers, while the white Arctic hares live on the open tundra.

Dall sheep and polar bear are the two most coveted trophies in the Northwest Territories. Other big-game species are mountain goat, grizzly, moose, caribou, black bear, buffalo, and possibly in the near future, muskoxen. For really unusual trophies, a hunter can stalk seals or go out with the Eskimos and harpoon a white whale.

Dall sheep are found over the entire range of the Mackenzie Mountains. On the other hand, mountain goats are found only in the southwest corner of the Territories. Moose are found throughout the forest lands, while barren-ground caribou range all over the open tundra areas through the spring, summer, and fall. Many of the herds migrate into forest cover in winter. Woodland caribou are found in the forests.

The Northwest Territories are the only place on this continent where the polar bear may be legally hunted. The big ice bears are harvested on a quota basis, with each Eskimo village receiving a quota of bears that can be taken. Two villages have received permission to sell part of their quotas to outside hunters.

This is a unique and top-quality hunt. The bears may be hunted only by the traditional method with huskies and sleds. Each non-resident hunter must be accompanied by an Eskimo guide on the hunt. The village also provides food and accommodation for the hunter. Incidentally, the hunt costs $3,000, with the hunter getting the skin and skull as trophies and the Eskimo village getting the meat, plus the cash income.

The grizzly bear and brown bear are two other bear species that can be hunted in the Territories. Both bears have wide distribution. The foothills of the Mackenzie Valley are the top area for grizzlies, while a hunter can run into a black bear just about anywhere. The great barren-ground grizzly, an endangered race of grizzlies that lives on the open tundra, is fully protected. Wolves can be taken by any hunter possessing a valid hunting licence.

Beluga or white whales and seals are two unusual trophies that can be hunted in the Territories. Hunting for both these marine mammals is done along the same basis as the polar-bear hunt. The hunter hunts out of an Eskimo village with Eskimo guides.

Buffalo may be hunted around the Wood Bison National Park in the southern region of the Northwest Territories. The buffalo from the park have overflowed the boundaries. There are a couple of outfitters who specialize in buffalo hunting. This continent's other shaggy bovine — the muskoxen — may soon be legal game in a very limited way. On some Arctic islands, muskoxen are so numerous that they are overbrowsing their winter range. Winter starvations have taken place. The territorial government is considering a limited open season on these big beasts.

The hunting seasons for all game begin on July 15 and generally end on November 15. However, the buffalo season opens on September 15 and closes on December 31, while the polar bear season opens October 1 and closes May 31. The sea mammal seasons are open during spring and summer, after the spring break-up and before the winter freeze-up.

Non-resident hunting-licence costs are: small game, $10; big game, including Dall sheep, mountain goat, grizzly, black bear, moose, and caribou, $150; polar bear, $250; buffalo, $150; seal, $25 white whale, $40.

NOVA SCOTIA

Division of Wildlife Conservation
Nova Scotia Department of Lands and Forests
Kentville, Nova Scotia

Where to Fish

Nova Scotia may be better known for its picture-postcard scenery than its fishing, but that is not because the fishing is not good. The province offers fine brook-trout angling plus a dozen good salmon rivers, brown-trout angling, some landlocked salmon, plus smallmouth bass and pickerel in its lakes. Its saltwater angling consists of top striped bass action plus bluefin tuna and swordfish for the big-game fisherman. Cod, pollock, and mackerel abound as well.

Wedgeport is the tuna capital. It hosts the annual International Tuna Cup competition, where teams of big-game anglers from all over the world compete. There are tuna fleets at Cape St. Mary, Chester, and Halifax. The world-record fish, a giant of 1,065 pounds, was caught off Cape Breton. The best tuna fishing is from July to October, depending on location. August is probably the peak month.

The best striped-bass fishing is in the waters of the Bay of Fundy. All the major rivers — Avon, Bear, Stewiacke, Shubenacadie, and others — get striper runs. The estuary of Annapolis Royal is another hotspot, as is the Minas Basin. The south shore and Northumberland Strait all get intermittent striper runs. The fish are not big — up to 25 pounds. They can be caught by casting from shore or from boats.

Such saltwater species as cod, pollock, hake, halibut, and mackerel can be caught from shore and from harbor installations around the entire coastline. Charter boats are available to take anglers out to inshore and offshore grounds as well. None of these fish is viewed seriously as sportfish.

The salmon is the king of Nova Scotia waters. There are about a dozen good streams and, since the ban on commercial fishing, the salmon runs have increased in strength. Salmon angling is restricted to flyfishing only. The best east-shore streams are West and Moser's, while the west shore has La Have and Stewiacke. Other good streams are St. Mary's and Phillip. Cape Breton Island has salmon runs in the North, Middle, and Margaree Rivers.

Brook trout are found in countless small creeks throughout Nova Scotia, with those in the more remote areas of Cape Breton being the best. Many of Cape Breton's lakes also have squaretails, with Lake Ainslie being the best. Sea-run brown trout ascend into many streams. Two of the best are Cornwallis and Mersey. Rainbow trout have been stocked in a number of lakes, with Rumsey and Sunken Lakes in the southwestern part of Nova Scotia being the best.

Smallmouth bass are found in Dartmouth Lake near Halifax, but they are more abundant in Elliott and Lily Lakes. One top smallmouth stream is the Black River. Pickerel abound in Lake Milo.

Fishing access is no problem in Nova Scotia. Even the small brooks which gurgle through pastures and farmlands are open to considerate anglers who ask for permission to fish. Accommodation, including campgrounds, is available in or near all the small communities. Nova Scotia is not a big place, so an angler can always find somewhere to stay and still be close to his chosen fishing water. The Department of Tourism, Box 130, Halifax, is a good source of information on both fishing and accommodation.

Where to Hunt

The white-tailed deer is the number-one big-game animal in Nova Scotia, but some bear are also bagged every year. Moose hunting is restricted to residents only and with only limited licences sold. The deer and bear season runs from mid-October to mid-November. The deer hunting is good on the mainland's 119 counties, but it is even better on Cape Breton Island. Bear are mostly confined to the wilderness areas.

Ruffed grouse is the most abundant game bird, being found province-wide. Hants, Colchester, and Pictou Counties have the top grouse gunning with Pictou being the best. The farmlands of the picturesque Annapolis Valley also have fine pheasant and Hungarian-partridge gunning. Woodcock hunting is good in many parts of Nova Scotia, particularly the woodlots of the Annapolis Valley.

The snowshoe hare is an important small-game species, and it is found over the entire province. Bobcats are also on the game list, with open seasons in the winter months.

Waterfowl hunting can be quite good in many areas of Nova Scotia. Black ducks are a very important game species, particularly in the inland marshes and estuaries. Of course, sea ducks are hunted around much of the coastline. Canada geese also stop over on their southward migration.

Nova Scotia is one of the few places where ducks are hunted by a technique called "tolling", where a dog is used to attract ducks to shooting range by running back and forth on shore near a blind. Ducks are curious creatures and swim close for a look. A breed of rusty-colored dogs called Nova Scotia Tolling Retrievers has been developed especially for this sport. The breed is recognized by the Canadian Kennel Club.

The opening of the small-game season varies: grouse, ducks, geese, and woodcock in early October; huns and pheasants in mid-October; and rabbits in mid-November. Most small-game seasons close in mid-December. Non-resident hunters must be accompanied by a licensed guide. Guides, including those who specialize in "tolling" for ducks, are available in most of the country towns. A non-resident big-game licence costs $40, while a small-game licence costs $15.

ONTARIO

Public Relations Branch
Ontario Ministry of Industry and Tourism
900 Bay Street
Toronto, Ontario

Where to Fish

It would take an entire book to describe Ontario's fine fishing. But alas, such a book will probably never be written, because describing the fishing in the province's 250,000-plus lakes and probably equal number of rivers, streams, and brooks would be a herculean task.

Ontario's piscaries offer everything from muskellunge to chinook salmon. Certainly, the savage musky must rate as the province's most glamorous fish. And Ontario may well have the best musky fishing anywhere. The biggest muskies come from the Thousand Islands area of the St. Lawrence River just east of Kingston. The Bay of Quinte around Adolphustown is another good water for monster muskies. Lake St. Clair, and Honey Harbour and Point au Baril on Georgian Bay are three other top-rated musky waters.

Muskies are even more abundant, but smaller in size, in several lakes and rivers of northwestern Ontario. Eagle Lake is probably the most productive, but Pipestone, Dryberry, and Lake-of-the-Woods all yield muskies to fishermen with the patience and perseverance to go after them.

The northern pike is distributed almost province-wide. The only place where this toothy brawler has not penetrated is the lakes of the Haliburton Highlands and the trout waters of Algonquin Park.

There is no accurate way to pick out top northern pike waters, but Lake of the Woods country and the myriads of lakes around Chapleau, Cochrane, Kapuskasing, and Geraldton all produce big pike. The better lakes are generally fly-in waters. The bays and inlets of Georgian Bay all yield northerns in great numbers, and they have the virtue of being accessible to every angler with an automobile and a boat.

The walleye — or pickerel as it is called in Ontario — also enjoys a wide distribution. All the watersheds in northwestern Ontario have good walleye fishing. So do the big lakes such as Nipigon and Nipissing. The Kapuskasing country and the vast wilderness northeast of Wawa offers unbelievable walleye action. Closer to the more populated southern part of Ontario, the French River is fine walleye water. The Kawartha Lakes, including Rice Lake, all yield many walleyes in spring. And since the commercial fishing ban in western Lake Erie, walleye have resurged there and may soon offer top angling.

Bass — smallmouths and largemouths — are found over much of the province as well. The smallmouth is much more widely distributed. It was stocked in many cold-water trout lakes in the north, and has become so overpopulated that its growth has been stunted. In some of these lakes, a 10-inch bass is a big one. Some of the top bronzeback waters in Ontario are found around Fort Frances, in the northwestern part of the province. The best water is probably the North Channel of Georgian Bay between Manitoulin Island and the mainland. The Thousand Islands area of the St. Lawrence River is also a smallmouth hotspot. Certainly more anglers go there to fish for bronzebacks than for muskies.

Some good bassing shoals lie in Lake Ontario in Prince Edward County. Indian Point and Hay Bay are two of them. The same applies to Lake Erie. There, the bass shoals are found off Points Pelee, Long, Turkey, and others. Some of the lakes in the Haliburton Highlands also yield good catches of small-mouths.

Largemouths are found in the more southerly lakes. The Land O' Lakes area and the Kawartha Lakes area both have largemouth-bass waters. Lake Scugog, almost on the doorstep of Toronto, is a much unappreciated and overlooked water where lunker largemouths lurk among the lily pads.

To complete the repertoire of Ontario's warm-water fish species, there is a host of panfish and catfish. Only locals who know how good catfish are on a dinner plate, angle for these whiskered fish. The top panfish are white bass, white and yellow perch, and black crappies. Of these, only yellow perch are important in terms of angling, and only in the southern Great Lakes or in the big inland lakes such as Simcoe.

The rainbow trout brings a gleam to the eyes of many Ontario anglers. These fine gamesters are found in a number of inland lakes, but it is the Great Lakes steelhead that offer the most sport when they ascend spawning streams in the spring and fall.

The top rainbow-trout streams lie in the Bruce Peninsula. The top rivers here are the Beaver, Saugeen, Sydenham, Big Head, Nottawasaga, and a few smaller ones. Manitoulin Island has a fine run of steelhead into Blue Jay Creek. This little stream also holds native brookies. All of these streams get heavy fishing pressure, particularly on weekends.

The bays and coastline around Goderich, Kincardine, and Owen Sound pro-duce fine steelhead for trollers. The former two areas also yield coho and chinook salmon with increasing regularity. The mouth of the Credit River, right in the Toronto suburbs, also produces coho in the fall.

However, in terms of numbers of fish caught, the two native trout species — brook and lake — still outrank the rainbow. Ontario has a number of fine brook trout streams. The Sutton and Winisk Rivers, both flowing into Hudson Bay, are top waters for trophy trout. However, brookies are found in nearly all the tributary streams of the rivers of the Hudson and James Bay drainage. A fine way to fish there is by canoeing and camping. The Sutton and Winisk are fly-in propositions. Both have lodges on them.

Many of the streams that flow into Lake Nipigon have fine brook trout fishing. Some of the lakes in Algonquin Park are still hard to beat for both brookies and lakers, right after ice-out. The better lakes in the park require canoeing and portaging in. No flying-in is allowed. This law has helped to maintain the fishery at a top level.

Anyone contemplating fishing in Algonquin Park should get a copy of the booklet *Fishing in Algonquin Park*, plus a map of the canoe routes in the park. These are available from the Sport Fisheries Branch, Ministry of Natural Resources, Queen's Park, Toronto, Ontario.

Aside from this, brookies are found in countless beaver ponds in the northern bush. Generally they are taken only by anglers who are not afraid to do a bit of walking and facing the bugs.

Lake trout are found nearly province-wide, particularly in the cold, deep lakes of the northern portion of the province. The country north of Sioux Lookout is tops for lakers. But there are also some good fly-in waters for lake trout north of White River. Lake Temagami, north of North Bay, yields good fish. It is popular with ice fishermen. Lake Opeongo in Algonquin Park produces some trophy trout every year. One surprisingly good and well-known producer of lake trout is Lake Simcoe, and hour's drive north of Toronto.

Fishing is an important tourist business in Ontario, and fishing lodges and outfitters proliferate throughout the better fishing areas. There are many fly-in operators with small seaplanes. A good source of information on fishing camps and lodges is the Northern Ontario Tourist Outfitters Association, R. R. 1, Alban, Ontario. Another good source is the Public Relations Branch, Ministry of Industry and Tourism, Queen's Park, Toronto.

Where to Hunt

Moose is Ontario's number one big-game animal, but the province also has fine waterfowl gunning and good grouse and woodcock hunting. The moose season north of Highway 11 opens on September 15, with the southern areas opening later. The top moose-producing area lies in northwestern Ontario in the Kenora-Sioux Lookout-Red Lake region. This area is a maze of waterways making it relatively easy to get deep into the bush. During the early season, the best moose hunting is on water, because moose like to feed on aquatic vegetation. The vast forests around Hornpayne, Geraldton, Hearst, and Cochrane have good moose hunting. Nakina and Armstrong on the CNR railway line are also tops. The hunters who fly deep into the wilderness for guided hunts have much better success than the road hunters.

By far the best deer hunting in the province is in the Fort Francis-Kenora region, but local pockets around Parry Sound and north of Tweed are also good. In the southern areas, deer are generally hunted with hounds in a manner similar to deer hunts in the southern United States. However, Ontario gets just a little too much snow to be top deer country. There is no doubt that there are better places to bag a whitetail than Ontario, except perhaps the Kenora-Fort Francis region. Deer seasons vary from zone to zone, but there is a deer season in some part of Ontario at all times from early October to mid-December.

Probably more black bear are bagged in Ontario than anywhere else. This is not because bears are more numerous than elsewhere, but because Ontario is easily accessible to large numbers of hunters. A week's bear hunt — including guide, room, and board — can be arranged for under $250. Spring is the best time to go on a bear hunt. The success rate runs as high as 40 percent in some areas. Moose and deer hunters may also take bear in the fall. The best bear hunting is around Mattawa, Chapleau, Wawa, and Kenora. The bear season in Ontario is open from September 1 to June 30.

Waterfowl hunting in Ontario is excellent in several localities. The outstanding area for geese and ducks is the bleak shoreline of James and Hudson Bays. The ducks are mostly pintails and mallards, while the geese are mostly snows in both the white and blue-color phases. Some Canadas are bagged as well. There are a number of goose camps operating on James and Hudson Bays. The ducks are mostly pintails and mallards, while the geese are mostly snows in both the white and blue-color phases. Some Canadas are bagged as well. There are a number of goose camps operating on James and Hudson Bays. The hunts are booked as a package deal, including air transportation into camp. Toronto and Timmins are the usual jumping-off points. The coastal mud flats on James Bay and Hudson Bay also offer outstanding snipe gunning.

Good duck shooting is available on many of the inland marshes and lakes. The best known are the Lake Erie marshes. But Georgian Bay, Lake Simcoe, Lake St. Lawrence, and the Ottawa River all have good pockets of duck hunting for both dabbling and diving ducks. Walpole Island Indian Reserve, on the doorstep of Detroit, offers fine duck hunting on a daily-fee basis. The cost includes an Indian guide.

Ontario has a variety of upland game birds, but only grouse and woodcock are numerous enough to attract visiting hunters. Ruffed grouse are found province-wide, but in the far north they are quite tame and make poor wing shooting. In southern Ontario the grouse are as wild as any in Ohio or New York. It is hard to pinpoint top ruffed grouse hotspots because there are so many, but the upper Bruce Peninsula between Lake Huron and Georgian Bay, Manitoulin Island, and the area around Parry Sound are all very good. Spruce grouse are also found in the wilderness areas of the province. They are generally encountered deep in the wilderness during a moose hunt. These "fool hens" make poor hunting.

Sharp-tailed grouse are also found in Ontario. The main range is the remote wilderness of the far north, but there is a huntable population around Fort Francis. Some scattered coveys also exist on Manitoulin Island. Willow ptarmigan are restricted to areas even further north than the sharptails. Sportsmen

All the flyways offer goose hunting, but probably the best snow goose and blue goose gunning comes in Louisiana, Texas, and the James Bay coast of Ontario.

seldom encounter them, but they can be hunted in the winter by taking long snowmobile trips into the open barrens from Moosonee.

Woodcock hunting in some areas is excellent and, luckily, the timberdoodles are not hunted by the average hunter. The Bruce Peninsula, Manitoulin Island, and the Ottawa River Valley are top woodcocking areas.

Pheasants, Hungarian partridge, and bobwhite quail are Ontario's other three game birds. The farmlands around the Lake Erie shoreline and the Niagara Peninsula are the main pheasant range. The hunting is not particularly good except for local pockets. Urban sprawl has swallowed up many of the best pheasant covers. Pelee Island in Lake Erie offers some of the best pheasanting on the continent, next to that of South Dakota. Only 1,000 licences are issued for a season which lasts for only two weekends.

Bobwhite quail are restricted to southwestern Ontario along the western half of Lake Erie. The birds are most abundant in areas of Kent and Elgin Counties. Hungarian partridge are found on the farmlands of eastern Ontario, with the town of Winchester being right in the center of the hun range. In the past this area has had very fine hun hunting, but the hunting has declined in recent years.

Cottontails, European hares, snowshoe hares, and gray squirrels are all on the hunting menu, but only cottontails are hunted much. The cottontails, squirrels, and European hares are found in southern Ontario, while snowshoe hares are found in the northern woodlots and forests.

Small-game seasons open in mid-September in the far north and early October in the south. Bobwhite quail, pheasants, and cottontail seasons generally open in mid to late October, again depending on areas. Most bird seasons close in mid-December but in some areas grouse stay open until mid-January. Generally pheasant and quail seasons last for only a couple of weeks.

Non-resident small-game and wolf licences cost $35; a deer, bear, wolf and small game licence costs $40; moose, deer, bear, wolf and small game $125. A non-resident spring bear is $15.50 with non-resident wolf being $5.25. Export tags are: moose, $15, bear, $10; deer, $10.

PRINCE EDWARD ISLAND

Wildlife Division
Prince Edward Island Department of Tourist Development
Charlottetown, Prince Edward Island

Where to Fish

Prince Edward Island may be Canada's smallest province, but it boasts the best big-game fishing. Indeed, it is the best place in the world to catch giant bluefin tuna. The annual catch of big tuna runs over 400 fish per season, the largest so far being 1,040 pounds. The community of North Lake, almost at the eastern tip of the island, is the main port for the charter tuna fleet. But nearby ports of North Rostico, Alberto, Covehead, and one or two others also have charter boats.

Besides tuna, Prince Edward Island has good fishing for such small saltwater species as cod, halibut, mackerel, and others. Some of these can be caught right from harbor installations, with the causeway in Charlottetown being a hotspot for the tasty mackerel. However, the best way to go after them is on a party boat. Party boats operate out of all of the bigger coastal communities, particularly near the prime resort areas.

The hottest of the small saltwater game fish is the sea-run brook trout which periodically enters fresh water. The best time to catch these saltwater brook trout is in May or June. They frequently run up to 5 or 6 pounds. Although many P.E.I. rivers get runs of these sea-going brookies, the best are St. Peter's Lake, West, Vernon, and Morell Rivers. The place to fish for them is at the mouths of these streams where the water is brackish.

Atlantic salmon also ascend several of the Prince Edward Island streams. The runs are not as strong as those of New Brunswick, but at peak times the runs can be surprisingly good. Top salmon streams are those that are tops for sea-run brook trout.

Other freshwater fishing is mainly for brook trout. Squaretails are found island-wide in many small brooks and creeks, plus in some seventy ponds, ranging in size from one to 50 acres. Some of the best trout ponds are Leard's, Witlock, Pisquid, Selkirk, Morrison's, and McPherson's in Kings County; Bonshaw, Kelly's, and Carragher's in Queens County; and Milligan's, Campell's, Banks, Blanchad's and Bonshaw in Prince County. Early spring is the best time to fish these small lakes.

Prince Edward Island has become a prime tourist area, famous for its fine sandy beaches, drama festivals, scenic countryside, and friendly people. Fishing access is no problem even on creeks flowing through farmlands. And if the fish are not biting at one end of the island, you can drive to the other end in about four hours. The Prince Edward Island Travel Bureau, Charlottetown, is a good source of fishing information.

Where to Hunt

The Gulf of St. Lawrence is a key waterfowl staging area along the Atlantic Flyway, and Prince Edward Island is strategically located to benefit from this. Almost all marshes, bays, rivers, and ponds have fine waterfowl hunting. But top goose hunting can also be had on the stubble and potato fields. Geese feed on the small potatoes left by the big harvesting machines.

Black ducks and teal are the main duck species and the geese are predominantly Canadas. Malpeque Bay, New London Bay, St. Peter's Bay, and Earnscliffe-Orwell Bay are four local waterfowling hotspots. Sea ducks are found in late season around the entire coast.

Ruffed grouse and Hungarian partridge are the two main upland-game birds. Grouse are found in woodlots over the entire island while huns are farmland game. The top hun hunting is around Earnscliffe and Kensington. Woodcock are also found in the moist woodlots. The island offers some outstanding snipe gunning along the edges of marshes and low-lying pasture lands.

The snowshoe hare is found in the forest lands, while fox are found over the entire island. Both have game status. There is no closed season on raccoons. Prince Edward Island has no big game.

The season for all game except rabbits opens in early October. The rabbit season begins in early November. First to close are huns at the end of October, followed by grouse at the end of November. Migratory birds stay open until mid-December, sea ducks longer. A non-resident hunting licence costs $10.

QUEBEC

Tourist Branch
Quebec Department of Tourism, Fish, and Game
930 St. Foy Street
Quebec City, Quebec

Where to Fish

"La Belle Province" is even bigger in land area than Ontario, and it probably has almost as many lakes plus many more rivers. Only the absolute fishing highlights can be touched upon here.

Atlantic salmon and trophy brook trout are the two top game fish in Quebec, but arctic char, lake trout, and landlocked salmon are also plentiful. Walleye (called "doré" in Quebec) and northern pike are widespread and extremely abundant. Trophy-sized muskies and bass complete the fishing picture. Although Quebec has a long saltwater coastline, the saltwater fishing has not even been explored. It offers possibilities for bluefin tuna and striped bass.

Quebec has about 90 salmon rivers, many of which have become world famous among the select group of anglers who pursue this outstanding game fish. Usually the beats on the rivers in the Gaspé Peninsula are reserved a year ahead. The rivers on the north shore of Quebec are harder to reach, and some are held by private lease. Anticosti Island, a huge island in the Gulf of St. Lawrence, also has some fine salmon fishing. The remote streams of the Ungava Peninsula get good runs of Atlantic salmon. The two best rivers here are the Whale and George; both can be fished from Eskimo-run fishing camps.

The Ungava streams get tremendous runs of arctic char. Again, the Whale and the George are top streams. But there are a number of others, including some on Baffin Island. The Finger Lakes, east of Fort Chimo on Ungava Bay, are top arctic-char waters. Eskimos operate fishing camps on all of the better char waters, offering the angler a unique fishing adventure. Fort Chimo is the

---

One of the most exciting ways to hunt moose is by calling during the rut. This spine-tingling form of moose hunting is practiced largely in Ontario and Quebec.

170

jumping-off point for the Ungava region fishing camps. There is daily jet service to Fort Chimo from Montreal. The flight is 2½ hours long.

Brook trout are found from the gurgling brooks of the Eastern Townships to the big rivers of the north. Several waters also have the Quebec red trout, a geographic race of the brookie. It is the big rivers that have made Quebec's trout fishing famous. An angler who wants to land a brook trout of 6 pounds or over, should head for such rivers as the Assinica, the Rupert, the Mistassini, and the Broadback. The Broadback produces brook trout of over 9 pounds every season.

Excellent trout fishing can be had in many of Quebec's provincial parks. The 55,000-square mile Parc des Laurentides, north of Quebec City, has some very productive trout lakes. In the early spring two of the top ones are Lac Dameau and Lac Levesque. The more remote Chibougamau Provincial Park offers even better fishing. The top water here is Mistassini Lake, which is a fly-in proposition from the town of Chibougamau. The lake has brook trout, lake trout, and northerns.

Lake trout, walleyes, and northerns are found in thousands of lakes across the entire forested area of northern Quebec. It is difficult to pick top waters because there are so many. Muskellunge, the northern pike's first cousin, also inhabits several of Quebec's waters. The biggest fish come from the St. Lawrence system right on Montreal's doorstep. The top waters are Lac St. Pierre, Lac St. Louis, and Lac Maskinonge.

Not all of Quebec's lakes and rivers are open to public fishing. Private clubs still hold leases in areas of the north. But a non-resident angler will find access to an unbelievable amount of fishing water. Camping facilities exist in all the provincial parks, while all the better fishing waters have lodges or a least seasonal tent camps. Anyone planning a salmon-fishing trip to one of the better rivers should make his reservations early. At peak times the demand is high.

Where to Hunt

"La Belle Province" is fine hunting country and, with its French-Canadian charm, is a unique province to visit. French is the official language of Quebec and it is also the main language outside the big cities. However, many Quebecois speak at least a little English, so non-residents should have no fear of a major language barrier.

Caribou and moose are Quebec's two big trophies. Chimo and Shefferville are two main jumping-off points for caribou hunters. Caribou hunting is largely a fly-in operation to camps on big lakes. Quebec has woodland and barren ground caribou, plus a hybrid between these two races which the Boone and Crockett Club lists separately for trophy evaluation. The hunter success rate on caribou runs about 75 percent.

Moose are found over most of Quebec's forest wilderness. However, the Abitibi region has the best moose hunting. This vast area has many outfitters. The town of Val d'Or is the main jumping-off point. Black bear are also found over much of Quebec. The Abitibi region is excellent, but other areas farther south are just as good. The white-tailed deer is Quebec's fourth big-game species but deer hunting is not particularly good. The only exception is Anticosti, an island 135 miles long and 40 miles wide in the Gulf of St. Lawrence. Anticosti Island is privately owned and offers outstanding deer hunting. The limit is two deer per hunter, with the season being from mid-August to mid-December.

The caribou season in Quebec begins in September. The moose season opens in late September and closes in mid-October. The black-bear season opens along with moose and closes in mid-November. There is also a spring bear season from May 1 to July 31.

Quebec has some fine wing shooting. Ruffed grouse, woodcock, and Hungarian partridge are the three main upland-game species. Ruffed grouse are found province-wide, but in the far north they are "fool hens"; easy to kill but no sport to hunt. However, in the woodlots of southern Quebec particularly in the eastern townships, they behave like "proper" ruffed grouse. Woodcock are mainly found in the woodlots of the St. Lawrence lowlands. Hungarian-partridge hunting is restricted to the farmlands of the St. Lawrence Valley with the valley of the Rouge River being one of the better areas. Quebec also has ptarmigan, sharp-tailed grouse, and spruce grouse. These birds are found only in the wilderness of the far north and are seldom hunted except by the odd moose and caribou hunter.

Waterfowling in Quebec can be nothing short of fantastic. The Canada goose hunting around Cape Jones of James Bay is, at times, outstanding. The trick is to catch the main migrations of geese from the Arctic. Cree Indians operate hunting camps around Cape Jones with fly-in package deals for sportsmen from Montreal, Quebec, or Hamilton, Ontario.

Another top waterfowling spot is the Ile aux Grues, Montmagny area. The tidal marshes on Ile aux Grues (Isle of the Cranes) and on the shores of the St. Lawrence River have outstanding greater snow goose hunting, as well as fine black duck and teal gunning. The edges of the marshes in this area offer some of the finest snipe hunting on the continent. Good waterfowling areas are also found in the lower Ottawa River and the St. Lawrence River. Both are important migration routes for ducks. Sea ducks are found around Quebec's coastal waters.

The snowshoe hare is the number-one small game mammal and it is found throughout the province.

The small-game seasons generally open in mid-September, but the waterfowl season in the far north opens on September 1. Non-resident hunting-licence costs are: small game, $17.50; deer, bear, and small game, $27.50; deer and bear, Anticosti Island only, $28.00; moose, caribou, deer, black bear, and small game $103.00; spring bear, $12.50.

Muskellunge

SASKATCHEWAN

Tourist Branch
Saskatchewan Department of Industry and Commerce
S.P.C. Building
Regina, Saskatchewan

Where to Fish

Saskatchewan is an outstanding fishing and hunting country. Usually the hunters cling to the wheat stubbles of the prairies in their quest for ducks, geese, and upland-game birds, while the fishermen head north. The northern half of Saskatchewan is a mosaic of forests and water.

The waters harbor tremendous schools of walleyes, trophy pike, and lunker lake trout. A growing network of mining and logging roads has opened countless lakes to anglers.

Northern pike are the main claim to Saskatchewan's fishing fame. They grow big. Fish in the 30 to 35-pound class are caught every year, while 15 to 20-pound northerns are common.

Lake trout are found in all the major lakes, such as Lac La Ronge, Waterbury, Pelican Narrows, Cree, Wollaston, Reindeer and, of course, Athabaska, where a 102-pound laker once enmeshed in a commercial fisherman's net. However, lake trout inhabit thousands of small lakes scattered throughout the north as well.

Northern pike and walleyes have an even wider distribution because both fish are found in rivers. The Churchill River offers outstanding walleye fishing plus northerns, while the lakes on the system have lake trout. A fisherman who wants to experience real angling adventure should consider making a canoe trip on the Churchill. The river flows through magnificent wilderness.

The walleyes in Saskatchewan do not run large, just good eating size, but the northern pike make up the difference. Such lakes as Wollaston, Waterbury, Lac La Ronge, Pelican Narrows, Nemeiben, and Reindeer regularly produce enormous northerns.

Grayling offer fine flyfishing in a number of northern Saskatchewan streams and lakes. Some of the top grayling waters are the Clearwater, Cree, Fond du Lac, and Black Birch Rivers. Downtown Lake, just a jump from the village of La Ronge, also has grayling, as do a number of other waters.

Although the prime fishing in Saskatchewan is concentrated in the northern half of the province, the southern half does have a couple of worthwhile locations. Diefenbaker Lake on the South Saskatchewan has become an important recreational area. This 50-mile reservoir has good walleye fishing. The Cypress Hills have a number of cold, clear streams that offer fine flyfishing for rainbows, brookies, and browns. Rainbows have been stocked in two or three dozen other waters as well.

All of the lakes and rivers in northern Saskatchewan are on public land, so access is no problem. Many of the top lakes are fly-in propositions. Fishing

174

lodges are located on nearly all of the better lakes. The Tourist Branch, Department of Industry and Commerce, Power Building, Regina, maintains a listing of all fishing lodges and camps.

Where to Hunt

The prairies of Saskatchewan offer some of the best small-game hunting in the world. In the uplands, sharptails and huns are the main game birds, with geese and ducks in the stubbles and sloughs. Some of the best Canada goose hunting on this continent is found in Cumberland House, Lost Mountain Lake, or the Quile Lakes areas of Saskatchewan. The hunting pressure in these areas is much lighter than in the famous Kerrobert-Kindesley region and the goose hunting is equally good. Duck hunting is also good in these areas, but ducks are found over the entire province wherever there is water. The Saskatchewan River country — both north and south forks — is good.

Incidentally, local hunters tend to ignore such duck species as gadwall, baldpate, teal, and even canvasbacks and redheads in favor of mallards. A wheat-fattened mallard has to be one of the finest ducks on the dinner table.

Sharptails and huns are found over most of the grain belt, with the better hun shooting found in and around the southern half of the province. Sharptails are found all the way north and in the parklands. They mix with ruffed grouse. Spruce grouse are also found in the vast northern forests of Saskatchewan, but they are not hunted. In the winter ptarmigan migrate into northern Saskatchewan from the far north. Probably the only other bird that is hunted in Saskatchewan, and only by a handful of hunters, is the lesser sandhill crane.

White-tailed deer, moose, and caribou are the main species of big game. Pronghorns, mule deer, and elk are found in Saskatchewan, but only residents can hunt these three species. Black bear is also found in fair numbers in northern Saskatchewan.

The vast forest region north of Cumberland House is one of the top moose hunting areas on the continent. But good moose hunting exists over most of the northern Saskatchewan woodlands. Woodland caribou in Saskatchewan are found in the far north and one can actually drive to some of the areas by car. The best white-tailed deer in the province are in the southern half. In the past the best deer herd was in eastern Saskatchewan around Yorkton, but now western Saskatchewan is better.

Non-resident hunters should familiarize themselves very thoroughly with the different wildlife management zones of Saskatchewan. Seasons vary considerably, as do shooting hours for waterfowl. Non-residents must have a guide when hunting moose and caribou.

The upland game and waterfowl seasons open in early September and generally close in mid-December. Moose, caribou, and bear seasons open in mid-September and close in early October, and then open again in mid-November and close in early December. The deer season opens in mid-November and closes in early December. Non-resident hunting-licence costs are: small game, $50; deer, $50; black bear, $40; moose, $100.

YUKON TERRITORY

Director
Yukon Game Department
Box 2703
Whitehorse, Yukon

Where to Fish

This vast northern territory is far better known to sportsmen for its big-game hunting than for its fishing; but the Yukon has outstanding, if unpublicized, fishing. Fish abound in all waters. Grayling are the Yukon's most widely distributed and abundant game fish. They are found in just about every stream. Most of the streams crossing the Klondike Highway offer grayling just by walking to the nearest pool.

The Yukon's other stream fish is the Dolly Varden. The best water for these trout (or, more correctly, char) is the Teslin system. Both the Teslin River and Teslin Lake have Dolly Varden, but the lake produces bigger fish, many in the 10 to 12-pound class. Teslin River also has some big grayling, up to 3 pounds.

Rainbow trout are found in many of the Yukon's lakes and rivers. Watson Lake is perhaps the top rainbow water. Lake trout are even more widely distributed. The fish do not run as big as in the great lakes of the Northwest Territories, but they are abundant. Just about every deep lake in the Yukon lowlands has lakers. Many of the lakes off the Alaska Highway from Haines Junction to the Alaska border offer good fishing. Other good waters are right on the Klondike Highway. All the major lakes — Teslin, Watson, Dezadeash, Laberge, and others — are loaded with lakers. The fish in these bigger lakes commonly run up to 20 pounds.

Northern pike are also abundant in many of the Yukon's lakes. They have a wide distribution in all the lowland waters. The northerns in the small lakes are always hungry, and it is not unusual to have several fish follow a lure on every cast. Generally the pike do not run as large as in the waters further south, but the bigger lakes do yield fish up to 15 pounds.

The Yukon's arctic char and salmon fishing have not even been exploited. Salmon run into all the major rivers such as the Yukon, Teslin, and Alseck. Char are found in the northern streams. One of the top char streams is Firth River on Herschel Island in Mackenzie Bay. This is a short flight from Inuvik in the Northwest Territories.

Fish are abundant in all the major wilderness areas such as the big-game ranges; the Stewart and Pelly Rivers area southeast of Dawson; and the Ogilvie Mountain range, including the Blackstone and Ogilvie Rivers north of Dawson. It is easy to combine a fishing trip with a big-game hunt. The fishing pressure in the Yukon is incredibly light, even on waters by the much-traveled Alaska Highway. Anyone contemplating a Yukon fishing trip should bring plenty of bug dope and a headnet. In the early summer insects can be devastating.

There is no closed access to the Yukon's fishing, other than distances and the wilderness itself. Accommodations are few and far between, so anglers should be prepared to camp. For more information, write to the Department of Travel Information, Whitehorse, Yukon.

Where to Hunt

The Yukon, like Alaska, is synonymous with big-game hunting. This does not mean that small game is not abundant. Grouse of four species — blue, sharp-tailed, spruce, and ruffed — are all found in the Yukon, as are all three species of ptarmigan. Waterfowl are also abundant along the waterways.

Sheep and grizzly are the glamor big-game species in the Yukon. Caribou, moose, and black bear are too abundant to hold that position, while mountain goats are found only in the southeastern Yukon. Dall sheep are more widely distributed than both Stone and Fannin sheep. The mountains in the drainages of the Bonnet Plume, Blackstone, and Wind Rivers are top areas for Dall sheep. The Ogilvie Range is also excellent. Stone and Fannin races of the Dall sheep are found in the southeastern Yukon in the Cassiar Range of the Yukon and British Columbia. And the high peaks of the Cassiars have mountain goats.

Grizzlies range over much of the Yukon, but areas north of Dawson and Mayo are generally regarded as the best. Black bear are common everywhere. Polar bear in the Yukon may be hunted by Eskimos only. Such animals as wolves and wolverines are also widely distributed and are regarded as predators.

Moose are found almost everywhere. The foothills of the Ogilvie, Selwyn, and Richardson ranges have excellent moose hunting. But there is good moose hunting within a short drive of Whitehorse, Dawson, and Mayo. Caribou are also numerous, with barren-ground caribou being found on all tundra of all the major mountain ranges.

The Yukon has a number of top outfitters who hunt in the traditional way with saddle and packhorses. This type of a hunt must rate as one of the finest hunting experiences. All non-resident hunters must book their hunt through a registered outfitter and must be accompanied by a guide. All big-game seasons open on August 1 and close in early or mid-November, depending on species. There is a spring bear season from April 15 to June 15. Small-game seasons, including waterfowl, begin on September 1.

Non-resident hunting licences are: small game, $10; non-resident all game licence, $100; spring bear, $50. Trophy fees are: grizzly, $65; moose, caribou, goats and sheep, $25 each; black bear, $5.

Dall Sheep

Mexico and the Caribbean

MEXICO

Bud Lewis Public Relations
Mexican National Tourist Council
Suite 500
8560 Sunset Boulevard
Los Angeles, California 90060

The beautiful sandy beaches, warm climate, relaxing atmosphere of a more leisurely lifestyle, and the antiquities of ancient civilizations, have made Mexico a prime tourist center. But to the sportsman, Mexico offers some of the best saltwater fishing and some of the best bird hunting on the continent.

For Americans or Canadians, traveling to Mexico involves little or no red tape with customs and immigration officials. Fishermen will encounter no serious problems in carrying in tackle or even boats and motors. Alas, this is not the case with sporting firearms. Taking a shotgun or a rifle into Mexico involves reams of red tape. No handguns are allowed, and rifles must not be over .30 caliber. Most tourists will find that renting a firearm from an outfitter is much simpler than trying to bring one into the country.

However, for those who want to bring their own rifle or shotgun, here is the current procedure.

Obtain a letter of good character from your local chief of police, sheriff, or mayor. Send this letter along with six passport photos (2" x 2"), plus the following information: full name and address, occupation, nationality, height, weight, build, color of eyes and hair, type of forehead, mouth, chin, distinguishing marks, plus a full description of the firearm(s) — make, model, serial number; amount of ammunition for each firearm; name of Mexican port of entry, and the area where you will be hunting, to the nearest Mexican Consul. The Consul will then issue you a Certificate of Good Conduct. The cost of this certificate is $16.00.

Mazatlan, on the west coast of Mexico, is one of the top ports for marlin and sailfish such as this one. Up to 5000 billfish are caught here in peak years.

On your entry to Mexico, the customs officers will impound your firearms. You then go and present the Certificate of Good Conduct to the commanding officer at the Military Zone or Garrison. In Mexico City the address is Seccion Sexta de Estado Mayor, Secretaria de la Defensa Nacional, in the Lomas del Sotelo.

Along with this Certificate of Good Conduct you must also present four passport photos, plus the letter from your local sheriff, police chief, or mayor. It is also wise to have the full description of the firearms with you as well. Then the military commander may issue you a permit to carry the firearms. The issuance of this permit is at the discretion of the military commander. No doubt, by now you have determined that it is better to rent firearms in Mexico. This is what I do.

Where to Fish

There are three top fishing areas in Mexico. The Gulf Coast is one, with the waters of the Yucatan Peninsula being the major area. The Pacific Coast is next, with most of the fishing centered around the resort areas of Acapulco, Puerto Vallarta, and Mazatlan. And then comes the Sea of Cortez, between Baja California and the mainland.

The Gulf Coast offers a variety of game fish. The open waters have billfish of four species — striped, blue, and black marlin and sailfish — plus such smaller species such as dolphin and wahoo. The northwest side of the Yucatan Peninsula offers excellent inshore fishing for bluefin tuna and king mackerel, plus offshore reef fishing for groupers and snappers. Tarpon is found almost along the entire Gulf Coast.

The east side of the Yucatan, including the waters around the Isle of Cozumel, harbors bonefish on the flats and groupers and snappers on the reefs. Permit, sailfish, marlin, and bluefin tuna are other game species.

The two main fishing centers on the Gulf Coast are the ports of Tampico and Veracruz. Both are fairly important ports, with a number of good hotels where anglers can stay. Charter boats are available.

The Yucatan Peninsula is a relatively remote and primitive area. But the Island of Cozumel is fast developing as a major tourist resort and has several hotels. Many of the hotels maintain charter boats for fishing.

For anglers who like permit fishing as well as snook and tarpon, Boca Paila in the state of Quinta Roo is hard to beat. There is a lodge there called Boca Paila Lodge which caters to fishermen.

For adventurous anglers, the waters around Isla Mujeres offer top fishing for tarpon, snook, permit, snappers, and groupers, plus outstanding sailfish in the spring. The way to reach this island is by air charter from Mérida or charter boat from Valladolid. Another excellent fishing area is Isla Aguada, with the lodge El Tarpon Tropical near Carmen being the fishermen's headquarters. Huge tarpon, snook, snappers of several species, groupers, and permit during early summer, provide hot action.

The fishing on the Pacific Coast centers around the big resorts. Acapulco is primarily known as a resort center with fine beaches and expensive hotels, but it also has good big-game fishing for striped and black marlin. Sailfish are very abundant during the winter and early spring. Up the coast, the budding resort of Puerto Vallarta offers a bit more Mexican charm, plus big-game fishing that may be even better than that of Acapulco. Both cities have charter boats.

However, the major fishing center on the Pacific Coast is the resort city of Mazatlan, where 5000 billfish are caught every year. This port lies at the mouth of the Sea of Cortez, across from the southern tip of Baja California. Sailfish and black marlin are abundant from spring to fall, while striped marlin come in from January to April. The small-game fish include dolphin, wahoo, roosterfish, yellowfins, and even snook in the estuaries.

The beautiful Sea of Cortez, cradled between Baja California and the mainland, is the third top fishing area in Mexico. It offers striped, black, and blue marlin, sailfish, and bluefin tuna for the big-game fisherman. Dolphin, wahoo, roosterfish, California yellowtail, pompano, and several other species offer fine sport for the light-tackle fan.

The Sea of Cortez can be fished from the mainland or from Baja California. La Paz is the biggest resort in Baja because of its commercial airport, but the billfish grounds require a long run out. However, good inshore fishing is closeby. Los Barriles, close to La Pas, has some of the best roosterfish angling anywhere.

The main big-game fishing center is San José Del Cabo on the very tip of Baja California. Here, sailfish and marlin can be caught right in the inshore waters. Tuna fishing is good as well.

Other Baja fishing centers are Loreto, north of La Paz, and Mulege, further north still. Neither are particularly good for billfish, despite the fact that marlin and sails are taken occasionally. However, both have top light-tackle fishing for California yellowtail, roosterfish, and dolphin in spring and summer, and for groupers, snappers, sierra, and black sea bass the year around. Both these centers have fine hotels and charter boats.

There is fine light-tackle fishing along the entire Baja coast, and increasing numbers of sportsmen from California are taking advantage of it. All an angler needs is a boat and a tent or camper. There are plenty of beautiful and empty beaches where anglers can camp. However, accommodation is available in a number of smaller communities along the coast.

The mainland side of the Sea of Cortez offers essentially the same fishing as the Baja side. The two main centers are Topolobampo and Guymas. Striped marlin and sailfish are caught from spring to late summer, with sailfish being the more abundant, but neither is as plentiful as further south. Both areas have excellent fishing for dolphin, California yellowtail, roosterfish, snappers, black sea bass, and snook in the estuaries. Hotels and charter boats are available in both ports.

Again, excellent light-tackle fishing can be had along the entire coast from Puerto Penasco in the very north of the Sea of Cortez right down to Mazatlan. The main fish species are: dolphin, roosterfish, yellowtails, snappers, groupers, and black sea bass; plus corvina, cabrilla, mackerel, pompano, and several other species. A fisherman will not have any trouble catching enough fish to feed a whole platoon of hungry mouths. And some areas are a clamdigger's paradise.

Several of the smaller communities such as Puerto De La Libertad and Bahia Kino do have charter boats and accommodation. However, many of the anglers from the southwestern states prefer to bring their own boats and camping gear. There are many fine beaches and scenic rocky coves where fishermen can camp.

Fishing in Mexico, whether out on a big charter-boat with accommodation in a posh hotel or, just from a beat-up cartopper while camping on a remote beach on the Sea of Cortez, is something every angler should try at least once in his lifetime.

Where to Hunt

Mexico offers some of the finest hunting — particularly upland bird and waterfowl shooting — in the world. The most coveted big game was, of course, the jaguar. This big, beautiful spotted cat is much harder to bag than the lion, tiger, leopard, or cougar. Today jaguar hunting, indeed hunting of all spotted cats, is illegal in Mexico.

But Mexico has other big game. The highly prized desert bighorns are found in Baja California. The white-tailed deer range extends over most of Mexico; while northern Mexico has mule deer, the diminutive Coues race of whitetail and, even some desert pronghorns. Javelina is also found in the north, while the jungles of the south harbor the white-lipped peccary, a bigger cousin of the javelina. The jungle country also has the tiny Brocket deer, the smallest deer of North America. A mature buck weighs a mere 40 pounds. Its antlers are two spikes, three or four-inches long. Because it lives in dense jungles, the Brocket deer is hard to hunt.

Rabbits, squirrels, and various rodents such as the paca are the principal small-game mammals. The iguana lizard is a highly regarded delicacy and has an open hunting season from November to March.

But it is the bird hunting that makes Mexico a hunter's mecca. Doves — mourning doves and whitewings — are extremely numerous in many areas. Band-tailed pigeons are found in the north, while scaled pigeons and the red-billed pigeon are found over much of the country.

The northern Mexican states have bobwhite, scaled, Mearn's, and Gambel's quail. In some areas these birds are extremely numerous. The tree quail is found in the south, while the state of Yucatan has outstanding gunning for Yucatan bobwhite. The city of Merida is the center for top quail hunting in Yucatan.

Other interesting upland game birds are the curassow, a game bird almost the size of a wild turkey; the crested guan; the tinamou, a cinnamon-brown bird about the size of a ruffed grouse; and the chachalca. In the north there are wild turkeys, while the Yucatan Peninsula has the very beautiful ocellated turkey.

Waterfowl hunting in Mexico is outstanding. The Pacific and gulf coast states, as well as the northern states of Mexico, are important waterfowl wintering grounds. The waterfowl season is from November to February. The ducks are mainly teal, pintails, gadwall, baldpates, and shovelers, plus the tree ducks and the Mexican ducks. Snows, whitefronts, and Canadas are the main goose species, with brant along the coast. Sinaloa is probably the best waterfowl hunting state. There are a number of ranches in the state that cater to visiting waterfowl hunters.

All the major tourist centers of Mexico, such as Mazatlan, Puerto Vallarta, and Acapulco have bird-hunting guides who can be hired. The general rates are $35 per half day — morning or evening shoot. Shotguns, generally semi-automatics or pumps, can be rented from the guides at $5 per day.

Hunting licences can be obtained from the Forestry and Wildlife Department Offices (Forestales y de la Fauna Silvestre) in most major towns and cities. In Mexico City hunting licences are purchased from "Direccion General de Caza", Aquiles Serda No. 28. A hunting licence costs 240.00 Mexican pesos, about $25 U.S. dollars.

To export game from Mexico you must have a Mexican export permit or your Mexican hunting licence must be stamped with an official seal endorsed by a game official, granting permission to export game. Migratory birds must be fully dressed before being imported to the United States, but one wing, fully feathered, must be left on each bird for identification purposes.

For additional information on hunting, contact the Mexican tourist offices, located in all major cities in the United States and Canada. To obtain a list of guides, you will have to write to the Tourist Department of the state in which you wish to hunt. Be sure to write early; it may take several months before you get a reply. After all, Mexico is the land of mañana.

THE CARIBBEAN ISLANDS

The islands in the sun — the Bahamas, Barbados, Bermuda, Jamaica, and several smaller ones — have become extremely popular resort areas. Sunshine the year around, warm water, and palm-fringed sandy beaches, are powerful magnets for the vacation-goer. But during the past couple of decades, these islands have also been attracting anglers. This part of the Atlantic Ocean is one of the top sportfishing grounds of the world. Billfish — white and blue marlin and sailfish — plus bluefin tuna offer superb big-game fishing. The abundance of bonefish, barracuda, dolphin, wahoo, permit, and assorted snappers and jacks, mackerel, and several other species, is pleasing to the light-tackle fan.

There is not much hunting in this part of the world, mainly because of the extreme difficulties involved in bringing firearms into these countries. When tourism was in full swing in Cuba, the island offered some superb bobwhite-quail gunning, plus pigeons, doves, and ducks. Guides with dogs were available. And, of course, anyone who has read the more recent works of Ernest Hemingway knows that Cuba has some outstanding saltwater fishing. Largemouth bass are also found in some of the inland lakes. The island of Jamaica has some fine bird

shooting. Haiti and the Dominican Republic have fishing and bird-hunting potential, but neither of these countries are prime vacation areas. However, tourism is beginning to develop in Haiti.

BAHAMAS

Bahama Islands Tourist Office
30 Rockefeller Plaza
New York, New York 10020

The Bahama Islands constitute a mass of about 700 islands off the east coast of Florida; but of these, only a small number are inhabited. The islands are the peaks of ancient mountain ranges, and deep channels exist between some of them. Myriads of coral heads are scattered throughout this area.

The fishing here, like saltwater fishing almost everywhere, can be divided into three classes — big game, reef fishing, and flats fishing, the latter two being done with light tackle.

Big-game fishing is primarily for white and blue marlin, sailfish, and bluefin and yellowfin tuna. Occasionally other species also occur. As an added attraction, big-game trollers also pick up dolphin, wahoo, king mackerel, bonito, and several other species.

Reef fishing, by casting or trolling, offers some of the hottest action anywhere. The primary quarries are five or six species of snappers (mutton, yellowtail, gray, and others), plus several species of jacks and the Nassau grouper.

Flats fishing means bonefishing with either spinning or fly tackle. Many light-tackle anglers consider bonefish to be the finest game fish in salt water.

Fishing is available throughout the entire Bahamas chain. Reef fishing is universally good. Some of the hotspots for bonefish are the flats of Andros Island, Cat Island, Long Island, and the east side of Grand Bahama. The area between Jacob's Cay to Little Abaco has tremendous flats.

Big game fish cruise the offshores around the entire chain, but Cat Cay, Walker's Cay, Freeport on Grand Bahama, Nicolls Town at northern Andros, the deep water off Little Cat Island, Exuma Sound, and a dozen other areas are generally considered the best big-game areas.

The Bahamas offer tremendous variety in accommodation.

Commercial jets fly daily from major North American cities to Nassau. All the major islands in the Bahamas are served by commercial aircraft from Nassau. Air charters are available to the small islands. There are Bahama Islands Travel Bureau offices in Boston, Los Angeles, Chicago, Miami, Dallas, Washington, D.C., and New York City, as well as in Toronto, Canada. These are a good source of information on fishing and accommodation.

The gaff strikes home and a fine amberjack is raised from the water. The amberjack offers fine saltwater fishing in the warmer waters from Barbados north to Bermuda.

Charter boats, big and small, are available to take anglers out for any type of fishing. Big-game charter boats always supply the tackle, although veteran anglers use their own. Light-tackle fans should bring their own, including a variety of spoons, spinners and of course, lead-head jigs with bucktails.

BERMUDA

L. S. Perinchief
Bermuda Fishing Information Bureau
Department of Tourism and Trade
50 Front Street
Hamilton, Bermuda

The semi-tropical island of Bermuda is another popular vacation spot. There are over 100 islands in this group, many nothing more than just rocks. The islands rest on a plateau which drops off rapidly.

The offshore fishing is mainly for yellowfin and blackfin tuna, plus big amberjack, dolphin, wahoo, and barracuda. Blue and white marlin are also caught during the summer. Bonefish, gray snapper, palometa, and a number of other small fish such as yellowtail snapper and sennet offer fine inshore angling.

The best fishing season is from April to November when the waters warm up. But some species of fish are available the year-around. The fishing in Bermuda waters during the summer is excellent. A couple of international fishing tournaments are held here every year.

Bermuda has a good selection of hotels. Charter boats are available. Commercial jets from New York, Boston, and Toronto make daily runs. American and Canadian visitors do not need passports or visas, only proof of citizenship.

JAMAICA

Jamaica Tourist Board
4 West 58th Street
New York, New York 10019

This Caribbean island has long been a popular tourist resort. It also offers superb fishing. It may have the best blue marlin fishing anywhere. Other offshore fish species are blackfin tuna, dolphin, wahoo, kingfish, common bonito, and oceanic bonito. Sailfish and white marlin are also taken.

Tarpon and snook offer good inshore fishing in brackish water near stream mouths. Bonefish are abundant, but good wading flats are not. Other inshore fish

---

Big-game fish such as this Allison tuna offer the supreme thrill of saltwater angling. Other species of tuna are caught from the Caribbean Islands north to Newfoundland.

are snappers and jacks of various species.

Anglers wishing to try something different should have a crack at mullet in some of the rivers. There are several species of mullet, some of which go up to 5 pounds. Rio Corbe and Rio Grande are the two best mullet rivers.

The main fishing centers are Port Royal near Kingston, Port Antonio, Montego Bay, Whitehouse, and Kingston. The harbor at Kingston is best known for its tarpon, but snook and snappers may also be taken. The best bonefishing is near Montego Bay.

All the top fishing centers in Jamaica have good hotels and charter boats. Kingston is served by commercial jets from all major North American cities. And since the island is only 140 miles long and about 70 miles wide, getting to the fishing centers is no problem. All the major hotels have bus services. No passport is needed for U.S. citizens for up to a 6-month visit, but U.S. visitors must have proof of citizenship.

PUERTO RICO

Director of Tourism
268 Ponce de Leon Avenue
San Juan, Puerto Rico

The U.S. possession of Puerto Rico offers some outstanding big-game fishing, with blue marlin being the most abundant. Other offshore species are white marlin, sailfish, yellowfin tuna, and dolphin.

The best big-game fishing is off the south and north sides of the island. The top big-game waters on the south shore are between Cabo Rojo and Guanica. Most of the big-game fishing on the north coast is around San Juan.

Small game fish include wahoo, king mackerel, barracuda, tarpon, snook, bonefish, and such reef fish as snappers and groupers. These fish are found around the entire island. The east coast has the best reef fishing.

Puerto Rico also has some fine largemouth bass fishing in a dozen or so impoundments. There are a couple of dozen rivers which get runs of tarpon and snook.

Accommodation is available in all the principal fishing centers, such as Parguera, Santa Isabel and of course, San Juan. San Juan is served by commercial jets from all major North American cities via Miami. Accommodation here is the cheapest in the Caribbean.

There is a charter fleet at San Juan and a few boats are available at some of the other centers. In general, the fishing is underdeveloped.

OTHER CARIBBEAN ISLANDS

Barbados and the Grenadines, and some of the other smaller islands of the West Indies, along with the Cayman and Virgin Islands, are becoming popular vacation resorts. But only the Virgins, Caymans, and Grenada offer good fishing.

Fishing in the Virgin Islands is excellent, with the island of St. Thomas being near the best grounds. Blue marlin offer excellent billfish action in spring and summer, with the peak in July and August. Blackfin tuna are a year-around proposton. Then there is a whole range of small game fish available, including big permit.

All the major islands — St. Thomas, St. Croix, St. John and the British possession of Virgin Gorda — have good accommodation, with a very good selection at St. Thomas and St. Croix. There is daily commercial jet service from Miami to St. Thomas. Charter boats are available on the major islands, with St. Thomas having one of the largest fleets in the entire Caribbean area.

Unfortunately, the unfriendliness and even hostility toward whites, as well as the high crime rate, mar vacationing on the Virgins. For detailed information on

fishing and accommodation, write to the Department of Tourism, St. Thomas, U.S. Virgin Islands.

The Cayman Islands have become a millionnaire's playground because of their tax-free money and numbered bank accounts. But the Caymans also have good offshore fishing for marlin and sailfish, tremendous wahoo, and the whole range of other species that are found in this area of the Caribbean. The flats on Little Cayman Island have good bonefishing.

There is a wide selection of accommodation on Grand Cayman. There is also commercial jet service to Miami, Puerto Rico and even the Bahamas. But the fishing facilities are not at all well developed. There are no big fleets but charter boats are available on Grand Cayman and on Cayman Brac. For additional information, write to the Cayman Islands News Bureau, Suite 2206, 1270 Avenue of the Americas, New York, New York 10010.

The charming island of Barbados has become popular among sun seekers, largely because of relatively inexpensive package vacations offered through travel agents. Billfish do not seem to migrate into Barbados waters, but the fishing for dolphin, bonito, and a variety of other small game fish is good. There are a few small charter boats operating off the islands.

The Grenadine Islands rank very highly among the most beautiful islands anywhere. The beaches are excellent and the mountainous scenery of Grenada is striking. The fishing is only now being explored, and excellent catches of sailfish plus fair marlin catches are being made. There is top wahoo action in Grenada waters, plus the whole range of other small game fish. Reef fishing is excellent.

Grenada can be reached only by a flight from Barbados or Antigua, but probably this will change in the near future. Tourism will grow here. For additional information, write to the Eastern Caribbean Tourist Association, 40 East 49th Street, New York, New York 10019.

Acknowledgments

My many thanks to all of the state and provincial fish and game departments across North America, Mexico, and the Caribbean for their invaluable assistance in the preparation of this book. Thanks are also due to the following agencies or persons for the photographs that illustrate the book:

Canadian Office of Tourism (10); New Mexico Department of Game and Fish (84); Susan Sosin (28); Information Canada (112); Ontario Ministry of Natural Resources (65, 104, 151); Jerome Knap (48, 69, 178); Mark Sosin (57); David Richey (60, 146); Ontario Ministry of Industry and Tourism (52, 78, 100, 115, 167, 171); Quebec Department of Tourism, Fish, and Game (154); Bermuda News Bureau (184, 186, 189).

Also from Pagurian Press

JEROME J. KNAP'S
THE COMPLETE OUTDOORSMAN'S HANDBOOK
A Guide to Outdoor Living and Wilderness Survival

There is an outdoor recreation boom sweeping the entire Western world and this continent in particular. There has been none like it in the past. The out-of-doors has always had an appeal for some, but they have been a small minority. Two decades ago, you could go on a canoe trip during the summer months in the wilderness of Quetico and not see another soul for an entire week. Not today. You are lucky if you see *only* three or four canoeing parties a day.

The reasons for this outdoor boom are many: a greater interest in wild life, more leisure time, a more affluent society, and better highways and transportation systems.

Every person who ventures into the out-of-doors should possess the basic skills for outdoor living. He should know about the natural world around him — how it lives and functions. He should know its moods, its sounds, and its signals. But above all, the outdoorsman must have a code, an outdoor ethic, to ensure that his life and travels in the out-of-doors are in harmony with nature. Man, like all creatures, is a user — that is how nature created him. Frequently, his use leaves wounds. Every campfire, every hiking trail, every fish caught, and every grouse killed, is a wound, but these are wounds that nature heals with ease. A true outdoorsman never leaves wounds that will permanently scar. That is what the outdoor code and the outdoor ethic — and this book — are all about.